THE DISCOVERY OF ILLUSION

THE DISCOVERY
OF ILLUSION

Flaubert's Early Works, 1835-1837

BY

ERIC LAWRENCE GANS

UNIVERSITY OF CALIFORNIA PRESS
BERKELEY · LOS ANGELES · LONDON
1971

University of California Publications in Modern Philology

Volume 100

Approved for publication May 15, 1970
Issued February 18, 1971
Price, $5.50

University of California Press
Berkeley and Los Angeles
California

❖

University of California Press, Ltd.
London, England

ISBN: 0-520-09371-2
Library of Congress Catalog Card Number: 70-631858

PREFACE

THIS STUDY is a slightly revised version of a doctoral dissertation presented to the Romance Languages department of Johns Hopkins University in October 1966. As such it should not be read as presenting definitive conclusions with regard to either its content or its methodology. My hope in publishing it some four years after first writing is that it will shed new light and provoke fruitful discourse in both these domains.

As regards its content—psychostructural analyses of twenty-four of Flaubert's earliest writings—this study atempts a systematic, holistic interpretation of works concerning which a great deal of critical material is already available, but of an unsystematic, fragmentary nature. I have sought to demonstrate the significance of each work in itself, both as a (synchronic) totality and as an element in a (diachronic) personal and literary evolution. At the very least these analyses demonstrate the birth and development of themes and structures—the heroine's "awaiting" role, for example—that later become fundamental components of Flaubert's mature works.

The question of methodology is more important. This study employs a Freudian terminology that may in some cases mislead the reader into viewing it as essentially an attempt to psychoanalyse the young Flaubert. Were I writing today my analysis would be couched more explicitly in *structural* terms; for whatever interest Flaubert's psychology may hold, the primary purpose and value of my work lies in its presentation of the structural evolution of these adolescent stories as consisting of the emptying-out of their Romantic forms in preparation for the subsequent transcendence of these forms in the author's maturity. The Freudian terms here employed should be taken only as referring to the basic structures of the youthful writer's human universe, and not as elements of a quasi-narrative account of his psychological problems. The ambiguity is not, however, wholly in the mind of the reader; and I readily admit, not so much to the "Freudian excesses" some readers of the manuscript have claimed to find, as to a certain lack of focus that obscures what I have always believed—now perhaps more clearly than at the time of first writing—to be the basic truth of this work. To illustrate by means of a brief example, the analysis of several of the stories involves the theme of fraternal rivalry, the source for which in Flaubert's personal experience seemed and still seems to me to be his feelings of jealousy toward his older, more conventionally successful brother. Criticism of these analyses has inevitably centered on the lack of evidence in Gustave's childhood of any *overt* hostility toward his brother (although evidence of feelings of compensatory contempt is not lacking in the later correspondence, and is made use of in Sartre's discussion of Flaubert's family relationships in the 1966 *Temps modernes* articles.) But what I feel to be lacking in my presentation is a clear positing of the structural parallel among the relationships: Gustave-Achille; hero-rival (in the stories); and "poète"-"bourgeois." Had this been more explicit, it would immediately have become evident that it is the parallel between the *last* two and not the first two of these terms that is the more significant for my analysis. But if I thus beg the indulgence of the reader, it is only because I believe that the essential relationships, though at times partially obscured, nevertheless are indeed defined and analyzed in these pages.

One further regret (which the reader may or may not share) is that the formal-aesthetic structures herein analyzed, while they are linked perhaps at times too obsessively with the psychological structures of Flaubert and his Romantic adolescent peers, are only in passing treated as homologous with the *socioeconomic* structures of the epoch. This is not to say that I would today espouse a strictly Goldmannian perspective; literary structures are in essence projective, not implicit; they cannot in my view be considered simply as isomorphic to wholly implicit (or "unconscious") social infrastructures. But the society does provide the primary stimulus for Flaubert's attempts at projective transcendence, and it might have been well, for example, to consider in the Conclusion the significance of the events of 1848–1852 as providing a precondition for the achievements of the mature Flaubert such as was not yet to be found in French society under Louis Philippe.

These post facto regrets are not alibis, and this study will stand or fall on its own merits. I hope only to have clarified here the fundamental intention of my analysis, and to suggest in what way it can be read most fruitfully.

I would like to express my special thanks to Mrs. Suzanne Shafner for her participation in the production of the original manuscript of this volume. She is indeed the virtual author of the plot summaries that appear at the head of each chapter, and her editorial and technical assistance in the spring and summer of 1966 is still deeply appreciated.

CONTENTS

INTRODUCTION

PROBABLY NO other important writer left behind so large and manifold a body of *œuvres de jeunesse* as did Flaubert. Beginning in his thirteenth year (1835) and continuing with various interruptions up to the first *Education sentimentale* (1843–1845), this series of works offers an insight unparalleled in French literature into the adolescent development of its author. And for Flaubert this development is all the more significant in that it makes visible his transformation from a conventionally Romantic youth into the writer who more than any other figure of European literature embodies the repudiation of the Romantic world view and the rejection of its literary forms.

It is not, therefore, surprising that since the *œuvres de jeunesse* were published in the Conard edition of Flaubert's works in 1910, they have been the object of considerable critical interest. Biographers, notably Maynial[1] and Shanks,[2] have examined these works for the revelations they offer concerning the author's adolescence; most scholars have dealt with them as evidence of Flaubert's long and difficult literary apprenticeship, leading from the first crude sketches to the careful craftsmanship of *Madame Bovary*.[3] But, because these works are clearly of a derivative nature and, particularly during the earliest years, have little value as literature, it has been the rule even for those who study them from a literary standpoint to treat them not as entities in themselves but as mere fragments, of interest only for specific descriptive details, stylistic devices or themes that can be related to those of the mature works.[4]

---

[1] Edouard Maynial, *La jeunesse de Flaubert*, 2d ed. (Paris, 1913).

[2] Lewis Paiget Shanks, *Flaubert's Youth, 1821–1845* (Baltimore, 1927).

[3] Such is the case in the studies of Antoine Y. Naaman, *Les débuts de Gustave Flaubert et sa technique de la description* (Paris, 1962), Germaine M. Mason, *Les écrits de jeunesse de Flaubert* (Paris, 1961), Jean Bruneau, *Les débuts littéraires de Gustave Flaubert* (Paris, 1962), et al. Bruneau's work contains reproductions of several previously unpublished early manuscripts.

[4] Jean-Paul Sartre has recently published seventy pages of extracts from his long-awaited work on Flaubert as well as a brief selection on the author's childhood ("La conscience de classe chez Flaubert," *Les Temps Modernes*, May 1966, pp. 1921–1951, and June 1966, pp. 2113–2153; "Père et fils," *Biblio*, January 1966, pp. 19–23). These partial studies put into practice the program for a Flaubert biography outlined in the "Question de méthode," the preliminary section of Sartre's *Critique de la raison dialectique* (Paris, 1960).

Sartre's primary interest is biographical rather than literary; for him the work is only of importance insofar as it contributes to an understanding of the author's life:

> La vie est éclairée par l'oeuvre comme une réalité dont la détermination totale se trouve hors d'elle, à la fois dans les conditions qui la produisent et dans la création artistique qui l'achève et *la complète en l'exprimant*. Ainsi

This study, which deals not with the whole body of the early works, but only with the efforts of the first two years of their author's career, does not share these objectives. By thus restricting my field I am able to consider in detail the individual structure of each of the twenty-four works written during this time span. The underlying assumption of this analysis has been that even the most immature of these works is a literary entity, a microcosm that, crude and imitative as it may be, cannot but reveal the basic structures of Flaubert's own consciousness. Those who have analyzed the thematic content of the early works have revealed to what extent the situations that interested Flaubert in his maturity already obsessed him in his adolescence. But these situations are not found in the early works in isolation. Just as in the mature novels, they are elements of an over-all structure and can only be fully understood in relation to the part they play in this structure. If, when we study *Madame Bovary,* we do not concern ourselves with the Vaubyessard ball, the boat ride with Léon, and the like, in themselves, but as parts of the universe of Emma's experience, then we should be ready to treat the ball or the boat ride in the same manner when they first appear in Flaubert's literary repertory. In this fashion we are able not merely to discover the differences in technique that separate the youth from the mature writer, but to trace the evolution of Flaubert's vision of the world as a continuous process.

The particular interest of this evolution in Flaubert's writing is that it involves not a simple linear development from imprecision and lack

---

l'oeuvre—quand on l'a fouillée—devient hypothèse et méthode de recherche pour éclairer la biographie.... (*Critique,* p. 90)
Sartre wholly neglects the early works in his analysis of Flaubert's youth; instead he seeks to relate the substance of the mature novels directly to the author's preadult *experience:* "Il faudra rapporter [*Madame Bovary*] à la réalité présente en tant qu'elle est vécue par Flaubert à travers son enfance ... son oeuvre exprime sous un masque à une génération dégoûtée du romantisme les désespoirs post-romantiques d'un collégien de 1830." (*Critique,* p. 48). Here the fact that the "désespoirs post-romantiques d'un collégien de 1830" were expressed before *Madame Bovary* in a whole series of youthful works is not considered worthy of mention. For Sartre the literary form springs directly from the author's unique historical and personal situation; he does not conceive the creation of form, as I do, to involve an initial acceptance and subsequent rejection of a preexisting tradition. Hence Flaubert's process of liberation from the Romantic forms of his youth is of no essential concern to Sartre.
Of course my conception of Sartre's method can be based only on the program outlined in the *Critique* and held to in the selections published until now (1966), which deal with Flaubert's social and familial position and scarcely mention his works or even his literary career; a definitive judgment will have to await the publication of his study in its completed form.

of integration to a mature grasp of one's subject matter, as with a writer like Balzac, but a process of negation whereby the Romantic world view, at first accepted unquestioningly, is eventually discredited and repudiated. This repudiation plays an important role in the mature works themselves: the Romantic desires and attitudes expressed by the heroes and heroines of the early works reappear in *Madame Bovary*, but in an ironic form, as illusions disavowed by the author himself. The celebrated conversation between Emma and Léon on their first meeting in the inn at Yonville, during which they exchange Romantic clichés while Charles and Homais converse in bourgeois platitudes, is a classic example of the mature Flaubert's ironic negation of Romantic conceptions: "Je ne trouve rien d'admirable comme les soleils couchants, reprit [Emma], mais au bord de la mer, surtout. — Oh! j'adore la mer, dit M. Léon."[5]

It is certainly feasible to investigate the contrast between the Romantic youth and the "Realist" adult by making thematic comparisons between the mature and the early works. For example, in the dance theme, it is easy to see the gulf that separates the Vaubyessard ball, which is treated as fascinating only to Emma, from the balls of the early works where the author participates in the excitement along with his characters. But such comparisons cannot reveal the over-all significance of Emma's Romantic illusions in the structure of Flaubert's mature world view. If the illusions that formed the basis for the early works have now been discarded, why have they been made the foundation for the career of the mature author's most illustrious heroine? This question is primary to any understanding of Flaubert; and its answer depends on our grasp of the evolution of the Flaubertian universe as a totality. The primary objective of the study of the early works must be the elucidation of the genesis not merely of the parts of this universe, but of the whole.

Yet we can only accept the necessity for examining the early works as structural entities once we are certain that the series of structures we uncover genuinely reflect the personal evolution of the author. This is not an idle question. A generation before Flaubert it would almost certainly have been impossible to find any genuine self-revelation in the works of an adolescent. The early works of Balzac (or those of which Sartre tells us in *Les Mots*) are no more than servile imitations. Any personal content such efforts may contain would be of an incidental nature in relation to the whole, and an analysis of any one of them would surely tell us little about the author's personal vision of the world. On

---

[5] Flaubert, *Œuvres complètes*, (Paris: Ed. du Seuil, 1964), I, 601–602.

what basis then are we justified in assuming that it was possible for an adolescent growing up in the French bourgeoisie in the 1830s to express his own personal attitudes in the literary forms at his disposal?

Louis Maigron in his *Le Romantisme et les mœurs* (Paris, 1910) has spared no effort in convincing us of the immense popularity of Romantic literature among the adolescents of Flaubert's generation. Flaubert himself, in his preface to the *Dernières chansons* of Louis Bouilhet,[6] recalls the impassioned Romanticism of the youths among whom he grew up:

Mais on n'était pas seulement troubadour, insurrectionnel et oriental, on était avant tout artiste; les pensums finis, la littérature commençait; et on se croyait les yeux à lire, au dortoir, des romans; on portait un poignard dans sa poche comme Antony.... (P. 475)

Such ardent participation in Romantic modes and such enthusiasm for the literature that inspired them cannot be imagined unless we assume that Romanticism embodied the fundamental world view of its enthusiasts. And if this is so, then the works of an adolescent of those times, however derivative they may appear, must be taken as expressing not a set of conventional attitudes derived from his elders but his own personal outlook. Nor is it necessary to assume that for this to be true, the individual youth must submerge his individuality in a purely collective expression of the ideals of his contemporaries. If we consider a broadly defined world view such as Romanticism to possess a "language" of forms, modes of behavior, and so forth,[7] it becomes clear that it generates enthusiasm in its adherents not by forcing them to conform to any specific formula, but by permitting those who accept its language as their own to express through it their own feelings and attitudes. Romanticism, like any vital cultural movement, offered its followers— the youth of Flaubert's generation—a set of categories in which they could formulate their own vision of the world.

Why does Romantic literature, in contrast to that of any earlier period (or indeed of any later one), have such a kinship with the outlook of the youth of its day? In essence Romanticism is the first "adolescent" world view because it prescribes outright rejection of the adult's determinate economic role in bourgeois society. In all literature

---

[6] Reprinted in the *Correspondance,* nouvelle éd. augmentée (Paris: Conard, 1910–1933), VI (1930), 473–487.

[7] The idea of treating cultural forms as languages originated among the Structuralist followers of Lévi-Strauss; in particular such an approach is formulated in *Marxisme et structuralisme* by Lucien Sébag (Paris, 1964).

before the Romantic era the problems that face the hero arise after, not before, his entry into the adult world. Even for a youthful hero like Hamlet, life becomes problematic only after his obligation to take action as an adult has been spelled out to him. Closer to the Romantic era, the works of the eighteenth century took considerable interest in the adolescent, but this interest centered primarily on his discovery of adult sexuality. The scene of sexual initiation which occurs repeatedly in the "licentious" works of this century, for example in the episode of Cécile in *Les liaisons dangereuses* or that of Chérubin in *Le mariage de Figaro,* prefigures the Romantic vision of maturation as a loss of innocence and a fall into a sinful world, but quite obviously the two ages give the pathos of the situation an altogether opposite emphasis.

The Romantics made the unworldliness of the adolescent a model of universal validity: initiation into the adult world was permanently refused. This is above all true of the French Romantics. In comparison with René, even Werther is quite a worldly figure; the German hero at least engages in a love affair, while the Frenchman's only affection is for his sister. For the uprooted aristocrats who, like Chateaubriand, were the founders of French Romanticism, the world outside their fondly remembered ancestral mansion is a barren place, occupied by the hostile forces of the Revolution. The love affair of Werther and Charlotte is the expression of a bourgeois sensibility wholly foreign to Chateaubriand's hero. René does not, like Werther, yearn for that which he cannot obtain; he can only regret what he has lost. His incestuous passion is the sign of his refusal to leave the home of his father and to make his way as an adult in a bourgeois world.

René is easy enough to interpret as reflecting the outlook of the aristocratic *déracinés* to which its author belonged. But its influence on the French Romantics and on Flaubert in particular requires us to seek for it a broader significance. The Romantic youth who kept a dagger in his pocket and affected to drink wine from a skull was more likely to be a purebred bourgeois than an aristocrat, and it was undoubtedly this bourgeois *jeunesse* to which Chateaubriand was referring in his well-known repudiation of his youthful imitators: "Il n'y a pas de grimaud sortant du collège qui n'ait rêvé être le plus malheureux des hommes..."[8] For, although Chateaubriand shared his influence on those of Flaubert's generation with bourgeois Romantics like Hugo and Dumas, *René* offered a clear-cut vision of the adolescent's confrontation

---

[8] Chateaubriand, *Mémoires d'outre-tombe,* Ed. du Centenaire (Paris, 1948), II, 43–44.

with the adult world that later writers could do little more than elaborate on. Other than the purely escapist modes inspired by the historical novel and drama, the "Realist" figures, created by Balzac and Stendhal, of the young bourgeois going out to conquer the world—Rastignac or Julien Sorel—offer the only real alternatives to René. Either the adolescent must accept the rules of adult society and renounce his preworldly "universality" to assume a *particular* place in the world, or he must remain like René an eternal outsider. French Romanticism lacks the optimistic universalism that finds expression in *Faust;* it does not believe in the possibility of grasping the universe as a whole through adult experience.

We now have a skeletal understanding of the adequacy of Romantic literary forms to express the world view of the adolescent of Flaubert's generation. But if these forms had been truly adequate to Flaubert's needs he would never have felt, as he did, the obligation to go beyond them. As my analyses demonstrate, the early works reflect a *continuous* development toward a final transcendence of Romantic forms; thus, their sequence must involve a progressive revelation of the inadequacy of these forms for Flaubert's purposes. How then can it be possible for Romantic forms to be the natural mode of expression for the adolescent Flaubert and, at the same time, for him to uncover through his own application of them their ultimate invalidity for his own efforts as a mature writer?

The answer to this question lies in examination on a deeper level of the relationship of the youth of Flaubert's time to Romantic literature. We have characterized this literature as "adolescent" because of its refusal to accept the realities of the contemporary bourgeois world, and explained in this fashion its appeal to adolescents like Flaubert. Yet Romantic literature was not written by adolescents but by adults; the nonacceptance of the world they glorified was not the normal preworldliness of the youth but the adult's heroic refusal of his assigned role in society. The originality of Romanticism could not, after all, consist merely in endowing adolescents with adolescent attitudes. In setting up the extraworldly adolescent position as a universal model, Romanticism was proclaiming to *adults* the necessity of refusing the bourgeois world. And the attraction of Romantic literature for the youth was precisely that it offered him examples, not of adolescents like himself, but of mature heroes who raised to a universal level of significance his own feeling of alienation from the narrowness of bourgeois society.

It is on the specific nature of this alienation that a contradiction develops between the adult Romantics and Flaubert, the most significant of their youthful imitators. These adults are already a part of the world; theirs is an attitude of "escapism" because they refuse to accept the reality around them. Historical dramas and novels are flights into a world in which adulthood is no longer problematical; works like *René* represent the author's disillusionment with the contemporary world as leading to a refusal of this world, even though this is not a genuine possibility for the author himself. For the adolescent, however, Romantic forms are only escapist insofar as he identifies with the adventuresome careers of the historical heroes. The "contemporary" works that glorify his own extraworldly position are, paradoxically, *realistic*. What for the adult is only an impossible wish is for the youth a reality. He already *is*, as the writer longs to be, outside the bourgeois world.

Yet quite evidently the Romantic youth is not himself satisfied with his extraworldly situation. He too experiences alienation precisely to the extent that he already possesses the desires of an adult for sexual satisfaction and social recognition without having, generally speaking, the facilities for satisfying either. These "worldly" desires are in no sense peculiar to the youth of Flaubert's generation; what is significant about them is their contradictory relation to the Romantic conception of the contemporary world as an essentially negative place.

Because they share the same worldly desires, the adult and the adolescent Romantic do not differ greatly in their attitudes toward the historical hero; both admire him as capable of an immediate self-realization in action that is no longer possible in the modern age. But it is a different story with the contemporary hero, the "René." The adult "René" is one who, as a result of his own disillusioning experience of the world, has come to find no possibility of satisfaction within it. The youth, by taking up the pose of this hero, is merely expressing the reality of his present state in which he stands, whether he likes it or not, outside the adult world of family and career. Rather than rejecting the world as a result of his own experiences, the adolescent refuses it a priori, basing his refusal on the sense of his own intrinsic superiority to the world that he has inherited from René.

Thus the relationship of the adolescent to Romanticism is a double one: on the one hand, his frustrated worldly desires are given expression in the "wish-fulfillment" identification with worldly historical heroes; on the other, he glorifies his own exclusion from the world by modeling himself on the contemporary sufferer from the "mal du siècle." It is this doubleness that eventually separates Flaubert from the Romantic forms he at first wholeheartedly adopted from his elders.

At this point I introduce a concept that is of great value in my analyses: the concept of *praxis*. By this term I designate the career of the individual or, in particular, of the literary protagonist, considered as a significant totality. If the term "totality" is taken in its broadest sense, the "praxis" of the hero can be said to be the subject matter of all narrative literature, all literature that tells a story. But if a totality is more strictly defined as requiring the organic relation of each separate episode of the story to the whole, we can restrict the application of this concept to the modern novel as it originated in the Romantic period. The old picaresque form that dominated the novel from its beginnings (*Lazarillo de Tormes, Don Quixote*) was, in a paradoxical manner, dependent upon the same "feudal" conception of duty that confronted the heroes of Renaissance tragedy. The picaresque hero was free to wander about, with his separate adventures never truly forming a praxial unity, so long as his position in the world represented a *negation* of the duty of the normal individual. Because he stood outside the economic structure of society, as a "rogue" like Lazarillo or a functionless feudal landowner like Quixote, he was bound by no divinely imposed duty and was free to experience from without the manifold of worldly existence. The traditional feudal framework that still surrounded the emerging bourgeois economy recognized the individual for what he *was,* not for what he could become. The career of a picaresque hero had neither beginning nor end because he had essentially no need of arriving anywhere—rogue or nobleman, he was already *there*. But with the destruction of this traditional framework and the formation of a truly bourgeois society, such as was instituted in France after the Revolution, the picaresque novel disappeared. Once the individual's choice of a career had become relatively free, he was forced to view his life as a whole from the standpoint of the goal he sought to attain, as a *becoming* rather than a *being*. Thus the picaresque hero's experience of life as a series of disconnected adventures gave way to the *praxis* of the modern hero—his unitary, unavoidably particular path through the world toward his goal.

It was the particularity, the nonuniversality of this necessary choice that troubled the Romantics. For man to remain a "universal" being and not a mere cog in the wheel, he was required to reject as unworthy of him, like René, all particular roles in society. Yet this rejection was experienced not merely as an *act* but as a process constituting the entire career of the hero: as his praxis. René's career is essentially a process of disillusionment with a world that has failed to offer him the satisfactions he needs and had originally hoped to find within it. Such a vision of worldly experience is consistent in an adult, who has lived through his own disillusionment with the world. But for the adolescent writer like Flaubert who, as I have said, is *already* René, the series of activities through which his own world-rejecting heroes reach their final disillusionment is not his own, but that of an *other*. The protagonist is merely finding out what the author himself already knows without ever having needed to experience it at first hand: the bourgeois world is a worthless place, offering no satisfaction to the superior soul who thirsts only for the ideal. Thus a significant contradiction arises between the writer and his hero. The hero is, by the very nature of the Romantic style, set up as an example of existential validity, a model to be imitated; yet the writer himself has no real desire to imitate his model, for his own superiority to the world exists a priori and needs not be acquired through a praxial totality of worldly experience.

Hence the Romantic hero begins to appear not superior, but actually *inferior* to the youthful writer. The Romantic forms, which by their very nature assert the superiority of the hero and set up his career as a model to be emulated, come into contradiction with the hero's participation in a praxis that the writer had always known to offer only illusory possibilities of satisfaction. This conflict is ultimately resolved in the post-Romantic forms of Flaubert's maturity: the dreams of Emma Bovary are revealed to be not the noble yearnings of a Romantic heroine, but the illusions of an *imitation* Romantic heroine, a woman living within the bourgeois world who falsely conceives of herself as standing outside it. Emma is an unidealized version of the praxial Romantic hero as viewed by the adolescent who is an a priori Romantic hero. Her praxis is not offered as a model. She does not merely, like René, overestimate the possibilities of the world; she overestimates her own capacity to transcend its unheroic banality.

Flaubert's mature conception that such illusions as Emma's are the necessary basis of worldly praxis cannot be derived from his repudiation as an adult of his own Romantic past; it has its source in an original "adolescent" intuition that, from the point of view of one who stands outside the particularity of the world, all praxis is based on illusion. The celebrated "impassibility" of the mature novels is, indeed, an expression of this adolescent outlook, which Flaubert was able to preserve in his maturity by adopting the "extraworldly" career of the writer. The illusory worldly activities of Emma, like those of the earlier Romantic heroes and heroines, retain their roots in the "worldly desires" of the author. But Flaubert knew that no praxis based on these desires could ever make anyone into a Romantic hero superior to the bourgeois world. This superiority was for the mature Flaubert only possible in the praxis of the artist.

It is during the course of the two years covered by this study (1835–1837) that Flaubert gradually came to realize the necessity of basing his protagonist's praxis on illusion. At first he too had written of Romantic disillusionment, of the hero's inevitable discovery that it is impossible for him to fulfill his desires in the world. For the adolescent's superior extraworldly status is, it will be recalled, only half the picture: the youth also possesses worldly desires that he hopes to satisfy vicariously through the activities of his heroes. The contradiction between the positive, exotic side of Romanticism and its negative "contemporary" side did not make itself immediately felt, and Flaubert did not become aware of the intrinsic validity—in Romantic terms—of his own adolescent position until the end of the first year of his career. And after this discovery there remained for him the still more important one that, as an adolescent, protected from the world by his secure position in the family, his own vision of the world could not in fact be embodied in a literary work because it was in its essence *nonpraxial*, external to the adult world of action. But in one of the last works of the second year, "Rêve d'enfer" (March 1837), Flaubert introduces his first "illusionary" protagonist, the heroine Julietta. By the end of two years of his adolescent development the fundamental structural difference between the mature Flaubert and his Romantic masters has already appeared. The contradiction between the extraworldly author and the Romantic hero has entered into the works themselves.

It would be a gross distortion to maintain that the development of Flaubert's post-Romantic vision is in any sense complete at this point. But from now on the early works no longer fit adequately into the Romantic forms the author is forced to find for them. After the first works of the third year, which develop to their limit the insights of "Rêve d'enfer," Flaubert's youthful literary development falls into a permanent state of crisis. In the autobiographical essay "Agonies" (April 1838), written near the end of the third year, Flaubert even despairs of ever being able to express himself through literary means:

Oh! si j'étais poète, comme je ferais des choses qui seraient belles! Je me sens dans le coeur une force intime que personne ne peut voir. Serai-je condamné toute ma vie à être comme un muet qui veut parler et écume de rage? Il y a peu de positions aussi atroces.[9]

And neither of the celebrated autobiographical works of the next years ("Mémoires d'un fou," "Novembre"), for all the literary value of their imagery or their descriptions, possesses a formal unity comparable with that of the works of the earliest periods. These later works, important as their content may be, do not face up to the formal objectives shared by both the earliest stories and the mature novels: the construction of a unified work of fiction around the praxis of its protagonist. Even the first *Education sentimentale* (1843–1845) fails to satisfy this criterion. Not until the appearance of *Madame Bovary* does Flaubert find an adequate fictional structure to replace the long-discarded forms of his Romantic youth.

The earliest stage of Flaubert's development is not, therefore, its most *crucial* stage. On the contrary, a sense of crisis can only arise once the contradictions of the author's early Romanticism have actually become explicit in his works. But the works of these early years are the most revelatory ones from a structural point of view because the evolution they embody is truly organic, determined by the gradual emergence of conflicts, as it were, unconsciously from within the Romantic forms themselves. In the analysis of this evolution we are able to observe in considerable detail the interplay between the writer's personal experience and the preexisting forms in which he seeks to incarnate it—the dialectic that is the source of all formal creation.

A few words remain to be said concerning the format of this study. From a chronological point of view, the works fall naturally into two periods corresponding to the two school years during which they were composed: 1835–36[10] and 1836–37. From a structural point of view, however, the second year also consists of two periods. I have chosen a tripartite structural division, because it fits Flaubert's literary develop-

---

[9] Flaubert, *Œuvres de jeunesse*, 3 vols. (Paris: Conard, 1910), I, 5. Subsequent references to this edition, abbreviated "OJ," will appear in the text.

[10] Two of these works were written in the early months of 1835, before the 1835–36 school year.

ment better than does a division based purely on chronology. Within
the parts each work has been treated in a separate chapter. Because
these stories are, although readily available, virtually unknown to any
but the Flaubert specialist, I have prefaced the analysis of each work
with a summary. A chronological table of the works is found in the
Appendix.

PART ONE

February 1835–June 1836

The literary production of the first period consists of sixteen brief works belonging to a diversity of Romantic genres such as "conte historique," "mystère," "portrait," and "conte fantastique." Of these, six were written as school assignments, five with subjects assigned by Flaubert's teacher.

Many of these works are highly dependent upon historical or literary source material. Where this material is known, it is possible to determine with reasonable accuracy which aspects of the works are original and which are borrowed; in the other works, it is impossible to ascertain how much of the work is attributable to Flaubert alone. But, except for the school assignments, the very choice of a subject is of great significance; furthermore, the author's immature style generally allows the reader to see how closely he identifies with his subject matter, and which aspects of it he finds most important. For instance, the emotionality of the following passage from "La fiancée et la tombe" could hardly be the result of mere imitation: "O pauvre Annette!... ô pauvre enfant tu souffres bien n'est-ce-pas. Si Paul était là, il te secourerait [sic]... ô si Paul était là..." (Bruneau, *Les débuts littéraires*, p. 163). Even in most of those assignments where the plot was predetermined, Flaubert has added incidents and psychological material of his own creation.

Because most of these works were not dated by the author, the exact chronology of the period is impossible to determine. To place the works in a generally reliable sequence, I have made use of handwriting evidence obtained by Bruneau from his study of the manuscripts; where doubt still remains, I have based the order of my presentation on the internal evidence of the works themselves. Specific problems of chronology are taken up in the chapters devoted to the works in question.

CHAPTER I

VOYAGE EN ENFER

January–March (?) 1835

THE NARRATOR is contemplating the world "[du] haut du mont Atlas" when Satan appears and invites him to come with him; "ensuite," says Satan, "tu verras mon royaume."

Satan shows him all human types: kings, pedants, courtesans, and wise men ("les plus fous"). Everywhere one sees unnatural violence: brother killing brother, a mother betraying her daughter, men destroyed by war. The narrator observes two giants fighting, one old and decrepit—"Absolutisme"—the other young and powerful—"Civilisation" (also called "Liberté"); Absolutisme finally succumbs. An old man appears, dressed in rags; he is "la Vérité," despised by mankind and cursing men in his turn.

"Et ton royaume?" the narrator finally asks of his guide; to which Satan answers, "C'est que le monde, c'est l'enfer."

"VOYAGE EN ENFER," the first surviving work of Flaubert's adolescence, is the first of two literary pieces contained in the author's "journal littéraire," *Art et progrès,* datable in the early months of 1835.[1] It is one of a series of "mystical" works in which the characters are confronted with universal forces in a supernaturally concrete form;[2] the figure of Satan, representing the controlling evil of the world, appears in all of these works save "La femme du monde," where he is replaced by the equally negative figure of Death. The style of "Voyage en enfer," more expository than fictional is, as Bruneau has noted, modeled on the *Paroles d'un croyant* of Lamennais. Bruneau, however, was unable to find any specific textual borrowings from this work.

In "Voyage en enfer" the evil of the world is viewed from above by the narrator. Satan does not play here the tempter role of the later works but acts only as a guide for the narrator, whose purely contemplative relationship to the world preserves him from any possible contamination by its evil.

In a highly schematic fashion, "Voyage en enfer" depicts the adolescent's falling from the innocence of childhood into the "guilty" knowledge of worldly evil. The narrator is not yet brought *into* the evil of the world, but neither will he be able to retain the original serenity of

---

[1] See Jean Bruneau, *Les débuts littéraires de Gustave Flaubert* (Paris, 1962), pp. 45–46.

[2] This series includes most notably "La femme du monde," "La danse des morts," "Smarh," and *La tentation de Saint-Antoine.*

[15]

his existence "au haut du mont Atlas." The knowledge that "le monde, c'est l'enfer," imparted to him by Satan's final aphorism, can only bring with it a fearful hatred for the world; the conclusion of the work on Satan's words is meant to convey precisely this feeling to the reader. The narrator-protagonist has not admitted the necessity of living in this "enfer"; but he has already lost his original innocence of its evil nature.

What is the basis for the young Flaubert's negative view of the world? In the broadest sense, all knowledge of the world which takes the place of innocence is essentially a knowledge of evil: the original paradise is itself the good, although it can only be known as such after one has been expelled from it. More specifically, we can see in this contempt for the world a manifestation of the Romantic's rejection, from a superior "universal" standpoint, of the narrow nature of individualist bourgeois society. The adolescent Flaubert applies this Romantic attitude to the world of his own experience, the world within which he has been forced to live, although he has not yet taken an active part in it. The earthly figure most deeply sympathized with by the author-narrator gives an indication of the author's own position in the world:

Et un homme, un pauvre homme en guenilles, à la tête blanche, un homme chargé de misère, d'infamie et d'opprobre, un de ceux dont le front ridé de soucis renferme à vingt ans les maux d'un siècle, s'assit là au pied d'une colonne.... Et il regarda les hommes longtemps, tous le regardèrent en dédain et en pitié, et il les maudit tous; car ce vieillard, c'était la vérité. (OJ I, 5)

Flaubert's identification with this twenty year old "vieillard" is evident:[3] he sees himself as "la Vérité," incarnating the truth of the still unworldly purity that is scorned by a cynical world. Compare with this the strictly autobiographical description of his schooldays in "Mémoires d'un fou:" "J'y vécus... seul et ennuyé, tracassé par mes maîtres et raillé par mes camarades" (OJ I, 490). But this unhappy worldly experience is as yet for him only secondary; his primary identification remains with the observer standing above the world. The same is true in the account of "Mémoires d'un fou": "Les imbéciles! eux, rire de moi!... dont l'esprit se noyait sur les limites de la création.... Moi qui me sentais grand comme le monde..." (OJ I, 490–491). Because he has

---

[3] Cf. this description of a later protagonist with whom Flaubert unquestionably identifies: "Sa taille était celle d'un homme de 20 ans; mais si vous eussiez vu ses joues creuses... *ce front chargé de rides,* vous eussiez dit: *C'est un vieillard*" ("Un secret de Philippe le Prudent, roi d'Espagne," OJ I, 64, italics mine').

not yet displayed a genuine concern for the objects of the world, Flaubert's inferior position within it is of no real consequence to him.

In contrast to this identification with "la Vérité" is that with "Liberté" in the following passage:

Et je vis deux géants: le premier, vieux, courbé, ridé et maigre, s'appuyait sur un long bâton tortueux appelé pédantisme; l'autre était jeune, fier, vigoureux, avait une taille d'hercule, une tête de poète et des bras d'or, il s'appuyait sur une énorme massue que le bâton tortueux avait pourtant abîmée; la massue, c'était la raison.

Et tous deux se battaient vigoureusement, et enfin le vieillard succomba. Je lui demandai son nom.

—Absolutisme, me dit-il.

—Et ton vainqueur?

—Il a deux noms.

—Lesquels?

—Les uns l'appellent: Civilisation, et les autres: Liberté. (OJ I, 4–5)

Here the young, vigorous "Liberté" triumphs over "Absolutisme" by making use of his weapon "la raison." The world may be an "enfer" but it is not invulnerable to progress: this represents the liberal, optimistic side of Flaubert's Romanticism.

Both "la Vérité" and "la Liberté" are prototypes of the author's later heroes—the first is the type of the victim, helplessly dependent on the evil world that mistreats and misjudges him, the second that of the active hero who upholds moral values by destroying the evil he encounters.[4] The underlying problems of these types are later revealed to be more personal and less purely social than their treatment in "Voyage en enfer" would imply.

---

[4] Of the first type, the female protagonists of "La grande dame et le joueur de vielle" and "Un parfum à sentir" are the clearest examples in this period; the second type appears in "Deux amours et deux cercueils," "Marguerite de Bourgogne," and "San Pietro Ornano," among others. Many of the later heroes combine the two types.

Chapter II

UNE PENSEE

February (?) 1835

THE NARRATOR is at a ball; he describes the mad pace of the dancers, the scent of the flowers, the dresses that brush by him. Amid all these whirling figures, one alone notices him, "un sein a palpité pour moi." He asks the girl to dance; they smile at each other, she sighs, and in her happiness she makes him forget the ball. Comes the morning and their farewell; the "pensée" fades away, for "une pensée d'amour, c'est une rose de printemps."

IT IS IN "Une pensée," the brief second piece from *Art et progrès,* that Flaubert first expresses the concern with worldly objects that was absent from the purely contemplative attitude of "Voyage en enfer." Here, the author recounts a personal sexual experience, an ephemeral "pensée d'amour."[1]

The dance, the scene of this momentary infatuation, plays an important role throughout Flaubert's career, most notably in the Vaubyessard ball of *Madame Bovary.* The dance offers Flaubert a vision of a "worldly paradise," an unreal, turbulent atmosphere of sexual freedom in which the cares of the everyday, evil world are swept away. It promises to the Romantic—the young Flaubert or his naïve heroine Emma—an infinity of guiltless love: "toutes ces robes, qui m'ont froissé en me faisant tressaillir d'envie..." (OJ I, 6).

The author retains here within a worldly environment the feeling of superiority to his fellows that was found in "Voyage en enfer"; the other dancers are in the opening sentence described as "fous."[2] But here he is not concerned with perpetuating this attitude of superior contemplation. In his relationship with his partner, the outside world is forgotten: "Je la regarde, elle est heureuse, et j'oublie la valse et le monde" (OJ I, 6). Here a sexual relationship serves the function of removing the author from the "enfer" of the world into a paradise of mutual concern. This is already a function of the dance itself, but it is intensified in the personal relationship: "Se penchant sur moi comme fatiguée, ses lèvres brûlantes me disent un soupir... et je comprends ce soupir" (OJ I, 6).

---

[1] The scene of this experience may perhaps be identified with a ball mentioned elsewhere in *Art et progrès:* "Le bal Lalanne a été magnifique, les toilettes étaient superbes et les costumes riches et frais" (OJ I, 7).

[2] "Des fous bondissent, s'élancent et se redressent, fiers et aigus, c'est la valse, c'est le galop" (OJ I, 6).

The unmistakably *maternal* attitude of the figure "se penchant sur moi" indicates the mutually protective nature of the love relation for Flaubert. He makes no active conquest of his partner; she comes to him and leans over him, protecting him from the world. At the same time, by understanding her "soupir," he consoles her from the worldly evils she has endured. In this brief fragment appears a prototype of the future love affairs of both the author and his male protagonists throughout his career, that of Flaubert for the maternal Elisa Schlesinger, and of Frédéric Moreau for Mme. Arnoux in *Education sentimentale*.

Whirling in the dance or soaring through the air, as in "Voyage en enfer," the author retains his unproblematic superiority. Sexuality, concern for worldly objects, has made its appearance, but Flaubert remains oblivious of any contradiction between the hell of the world as a whole and the paradise of the dance. It is not difficult to understand why. These two visions of life, as hell or as paradise, are dependent upon two separate attitudes: in one, the world is observed from without by a being who feels himself superior to desire; in the other, he experiences the dance as arousing and temporarily satisfying his sexual interests, and thereby as *taking him out of the world*: "j'oublie la valse et le monde." In either case the narrator stands outside the alienation of the "enfer." There is, of course, a contradiction between the superiority of the narrator of "Voyage en enfer" and his submission to desire in "Une pensée," but it cannot reach the notice of the author until the undeniably *worldly* nature of the "paradise" has been recognized. This development is first seen in the scenario "Deux amours et deux cercueils."

CHAPTER III

MATTEO [*SIC*] FALCONE, OU DEUX CERCUEILS POUR UN PROSCRIT

August–September (?) 1835

Argument.[1] un enfant se joue [*sic*][2] dans les champs il entend des coups de fusil. Un homme poursuivi arrive. Il le cache grâce à une pièce de monnaie. Ce même enfant séduit par les promesses d'un garde le livre. Matteo le père de cet enfant apprenant cette lâcheté le couche en joue et le tue. (Bruneau, p. 63)

ALBANO, a dreamy, charming Corsican lad, is playing on a heap of straw when a wounded man appears suddenly. He begs Albano to hide him and, after tossing the boy a coin, crawls under the straw. A few minutes later Albano is surrounded by a dozen guards who ask him if he has seen anyone run past, but the boy plays dumb. Finding that threats are of no avail, the head officer offers Albano a watch, and after a short struggle between his conscience and his desire for the watch, the boy glances pointedly at the heap of straw. As he takes his reward, his father arrives. The officer informs Matteo that his son has helped capture an escaped prisoner, and the fugitive, whose only crime was that of avenging his daughter, angrily threatens to tell everyone "que Matteo est un traître."

That evening Matteo orders his son to follow him; taking his rifle he sets off for the hill, after ignoring his wife's pleas to be permitted to come along. She watches them leave, and soon hears a gunshot; she collapses, groaning, and then rises with a strange smile on her lips.

The next day a child is pulled from the river, his hands tied together with a rosary and his chest pierced by a bullet. A woman hurries up, crying "Mon enfant, mon enfant," and falls to the ground. When the gravedigger arrives with only one coffin, he is told, "vous vous êtes trompé... il en faut deux!"

"MATTEO FALCONE," an adaptation of Mérimée's famous story to which Flaubert has added a characteristic subtitle, is the first of six school compositions ("narrations") written for the author's professor in *Quatrième*, Gourgaud-Dugazon. These brief works are all found in a single manuscript entitled "Narrations et Discours, 1835–1836," described by Bruneau in *Les débuts littéraires* (p. 52) as "un cahier assez épais et de petit format" in which the stories appear to have been copied in the order of their composition. Each "narration" is preceded by a short

---

[1] The significance of the "argument" is explained on p. 21.

[2] The misspellings, errors in punctuation, etc., that are found in the texts quoted from Bruneau, are reproduced from Flaubert's original manuscripts. The texts in the Conard edition of the *Œuvres de jeunesse* lack any such errors because these texts were edited before publication.

summary or, following Bruneau's usage, "argument": "Avant chaque texte, Flaubert a recopié le sujet, donné sans doute par Gourgaud" (p. 54). These "arguments," each of which is reproduced here, pose an interesting problem. In Bruneau's opinion they were dictated to Flaubert by his teacher and employed by him as the unique source of the "narrations."[3] But this is evidently not true; with regard to "Matteo Falcone" in particular, Flaubert employs an abundance of details taken from the Mérimée original which are not mentioned in the "argument," such as the hay pile, the watch, the bandit's wound. It seems evident that here Flaubert had access to either the original story or a thorough summary of it, and that the "argument" is only a summary of either the source or Flaubert's own version. It is clear from this example that we cannot rely on the "arguments" to furnish an accurate idea of what source materials Flaubert had on hand during the composition of these stories.

Bruneau has dated the narrations, for which the manuscript itself gives no dates, by comparison of their handwriting with that of other dated works written during this period. It appears from his investigations that "Matteo Falcone," as well as the following work, "Chevrin et le roi de Prusse," was probably written in August or September 1835.[4]

Flaubert's personal contribution to "Matteo Falcone" is relatively small; most of his story merely summarizes the original. Nor are all the changes he makes necessarily his own and not those of his professor. Nevertheless, the major changes are sufficiently characteristic of Flaubert's method throughout this period to indicate a significant degree of personal involvement. The theme of Flaubert's story is not identical with that of the original. Whereas for Mérimée Mateo was the chief protagonist and his brutal adherence to the unwritten laws of Corsican justice the central idea, Flaubert makes Albano[5] the hero and treats his unhappy fate as a tragic misfortune. This change of emphasis is made clear in his description of Albano's body after his execution by Matteo—a passage with no foundation whatever in the original:

Oh! le pauvre enfant! de beaux cheveux blonds tombaient sur ses épaules, ses lèvres étaient tachetées de noir... sa poitrine était percée d'une balle et l'on distinguait encore sa sanglante trace.... (OJ I, 17)

---

[3] This is implicit throughout his discussion, and nowhere more clearly stated than in the discussion of the present work: *"Mais [Flaubert] ne connaissait pas le chef-d'oeuvre du conteur* [Mérimée's story] qui devait lui servir de corrigé" (Bruneau, *Les débuts littéraires*, p. 63; italics mine).

[4] See *ibid.*, p. 53.

[5] This name is substituted in Flaubert's version for the original "Fortunato."

Here Flaubert does not hide his identification with Albano as the victim of his cruel father. To this we should contrast the description of Albano which opens the story:

C'était en Corse, dans un grand champ, sur un tas de foin que, à moitié éveillé, Albano, couché sur le dos, caressait sa chatte et ses petits, tout en regardant les nuages qui passaient sur le fond d'azur et le soleil qui... dardait ses rayons sur la plaine bordée de coteaux. C'était un bel enfant qu'Albano: de longs cheveux tombaient en boucles sur ses épaules, à chaque sourire vous auriez dit une parole de joie... (OJ I, 14)

The serene unity with nature depicted in this opening scene is that of a childhood "paradise," an innocent, inactive state uncomplicated by the sexuality of the "worldly paradise" of "Une pensée."[6] We can thus interpret Matteo's execution of Albano as a form of the "expulsion" from childhood that was alluded to in the discussion of "Voyage en enfer."

But these passages represent only a relatively minor deviation from the original. Of deeper significance is Flaubert's addition of an episode entirely absent from both the original story and his "argument": the death of Albano's mother. True, the mother appears in the original as begging for mercy for her son.[7] But she remains in the end submissive to the will of her husband, and makes no display of grief for her son. In Flaubert's version, however, the final scene is devoted to the mortal grief of the mother:

Une femme accourt, pâle, échevelée, et regarde longtemps fixement le cadavre; elle se cramponna aux barreaux de la morgue et répétait avec douleur:

— Oh mon enfant! mon enfant!

Puis elle tomba par terre en poussant un cri d'agonie...

Aussitôt arriva le fossoyeur apportant un cercueil.

— Vous vous êtes trompé, dit quelqu'un de la foule, il en faut deux! (OJ I, 17)

Flaubert thought his conclusion of sufficient importance to warrant announcing it in his subtitle "Deux cercueils pour un proscrit." What is the significance of this profound modification of the original plot?

"Matteo Falcone" is the first of Flaubert's works to represent a family situation. The family setting is not, of course, of his own invention, since it is given in the original; what is important is the way in which

---

[6] Cf. Flaubert's quasi-autobiographical characterization of Smarh's childhood: "[Il mena] une vie molle et paresseuse; il vécut commes les fleurs elles-mêmes, vivant au soleil et regardant le ciel" ("Smarh," OJ II, 108).

[7] "Giuseppa courut après Mateo et lui saisit le bras.—C'est ton fils, lui dit-elle d'une voix tremblante" (Mérimée, *Romans et nouvelles* [Paris: Ed. de la Pléiade, 1951], p. 206).

he expresses in this fictional setting attitudes undoubtedly derived from his experiences in his own family. By having the mother die of grief for her son, Flaubert places her in the position of supporting Albano against the "persecution" of his father. In "Une pensée" the author's passive attraction to a quasi-maternal love object who protected him from the "enfer" of the world is seen; here the familial derivation of this attitude is made more explicit. It is the father who forces the "enfer" upon his son, who expels him from the childhood paradise— in this case by killing him—and the mother who seeks vainly to protect him and whose suffering expresses the "injustice"of the father's action. This common element of protection links the paradise of childhood with that of the dance; the latter can be looked upon as a worldly repetition of the former, an attempt to retrieve a lost unalienated state. But here the mother's protection must fail: because the son has committed a crime, his death in itself is not truly unjust. It is noteworthy that while Mérimée emphasizes Fortunato's pleas for mercy from his father,[8] Flaubert eliminates these entirely. This omission cannot be attributed to chance; it is evident that Flaubert considered his hero's own suffering to be rendered unworthy of sympathy by the fact of his guilt. The mother's suffering, however, is as if a *redemption* of her son; her grief at losing him affirms the positive necessity of his presence in the "paradise," just as did the "soupir" of the narrator's dancing partner in "Une pensée."

This interpretation need not be founded on the analysis of this story taken in isolation. "Matteo Falcone" merely fits into a pattern that is repeated throughout the period. "La grande dame et le joueur de vielle" ends in exactly the same fashion as this story, with a mother dying of grief for her dead son;[9] and in "La fiancée et la tombe," it is the hero's fiancée who dies after a vain effort to bring him back to life. In both these later works the male protagonist with whom the author identifies is given a merely secondary role, while the innocent suffering of the female figure receives the greatest emphasis.

The limitations of the assigned plot of "Matteo Falcone" only let through a glimmering of the Oedipal family structure of the later

---

[8] For example, "Mon père, mon père, ne me tuez pas.... Oh! mon père, grâce! pardonnez-moi! Je ne le ferai plus!" (*Ibid.*, p. 206).

[9] "Elle resta muette quelques [*sic*] temps puis [elle] se releva en riant d'un rire de Satan; elle était folle" (Bruneau, *Les débuts littéraires*, p. 126). Cf. OJ I, 17: "Elle... s'affaissa par terre, puis elle se releva et un rire étrange contracta ses lèvres."

works. Here the father's "persecution" of the son has a concrete justification, while the son shows neither the attachment to his protective
mother nor the hatred for his cruel father which characterize the classical Oedipal situation. At this point Flaubert is content to give his hero
the role, indicated by the source, of the guilty yet too-cruelly-punished
victim, without concerning himself with the victim's own reaction to
his persecution, or with the profound necessity that is seen in the later
works to underlie the son's crime itself.

CHAPTER IV

CHEVRIN ET LE ROI DE PRUSSE, OU L'ON PREND SOUVENT LA TETE D'UN ROI POUR CELLE D'UN ANE

August–September (?) 1835

Argument. Frédéric donne à un de ses courtisans une boîte dans laquelle est le portrait d'une tête d'anne [*sic*]. Chevrin y substitute celui du roi, et le passe à table. Voltaire le prend et jure qu'il n'a jamais rien vu de si ressemblant. Le roi qui ne connaissait la boîte [*sic*] est outré de dépit se jette dessus et reconnaît ses traits. (Bruneau, p. 64)

KING FREDERICK of Prussia, that great man who could not only find time to correspond with Voltaire but to jest with his courtiers, one day presents a magnificently jeweled box to Chevrin, who takes it home and opens it, hoping for a decoration, or some money. Instead the box contains a miniature: with turned-down ears, an open mouth, and flared nostrils, it is nothing less than the head of an ass! Chevrin is crushed—"combien d'illusions, d'espérances, de rêves d'ambitions se sont évanouis devant... une tête d'âne!" At first Chevrin thinks the king has forgotten all his services, and he weeps; then it occurs to him that perhaps the king is only jesting.

Several months later at the king's table, Chevrin draws out of his pocket the same little box; it passes from hand to hand, and each guest in turn praises the portrait's resemblance to the king. Frederick, remembering the present he had given Chevrin, grows angrier and angrier till finally he grabs the box—and admits that he mistook his own portrait for that of an ass. "Or on convient," concludes the author, "qu'il n'y a pas grande différence entre la tête d'un roi et celle d'un âne, puisque le possesseur s'y méprend."

"CHEVRIN," written after but at about the same time as "Matteo Falcone," was also composed to an "argument" of Gourgaud, although here too it is likely that Flaubert had more information than his outline would imply.

Although it is written with considerable skill and charm, this story remains the most insignificant of the *oeuvres de jeunesse.* There is little attempt to go beyond the given facts of the plot. But even in this story a few themes of future significance can be unearthed. In the negativity of the characterization of King Frederick, who at the conclusion of the story "trépignait d'indignation, était rouge de colère," and who became the object of the disrespectful epigram that ends the narrative (see the summary), there is made visible the connection between the generalized

contempt for worldly authority expressed in "Voyage en enfer" and
the "son's" justified hatred for the "father figures" of the later works.[1]
The extreme disappointment that Flaubert attributes to his hero—
"Chevrin resta muet... toutes ses espérances déchues, toutes ses illusions
envolées comme un brouillard"—is not at all to be found in the "argument"; it can be linked to the tendency of many of the first-period
works, "Matteo Falcone" among them, to blame the father for the hero's
expulsion from the childhood paradise. But these themes are only indicated here, not developed; my analysis of them must accordingly await
the appearance of more personal and substantial works.

---

[1] The terms "son" and "father" will recur throughout my analyses, but are not
generally put in quotes except when they might otherwise be misinterpreted. They
refer not, of course, to the actual family situation of the characters, but to their
possession of certain traits characteristic of the roles of son and father in the
Oedipal family structure.

Chapter V

DEUX AMOURS ET DEUX CERCUEILS: DRAME EN CINQ ACTES

Summer (?) 1835

I. *Le mariage du Duc:* Louisa is married to the Duke Henri d'Harmans; the husband is indifferent to the marriage, but she is warm and affectionate.

II. *Au bal:* One of her admirers (Ernest) whom she receives becomes drawn to her, originally out of compassion and then out of love.

III. *Pitié:* Louisa at first repulses Ernest but finally permits him to remain "à titre d'ami."

IV. *Amélie:* The Duke's mistress Amalie [*sic*] is terribly jealous of Louisa and steals from her "tout ce qu'elle possède."

V. *Empoisonnée!!* Amalie puts arsenic in Louisa's milk every day; finally the legitimate wife dies. She is avenged by Ernest who kills not Amalie but the duke, who had accused Ernest himself of the poisoning; "tu es l'assassin," Ernest tells the duke, "et je suis le Bourreau."

THIS BRIEF sketch—the plot outline for an (unwritten) drama—is the first of six early works of Flaubert first made available to the public in Bruneau's study.[1] By virtue of the similar format and handwriting of the manuscripts, Bruneau has dated this fragment in the same period as the earliest "narrations" ("Matteo Falcone," "Chevrin," "Le moine des Chartreux") and the "Mort du duc de Guise,"[2] although its precise location in the series of works is uncertain. We know only that it was written at some time in 1835, before the modification of the author's handwriting, which dates from the last months of the year. I have chosen to treat it at this point because it reveals a deeper concern with certain problems that were only hinted at in "Voyage en enfer" or "Une pensée." "Matteo Falcone" and "Chevrin" are too insignificant to give any real insight in these matters, and the chronological position of "Deux amours" in relation to them is of little importance.

Bruneau suggests no source material for the plot outlined here by Flaubert. There seems no reason to doubt the originality of this plot although, as Bruneau points out, it shares its theme of adultery with Dumas's *Antony* as well as with numerous other Romantic dramas. But this theme, with its Oedipal implications, can hardly be seen as an externally imposed limitation on the author.

---

[1] "Deux amours" appears in Bruneau, *Les débuts littéraires,* on pp. 122–123.

[2] See *ibid.,* p. 122.

The relationships between the characters of "Deux amours" closely reproduce the classical Oedipal situation. The protagonist (Ernest) loves a married woman—although without possessing her—and in the end kills her husband; the plot could scarcely be more explicit in its Oedipal content. Yet it is not sufficient merely to uncover this content; my chief concern is to uncover the manner in which the work embodies a vision specific to the author.

I have not yet brought into my analyses the conception of "praxis" as the mode in which the characters of a literary work incarnate the writer's fundamental vision, for in the preceding works either no real praxis appeared ("Voyage en enfer," "Une pensée") or the protagonist's activity was wholly dictated by Flaubert's source material ("Matteo Falcone" and "Chevrin"). In the plot of "Deux amours," schematic as it is, the protagonists live and act in the world and thereby carry out a praxis. Their acts and relationships must be viewed within the over-all framework of this "worldly career."

The praxis of the "son" Ernest has clearly shown its roots in the crimes of the classical Oedipus legend. These deeds have a fundamental significance because they "praxialize"—that is, they express in praxial terms—the process repeated by every adolescent entering the world: the establishment of *his own* place in the world in emulation of the father, and the assumption of the father's adult sexual privileges in his choice of a love object with whom he seeks to reinstitute the unalienated nature of the original mother-son relationship.

These acts of entering the world are not simply "natural"; they are, as the legend shows us, *criminal* acts, crimes against the already established parental order. At the same time, they are a necessary aspect of the child's entry into the world. In each historical period the problem of this crime and this necessity is solved in a different manner. My question here can only be: how is this problem to be solved for Flaubert?

For Flaubert as an adolescent in the Romantic era, the painfulness, if not the criminality, of the original praxial act—the entry into the world—could not be hidden. To enter the adult world was, for the Romantic, to leave the unity of the childhood "homeland," to *fall* into the world of action, the bourgeois world in which praxis has merely an economic significance. This Romantic conception is the source of the vision of "Voyage en enfer." The adult state is felt as one of unideality, of alienation from the original paradise of childhood. At the same time, the necessity of finding a place in the world is not simply to be brushed aside. In particular the sexual aspect of entering the world is of critical importance. The "necessity" of sexuality is experienced most strongly by the adolescent, forcing him to face the fact that he is *already* willy-nilly alienated from his original innocence. This alienation can only be removed in an ideal love relationship that, like the "pensée d'amour," can shut the individual off from the evil world that surrounds him. From this standpoint the only valid praxis is the search for a sexual "paradise" that can "dis-alienate" the individual and thereby reproduce in a worldly form the original, unalienated state of childhood. This ideal love contains two equally important components: it is an adult sexual relationship, a satisfaction of desire; but it is also—and this second element should not be overlooked—the adolescent's way of asserting his superiority over the "bourgeois" father-world. Thus ideal love solves not only the problem of sexuality, but that of recognition as well. By asserting his superiority to the everyday world, the Romantic hero attains a status a priori higher than that attainable through bourgeois worldly achievements.

At the same time, the adultery theme of "Deux amours" demonstrates that the superiority of the Romantic hero is intimately bound up with the criminality of his love. The adultery theme itself is no invention of the Romantics but can in fact be found at the roots of modern Western culture—the culture that Hegel called "Romantic"—as Rougemont, for one, has ably shown.[3] What is new in the Romantic treatment of this theme is the attempt to justify the crime on the grounds of a "universal" morality that transcends the evil social structure of which marriage is a part. The criminal need feel no guilt; it is the legitimate husband who is really guilty because he makes use of unjust social conventions to tyrannize his wife. Rather than being a guilty act, the adulterer's crime is precisely what insures his superiority to his bourgeois environment.

These generalizations are evidently true for Ernest, in whose relationship to Louisa Flaubert combines the sexual paradise of the dance with the moral superiority of "Voyage en enfer." Ernest meets Louisa "au bal" in the second act; he is primarily attracted to her through pity at the "mauvais traitements de son mari." The "soupir" of the dancing partner in "Une pensée" is now concretely associated with the marriage relationship; the woman needs the ideal love of the hero as a compensation for her unideal relationship with her husband.

The establishment of an "amitié" with Louisa is only the beginning

---

[3] Denis de Rougemont, *L'amour et l'occident* (Paris, 1940).

of Ernest's praxis; his most meaningful act is his execution of the duke
for his indirect role in Louisa's death. Here the Oedipal act of "killing
the father" is given a full moral justification; in true Romantic fashion
its original criminality is altogether eliminated. How does this execution interpret the problem of worldly praxis? By killing the duke,
Ernest is destroying the evil worldliness that led to the death of the
innocent Louisa. The duke's illicit relationship to his mistress, who was
in fact the assassin of Louisa, is an example of the evil, worldly
adultery castigated in "Voyage en enfer":

Là un roi savourait, dans sa couche d'infamie où de père en fils ils reçoivent des
leçons d'adultère, il savourait les grâces de la courtisane favorite qui gouvernait la
France. (OJ I, 4)

Amalie, like the "courtisane favorite," is allowed to dominate the duke's
household. Here too the "son" Ernest, in becoming the "ami" of
Louisa, is certainly learning "des leçons d'adultère" from the "father,"
the duke—but Flaubert is not yet ready to admit this. The sexuality of
the duke as manifested in his adulterous love is evil, while that of Ernest
is represented as wholly virtuous.

The son's praxis is thus intrepreted not as a criminal entry into the
world, but a virtuous destruction of the worldly. In a very real sense
this destruction represents an *escape* from the world. Ernest's final
declaration, "tu es l'assassin et je suis le Bourreau," is no mere cry of
vengeful triumph. In becoming the "Bourreau"—with a capital "B"—
Ernest has set himself above the world in the condemning position of
the narrator of "Voyage en enfer." As "le Bourreau" he carries out not
any narrow desires of his own, but the exigencies of a transcendent
morality. Instead of dying at the end of the play as might be expected,
he is lifted out of the worldly realm and placed in a superworldly
position. What is there in this praxis that is specifically Flaubertian?

To answer this question we must examine not only the actions of the
hero, but the career of the heroine as well. Indeed, it is Louisa and not
Ernest who is the center of attention throughout the first four acts of
the play; her name heads Flaubert's list of "Personnages"; it is her
story, far more than Ernest's, that "Deux amours" seems designed to
present. What does Louisa's career consist of? Like the mother in "Matteo Falcone," she exists above all by suffering—from the "mauvais
traitements de son mari" to the thefts and finally the poisoning by
Amalie. Why does Flaubert, here as in "Matteo Falcone," take such an
interest in the woman's misfortunes? These misfortunes are the result of

the evil worldliness of the father Henri; in them is demonstrated the negativity of the "enfer." It is in compensation from them that Louisa must turn to the "ideal" lover Ernest, who becomes her *ami* and avenges her unjust death. Thus the woman's suffering is the real source of the man's praxis. It is her alienation, not his, that is primary. This pattern is repeated in many of the early works, and finds its mature realization in *Madame Bovary*, where, however, the "ideal" hero never arrives, because he exists only as the illusory object of the woman's passive awaiting.

Because of the emphasis placed on the woman's alienation, the male hero of "Deux amours" finds his role reduced essentially to that of an ideal *negation* of the worldly cause of this alienation. The son does not take over the father's place in the world—he merely destroys it. Consequently, the son never truly becomes a part of the world; his most significant act is not that of a worldly lover but of "le Bourreau." This reluctance to choose a truly worldly hero is symptomatic of the predicament of the romantic youth of Flaubert's generation; if the world is a priori an evil place, what is the point of seeking within it a "paradise" that cannot endure? This question only receives its difinitive answer in the *Education sentimentale* of 1845, with the removal of the hero (Jules) from the world of action to the contemplative sphere of the artist. Until then the problem of the romantic hero's worldly praxis continues to haunt the early works. The criminal side of Ernest's adulterous love, which Flaubert is able to disregard in "Deux amours," forces itself upon him, while the need to represent a truly worldly, adult hero makes itself more explicit.

CHAPTER VI

MORT DU DUC DE GUISE
September 1835

I. *Le Club du Guisard:* Surrounded by the noisy toasts of a crowd of well-wishers, the duke of Guise is handed a note of warning: "Donnez-vous de garde; on est sur le point de vous jouer un mauvais tour." Carelessly he traces an answer with the tip of a dagger: "On n'oserait." His friends attempt to impress upon him the danger he is exposed to at Court; he is detested by Catherine de Médicis, the true ruler of France, while Henri III bitterly envies his "gloire." The duke considers spending a few days away from Court, but the archbishop of Lyon protests: how can the duke think of leaving now, when all his plans for taking over the throne are just coming to fruition! Guise assents, and adds, characteristically, "je la verrais [la mort] entrer par la fenêtre [que] je ne voudrais pas sortir par la porte pour fuir." The duke's friends cheer, and all exit.

II. *Charlotte de Beaune:* A disheveled young woman enters, her teeth chattering from fear; she brings no news of a throne for Guise, she says, but has come to warn her lover that his death is imminent: "Demain, tu dois mourir." At his council tomorrow, Henri is going to propose the duke's assassination. Guise brushes off her urgent pleas for him to escape, and asks only for "un baiser avant la tombe."

III. *Le Conseil du Roi:* Henri III convokes the council: "Mes chers amis, il y a trop longtemps que le duc est roi et le roi duc." With Guise's murder, everything will return to its natural order. The king's advisers suggest instead imprisoning the duke for life, but Henri insists that the only sure method is assassination. Eight of his men offer their services.

IV. *Un Assassinat par un Roi:* The king assigns the men their places and retires to his chamber. Thirty guards have been posted on the stairway, and the eight assassins wait in the king's chamber—all for the killing of a single man! In the morning Guise is stopped outside the castle gate by a man who warns him, with tears in his eyes, that he will not leave the castle alive. The duke, thanking him but ignoring the advice, makes his way up the stairs; he is informed that His Majesty is asking for him. Guise enters the chamber but instead of the king he sees the assassins posted there; they pounce on him. Dying, Guise collapses on the king's bed. Henri enters, kicks the body and spits in his face. But then, for an instant, "Henri trembla devant le cadavre du duc de Guise."

"DUC DE GUISE," dated by Flaubert himself September 1835, was apparently not written as a school assignment.[1] But it is if anything less original than any of the "narrations" for, as B. F. Bart[2] has shown, the work is almost entirely plagiarized from the account of Guise's assassination

---

[1] "Le manuscript ne figure pas dans le Cahier des *Narrations et discours,* et ne porte aucune indication qui pourrait mener à y voir un exercice scolaire" (Bruneau, *Les débuts littéraires,* p. 81, n. 8).

[2] "Flaubert, plagiarist of Chateaubriand," MLN, May 1950, pp. 336–339.

by Chateaubriand in his *Analyse raisonnée de l'histoire de France*,[3] with Flaubert's sole contribution to the text being limited to a few added exaggerations.[4] Thus the most significant aspect of this story for my purposes is the choice of the subject matter itself.

Taken from the dramatized Romantic history of Chateaubriand, "Duc de Guise" relies heavily on the historical prestige of its hero to impress us with the significance of the events it narrates. This technique is highly characteristic of the Romantics; as Bruneau points out, "Flaubert a transformé le récit de Chateaubriand en une suite de 'scènes historiques,' genre littéraire très à la mode à cette époque" (*Les débuts littéraires*, p. 82). It is an aspect of the Romantics' nostalgia for temporally (or spatially) distant milieux in which the individual was not yet alienated from the world, but where an "ideal" state of identity still subsisted between his being as an individual and his worldly praxial position. This historical or exotic return to a lost "land of the ideal" may be called *idealization*. Rather than representing contemporary man *seeking* a praxis in which to fulfill his being, the writer accepts the identity of praxis and individuality in a ready-made form in the historical heroes of a more "natural," prebourgeois society.

This "land of the ideal" is not identical with the "worldly paradise" of "Une pensée." This paradise is not praxial; it is a timeless, disalienated state that corresponds to the dreams of the "son" for a solution to his alienation. The historical ideal is, on the contrary, a world in which the characters act, have goals, and the like, without being alienated from their position in the world. Rather than a possibility of the son, it is a positive vision of the world of the father, but one where the adult's established position in the world is not an object of negation, as in the contemporary world of "Voyage en enfer" and "Deux amours," but of admiration.

The specific attraction of the idealized subject matter of "Duc de Guise" for Flaubert is consequently that it allows him to glorify or "idealize" the worldly existence of his hero. The same is true in Chateaubriand's text, but, as Bruneau observes,

[On] peut penser que les raisons de l'admiration de Flaubert sont bien éloignées de celles de Chateaubriand. Pour ce dernier le duc de Guise représente la catholicité; pour Flaubert le duc est avant tout un "héros," un "Titan" dont la glorieuse destinée est tragiquement brisée par un de ces êtres hypocrites et méchants [Henri III] qui hantent les drames et romans historiques de l'époque romantique. (P. 82)

---

[3] Chateaubriand, *Œuvres complètes* (Paris: Garnier, 1860), X, 282–290.

[4] For example, substituting "poignard noirci" for "crayon" as the duke's writing implement (Bruneau, *Les débuts littéraires*, p. 83).

If we assume that Flaubert's choice of Guise as a hero was genuinely his own, what specific characteristics of this "Titan" are likely to have attracted his interest? The duke is essentially a father figure, destroyed by the envious "son" Henri. Although this correlation is already strongly suggested in the text of Chateaubriand, Flaubert seems concerned to emphasize it. Thus, where in Chateaubriand the king is called simply a "fou," Flaubert makes him into an "enfant," a "roi faible et imbécile."

Chateaubriand:

Mendreville déclara... que l'archévêque de Lyon parlait du roi comme d'un prince sensé et bien conseillé, *mais que le roi était fou, qu'il agirait en fou.*[5] (Chateaubriand, X, 283)

Flaubert:

Croix-Dieu! dit Mandreville [*sic*]... *Henri est un roi faible et imbécile; c'est un enfant que votre roi,* chétif arbrisseau qu'emportera le premier souffle d'une révolution.[6] (OJ I, 35)

And at the end of the story Flaubert adds a paragraph describing a guilt never felt by the murderer in the original:

Un instant pourtant, ayant bien considéré toutes ces plaies profondes, cette terrible et mâle figure et dont les yeux ternes et livides *semblaient lui reprocher son crime,* oui, un instant, Henri trembla devant le cadavre du duc de Guise. (OJ I, 39)

Why does Flaubert outdo Chateaubriand in enthusiastically taking the part of the father against the son? In the idealized universe of this historical narrative, as opposed to the "enfer" of the present, the son's Oedipal attempt to overthrow the father's authority has lost the redeeming features of an opposition to worldly evil. If in "Deux amours" Flaubert took the position of an adolescent forced to enter an evil world of which the "father" was the chief representative, in "Duc de Guise" there is no such problem; paternal authority, as represented by Guise, should rightly be imposed on the "enfant" Henri. The triumph of the son here is thus truly a crime. Flaubert's identification with the father serves to bring out the guilty aspect of the Oedipal confrontation that was absent in "Deux amours." Although the adult in the contemporary world lacks the solid righteousness of the Duc de Guise, he does have a social function, a recognized place in the world that Flaubert envies and admires at the same time that he condemns it. In the following work, "Le moine des Chartreux," the complex structure of the son's crime against the father is more explicitly revealed.

---

[5] Italics mine. Henceforth all italics in quoted passages are mine, unless otherwise indicated.

[6] Flaubert also makes the archbishop of Lyon, who in Chateaubriand's text spoke of the king as "un prince sensé," call him nothing more than "un enfant qui menace."

CHAPTER VII

LE MOINE DES CHARTREUX, OU L'ANNEAU DU PRIEUR

September (?) 1835

Argument. Un prieur est enterré avec une bague d'un prix considérable. Un moine désire s'en emparer; Pourquoi?...

Il va au caveau... sa terreur, les combats de sa conscience, bref il prend l'anneau [*en note:* avec peine], le passe à son doigt, recloue le cercueil mais il n'a pris garde à sa robe qui reste accrochée dedans. Il veut s'en aller, se sent retenir, tombe et meurt. (Bruneau, p. 61)

EIGHT DAYS ago the prior of the Grande-Chartreuse was buried; Brother Bernardo still remembers all the details of the interment—the prior's long gown, his white beard, his folded hands. Here his thoughts stop: it is the image of the old man's ring that tortures him. Not even the silence of the night can bring repose, not even prayer! and yet all of nature is at rest. To possess it, to be able to dream of the world: thus thinks Bernardo. "Oui, j'irai, je le prendrai, cet anneau!" And is it not only natural that a man deprived of reality will seek his pleasures in illusion? Bernardo knows that "cet anneau de prieur se [rattache] à des souvenirs de jeunesse et d'amour." The monk dreams of those who enjoy worldly pleasures; he sees the nearby castle and imagines the gaiety of the *bal*. But the thought of the ring never leaves him.

At midnight everyone is asleep; now is the time, he thinks. Bernardo takes a lantern and, shivering with fear, hurries to the church and descends into the vault. He must find it quickly, or his absence will be noticed. Trembling, he starts to read the inscriptions on the tombstones; "à chaque marbre qu'il touchait, il lui semblait que le mort allait se réveiller pour le damner et le maudire." Finally he finds the prior's tomb, opens it, removes the winding sheet: there is the ring. Bernardo justifies his action—what need has a dead man of a ring?—and puts it on his own finger. Just then the bell chimes for the night prayer. Bernordo tries to rise up, but something is holding his robe; as he lurches backward, his head strikes the stone wall.

Several years later, the vault is opened again for an interment. A skeleton with a broken skull is found, his robe caught in the nails of a nearby coffin. The monks bury him where he lies and chant a *De Profundis* for the repose of this unknown soul.

"Eh bien," concludes the narrator, "il avait voulu l'anneau pour avoir la vie;... il avait vécu, car rêver, craindre, attendre, posséder à l'agonie, c'est vivre."

WITH "Le moine" we return to the series of "narrations." According to Bruneau (*Les débuts litteraires*, p. 53), the handwriting of all but the last paragraph of this story resembles that of "Duc de Guise," while this conclusion is written in a more mature hand similar to that of the later "narrations" ("Dernière scène de la mort de Marguerite de

Bourgogne," "Portrait de Lord Byron," "San Pietro Ornano"). Thus I assume this narration to be more or less contemporary with "Duc de Guise."

The sources made available by Bruneau[1] indicate that Flaubert has made much freer use of his material here than in the preceding imitative works. Whereas in the "argument" (and, somewhat less explicitly, in the original plot of Filon) the monk steals the prior's ring out of cupidity, solely for its monetary value, Flaubert makes the ring a symbol of liberation from "imprisonment" in the monastery, and supplies a page-long description of Bernardo's longings for the joys of the world outside, as well as a conclusion justifying his ill-fated act.

The cloistered frustration of the monk has given Flaubert the opportunity to describe his own adolescent frustrations with greater explicitness than in any other work of the period. From within his cell Bernardo looks out with envy on the world and its freedoms:

> Oh! continuait Bernardo en regardant la forêt, là dedans peut-être se promène un jeune homme qui aspire à longs traits sa vie de bonheur; contemplant avec amour et extase un ciel pur et azuré... il peut porter au loin ses yeux où respirent la vigueur et l'avenir, sans qu'ils retombent avec dédain sur les barreaux de la cage d'un homme! (OJ I, 28)

Here, from the standpoint of the monk unable to enter it, the world appears not as an "enfer" but a paradise. The "ciel pur et azuré" is reminiscent of the opening of "Matteo Falcone": "Albano, couché sur le dos [regardait] les nuages qui passaient sur le fond d'azur" (OJ I, 14). But now the youth is not simply lying half asleep but breathing in deeply "sa vie de bonheur"; he is not a child like Albano but a "jeune homme" already part of the world.

Further on Bernardo's dreams grow more sensual:

> Puis regardant le château:... La valse peut-être bondit sur le parquet, saccadée et délirante! Il y a des femmes qui tourbillonnent entraînées dans les bras de leurs danseurs; il y a des laquais aux livrées d'or... il y a des lustres aux mille reflets, des diamants qui brillent dans les glaces; il y a des roses de la vie! (OJ I, 28)

Flaubert here duplicates the "paradisial" dance scene of "Une pensée."[2] There is no more guilt inherent in the dance than in the young man's

---

[1] The original plot, reproduced by Bruneau, is taken from the *Nouvelles narrations françaises* of Auguste Filon (Paris, 1834), p. 110. The "argument" assigned by Gourgaud was probably an outline of this plot (Bruneau, *Les débuts littéraires*, pp. 59–62). In the absence of any indication to the contrary, I assume that Flaubert had access only to the "argument."

[2] Cf.: "toutes ces femmes qui tourbillonnent et ces glaces qui reluisent et ces lumières qui flamboient (OJ I, 6).

walk in the forest; both are depicted as parts of a guiltless world, the fusion of the paradise of "Une pensée" with the idealized adult world of "Duc de Guise." It is in Bernardo's desire to escape his prison ("la cage d'un homme") and enter this world that the guilt resides. For it is this desire that will make him commit the fatal crime of stealing the prior's ring.

In what way is the ring connected with Bernardo's deams of freedom? " 'Oh!' " exclaims the monk, " 'l'avoir! le tenir! le posséder! rêver un monde dans une prison, penser à la vie dans un sépulcre! Oui, j'irai, je le prendrai, cet anneau!' " (OJ I, 28). Here the ring is equated with "la vie"; Bernardo dreams of an idealized life that he will possess by stealing the ring. But what will be the sense of this "possession"? Flaubert explains:

En effet, n'était-il pas naturel que ce pauvre homme, qui n'avait pas la réalité pour jouir, souhaitât des illusions pour rêver? Et on savait dans le couvent que cet anneau de prieur se rattachait à *des souvenirs de jeunesse et d'amour, dont sa piété n'avait pu se défaire,* car après la passion abattue il reste dans le coeur de l'homme des racines inviolables qui se rattachent à d'anciens souvenirs comme le lierre qui, pourtant mort, embrasse le chêne sur lequel il a grandi! (OJ I, 28)

The ring is associated with the prior's "jeunesse et amour"; by taking it, Bernardo will possess "des illusions pour rêver" based on the prior's past experiences—these are not wholly without guilt, as the phrase "dont sa piété n'avait pu se défaire" indicates. There is, however, a certain ambiguity in the attribution of these "souvenirs" which cannot be accidental; although in reality belonging to the prior, they are also Bernardo's own memories of his "pensée d'amour." And further on the ring is described without reference to the prior as a "souvenir du monde, qui allait habiter avec lui [Bernardo] dans le tombeau de sa vie" (OJ I, 29). Thus Bernardo's own "souvenirs" are no longer really his, but are attached to the prior's ring. His "pensée d'amour" was but a glimpse of a world that cannot be his own.

Although the theft of the ring is the basis for the plot assigned to Flaubert, this association of it with "souvenirs de jeunesse et d'amour" is wholly his own invention. The Oedipal significance thus given the ring is so striking that Theodor Reik singled out this story for particular attention in his study of Flaubert:

It is truly astonishing what richness in inner experience this apparently innocent story of a thirteen year old possesses. He is the Monk (chaste and solitary), he desires the ring (=marriage-ring) of the Prior (=Father). With it is bound up sexual pleasure (with the mother).[3]

The ring is the symbol of the father's sexual privileges, of a *legitimate* worldly sexuality with which the monk's dreams of freedom are associated, and which his own "souvenirs" never really possessed. And Bernardo's guilt for his crime is indeed strongly associated with fear of the "father":

Où donc est le forfait, disait-il, de prendre quelque chose à un cadavre? En jouit-il de son anneau, puisqu'il n'a plus ni vie, ni souvenir, ni monde à rêver?" et il saisit cette main froide et décharnée, s'arrêta encore un instant et *regarda avec peine cette barbe blanche, cet air de majesté répandu sur le visage du vieillard. Oh! c'est alors qu'il aurait voulu qu'il n'y eût dans le coeur des hommes ni remords ni conscience,* qu'il aurait voulu oublier le passé, le présent même, et ne penser qu'à l'avenir et à ses rêves! Et il touchait la main d'un cadavre! (OJ I, 30)

The corpse of the prior haunts Bernardo just as that of Guise, "cette terrible et mâle figure... dont les yeux ternes et livides semblaient lui reprocher son crime" (OJ I, 39) had terrified Henri; the son trembles at this vision of the father whom he must despoil of his worldly being.

How is the monk's crime to be related to the son's praxis in the preceding works? As in "Duc de Guise" the crime is the son's attempt to replace the father in his worldly position, but now this "position" is not seen as a social dignity but as an adult experience of sexuality, "des souvenirs de jeunesse et d'amour." The son's own memory of his fleeting experience of the worldly paradise in "Une pensée" is now associated with such adult experience; the train of thought that carries Bernardo from the ring to the vision of the dance can only be understood in this light. In "Deux amours" we were confronted with a similar situation. Louisa was already the wife of the "father," the Duke Henri d'Harmans; in becoming her "ami" Ernest was taking the father's sexual position for himself, the equivalent of Bernardo's theft of the ring. But in "Deux amours" Flaubert did not dwell on the guilty nature of Ernest's activity; it was justified by the duke's cruelty to his wife. Here, where the father-son relationship is considered without reference to the woman, the son's act can have no justification in her need for him; it becomes a selfish, worldly deed, a crime against the father. And yet, as is seen in the final paragraph, it is in this crime that life consists:

Eh bien! il avait voulu l'anneau pour avoir la vie, lui; il avait vécu, car rêver, craindre, attendre, posséder à l'agonie, c'est vivre. (OJ I, 30)

---

[3] Theodor Reik, *Flaubert und seine "Versuchung des heiligen Antonius"* (Minden, 1910), p. 96. Translation mine.

This is an explicitly *praxial* view of life, not as a return to a state of moral equilibrium, but as a worldly effort at grasping the object of one's desires, regardless of the guilt that may be attached to this action. In daring to commit a crime to attain the disalienation he seeks, Bernardo has uncovered the essentially criminal nature of the son's praxis.

The contradictory relationship between the "worldly paradise" and the "enfer" is now brought into sharper focus than in the preceding works. The prior's "souvenirs... dont sa piété n'avait pu se défaire" are to offer Bernardo, through the symbolic intermediary of the ring, a substitute for the paradisial existence from which his imprisonment separates him. But what is the meaning of this "imprisonment"? It is not a mere external constraint; it is imposed on Bernardo by his conscience, separating him from the inferior but happy beings in the outside world:

Maintenant, pensait-il en regardant la lune qui se reflétait sur les barreaux de sa cellule et sur le christ d'étain suspendu à son lit, maintenant il y en a qui vivent heureux et contents, sans penser à la veille, au lendemain, à la vie, à l'éternité, et qui vivent pour le jour dont il recueillent les joies comme le parfum qui s'exhale d'une fleur. (OJ I, 28–29)

It is the worldly life of these "heureux" that was designated as the "enfer" in "Voyage en enfer"; and it is still an "enfer" in the sense that Bernardo must look upon it as a *temptation* into which he is obligated not to fall. How does the ring offer him a possibility of overcoming the guilty nature of this paradise? Through the ring he will possess the "souvenirs" as *already* experienced by the prior, without having to act in the world on his own. That the precise mechanism of this transfer of the "souvenirs" is never made clear is not an accident; it is impossible to explain the symbolic function of the ring in "realistic" terms. Its existence provides for something inconceivable in the real world: the transfer of the father's adult experience to the son without the latter's having to go into the world to get this experience for himself. It is in this sense that Bernardo's interest in the ring is explained as stemming from his desire for "des illusions à rêver."

In "Le moine" the criminal nature of the son's praxis is made explicit, but the crime is kept outside the world, wholly within the father-son relationship. What does this reveal about Flaubert's vision of the son's position? The father already possesses worldly being (the "souvenirs de jeunesse et d'amour"). The son cannot establish *his own* being in the world independently of the father's: for this it would be necessary for him to obliterate his consciousness of the evil, unjustified nature of this being. He can only desire to "be" the father, to step into the father's place in a single concrete act; this he hopes to do by stealing the ring.

The son's praxis is thus no longer a negation of evil, as it was in "Deux amours" where Ernest's replacement of the Duke through his *amitié* with Louisa was treated chiefly from the *woman's* point of view, as a consolation, not a crime. This praxis must now involve the acceptance of the father's worldly being. But Bernardo's desire through an instantaneous act to step into the father's ready-made position is a sign of the superficiality of this conception of praxis. The temporal nature of action in the world is bypassed in this act, which breaks the continuity between present and past: "Oh! c'est alors... qu'il aurait voulu oublier le passé, le présent même, et ne penser qu'à l'avenir et à ses rêves" (OJ I, 30). This praxis is not *in* time, it is an attempt to *get out of* time. In his refusal of the normal temporal structure of praxis, Bernardo prefigures Frédéric Moreau, the hero of *Education sentimentale*, for whom any continuous effort toward a worldly goal is impossible; the difference is, of course, that in this early Romantic work an *ideal* goal— the ring—does exist in a concrete, immediately graspable form.

Thus the outlines of the author's mature conceptions of praxis are already visible in these early efforts. The woman—Louisa in "Deux amours"—suffers from the negativity of the world and *awaits* an ideal lover; the man—Bernardo—for whom such passivity is impossible seeks to disalienate himself through action, but without accepting the temporal continuity of worldly praxis. Each character seeks a kind of ideal being that stands outside of time, the Romantic "worldly paradise."

But if the goals of Flaubert's protagonists are Romantic, in what sense do these works foreshadow the mature, post-Romantic novels? Is it not simply that in these later works Flaubert revealed the falsity of his earlier, Romantic efforts?

In the broadest sense I am saying no more than this. But this statement contains more than appears at first glance. If these early works can later be revealed as false, then the falsity must have already been present at the time of their writing. Flaubert, as a youthful Romantic, already expressed in spite of himself the falsity of Romantic structures. In the great novels of the Romantic period, worldly temporality may be renounced (as in *Le Rouge et le noir* or, on a more abstract level, in *René*), but only as a result of the worldly experience of the hero. In Flaubert's early works this temporality is rejected a priori; the protagonists reach for a concrete "ideal" that will disalienate them instantaneously, and for one reason or another fail to attain it. The weakness of these youthful works lies in this "for one reason or another"; if the ideal has a concrete existence, as it does in the present story, then why must the protagonists *necessarily* fail to grasp it? Throughout the stories, Flaubert seeks a means of revealing this necessity in Romantic literary terms. Only by the end of the third period (Spring 1837) is necessity given a firm basis in the radical incompatibility of the ideal with the worldly—the rejection of the Romantic conception of a "worldly paradise." Even when this has been accomplished, Flaubert still, of course, faces the task of embodying this incompatibility in the temporal experience of the characters themselves; this will be the achievement of the masterpieces of his maturity.

CHAPTER VIII

DERNIERE SCENE DE LA MORT
DE MARGUERITE DE BOURGOGNE

September 1835–January 1836

Argument. Ce sujet peut faire suite à la *Tour de Nesle* et même il est difficile de le comprendre sans avoir lu ce drame. Buridan [Lyonnet] vient au château Gaillard, et étrangle Marguerite avec ses cheveux; elle avait été son ancienne amante. (Bruneau, p. 64)

"CONNAISSEZ-VOUS la Normandie" where each castle evokes such famous names; the Château-Gaillard is in ruins now, but in 1316 it was still young. Locked in its dungeons at that time was a young woman "qui gémissait et regardait le soleil couchant d'un air d'adieu, de rage et de désespoir"—Marguerite de Bourgogne, queen of France. She was twenty-six then, and perhaps the number of her crimes already surpassed the number of her days.

On this particular day Marguerite begs the guard to let her look out through the bars for just a few more minutes. In the distance she perceives a rider galloping toward the castle. It is Lyonnet; as he enters the dungeon Marguerite, startled, recognizes him: "Oh! Lyonnet, il faut que tu sois mon démon pour me poursuivre ainsi."

Lyonnet begins to confront her with her crimes: first, the murder of her father. Marguerite objects that Lyonnet was the one who did the deed. True, he answers. But in the beginning she was pure and he loved her; now he despises her as "la femme adultère." Denying her accusation that he never really loved her, Lyonnet pours out his wrath: because of her he has lost his faith and become ridden with vice. But now he will strangle her with her own hair. Times have changed; now *he* is the master.

Marguerite resorts to pleading; they can still run away, forget the bloody past, return to the love they once shared. No, Lyonnet says; did she ever spare her victims who begged for their lives? Let her make her final prayer; the last hour has come. Marguerite kneels and stammers a few words. Arise, commands Lyonnet; "bien d'autres... me demandent successivement une heure, une demi-heure, une minute, mais je donne plus: l'éternité!" He orders her to let down her hair, her beautiful hair! "Aussitôt il en prit deux mèches et en entoura le cou de Marguerite."

Marguerite was buried the next day; the inscription on her tombstone has worn away: "le temps efface tout, les rois eux-mêmes; mais leurs crimes—oui—mais plus tard."

WITH "Marguerite de Bourgogne," Flaubert returns to the historical genre. Here the "argument" provided him with no more than the bare outline of the action—and in contrast to "Matteo Falcone" or "Le moine," no more detailed sources have been found which he might have consulted. There is, however, little basic material in this story that is not already given in Dumas's drama. The conflict between Lyonnet (Buridan) and Marguerite is a central theme of *La Tour de Nesle,* despite the fact that Dumas ends his story with a reconciliation of sorts between the two principals.

Since Lyonnet's execution of Marguerite is a part of the "given," Flaubert's own contribution to the story consists largely in finding the sources for his action in the earlier relationship of the couple. What are these sources? According to the account of *La Tour de Nesle,* Marguerite had engaged in a secret love relationship with Lyonnet, then a page in her father's service. When Marguerite's father, the duke of Burgundy, discovered the affair and was about to send her away to a convent, Marguerite persuaded Lyonnet to kill the duke so that their love could continue; but after the deed was done, she changed her mind and sent Lyonnet away.[1] In Flaubert's story Lyonnet hates Marguerite for having thus destroyed his innocence and led him into crime:

En commençant à t'aimer j'avais aimé une enfant pure et candide, et... maintenant, Marguerite, je hais l'enfant qui est la femme adultère.... Je t'aimais et je t'ai donné mon bonheur, car je me suis étourdi sur le crime de ton père, et j'ai perdu ma foi, et maintenant tout mon être est le mélange de tous les vices... (OJ I, 23)

Lyonnet's execution of Marguerite is here treated as a revenge for her corruption of him.

But beyond this personal revenge, Lyonnet is shown as enforcing a universal moral code against Marguerite the murderess:

à toi les cadavres que la Seine chaque matin roulait dans son lit; à toi la honte, à toi l'ignominie, à toi la mort... (OJ I, 23)

In this act he is no longer a private individual; he has become a *public* executioner, giving death as punishment for all crime:

— Relève-toi, dit Lyonnet en la prenant par le bras; bien d'autres me font attendre comme toi; ils me demandent successivement une heure, une demi-heure, une minute, mais je donne plus: l'éternité! (OJ I, 24)

Thus Flaubert's conception of Lyonnet goes beyond his source material; Lyonnet had been given no public role in the "argument," which states only that he "étrangle Marguerite avec ses cheveux." What is the author's purpose in treating the execution as both a personal and a public matter? Compare Ernest's statement upon his own "execution" of the duke in "Deux amours"; "Tu es l'assassin et *je suis le Bourreau.*"

---

[1] This sequence of events is related in Act III of Dumas's play in the form of a long monologue by Lyonnet-Buridan himself. See Alexandre Dumas, *Théâtre romantique* (Paris: Firmin-Didot, n.d.).

In both stories the act of the "Bourreau" both avenges a personal crime and upholds the moral law; the personal satisfaction of the revenge is given a universal justification. In "Deux amours" I interpreted the murder of the duke as a negation of the worldly "father" by the "son" who thereby detaches himself from the evil adult world. The duke is an adulterer whose crime leads to the murder of his wife Louisa. Marguerite's crimes are the same: adultery and murder. But, although Marguerite herself has committed many murders, the specific crime of killing her father, which Lyonnet first seeks to attribute entirely to her, was in fact his own deed:

— Eh bien, Marguerite, toi tu as tué ton père et tu es reine de France; moi je n'ai tué personne et je ne suis rien.

— Tu m'accuses de la mort de mon père, Lyonnet, tandis que c'est toi, au contraire, toi qui as pris le poignard. (OJ I, 22)

Flaubert's hero, following the original, casts the entire blame for the murder on Marguerite.[2] But it is Flaubert who chooses to emphasize the guilty degradation that has resulted from this crime ("tout mon être est le mélange de tous les vices"). Lyonnet accuses Marguerite in order to acquit himself of his own guilt. Thus in "Marguerite de Bourgogne" the male "executioner" is himself overtly guilty, as he was not in "Deux amours"; although he seeks at first to escape it, Lyonnet must accept this feeling of guilt and can only seek to *disculpate* himself by executing Marguerite, the seductress. This development completes the lesson of "Le moine." Like the thief of the prior's "souvenirs de jeunesse et d'amour," Lyonnet cannot affect innocence of his crime; he can only seek to blame it on the woman as the object of his sexual desire.

In "Marguerite de Bourgogne" as in "Deux amours," the hero's final act places him outside the world as the upholder of moral law against worldly evil. Lyonnet never speaks of any future worldly career but only of the *past* guilt that his execution of Marguerite will abolish; this is the sense of the impersonal executioner role he assumes near the end

[2] Cf. Lyonnet's own account in Dumas (*ibid.*, p. 399):
Elle [Marguerite] tenait un poignard et elle disait: "Lyonnet, Lyonnet, si, d'ici à demain, mourait mon père, il n'y aurait plus de couvent, il n'y aurait plus de séparation, il n'y aurait plus que l'amour." Je ne sais comment cela se fit, mais le poignard passa de ses mains dans celles de Lyonnet de Bournonville; un bras le prit, le conduisit dans l'ombre, le guida comme à travers les détours de l'enfer, souleva un rideau, et le page armé et le duc endormi, se trouvèrent en face l'un de l'autre. C'était une noble tête de vieillard, calme et belle, que l'assassin a revue bien des fois dans ses rêves, car il l'assassina l'infâme!

of the story. Flaubert interprets Lyonnet's act, like that of Ernest, as a return to an extraworldly moral equilibrium through the destruction of the worldly. The hero's own guilty "worldliness" is no longer denied—Lyonnet's crimes have made him a "mélange de tous les vices"— but this worldliness is nevertheless overcome through his final deed.

In "Deux amours" the "execution" was identical with the Oedipal murder of the father. In this story it has become a *negation* of the original Oedipal murder, represented by Lyonnet's assassination of Marguerite's father; it is as if Oedipus had expiated the murder of Laius by executing Jocasta. And this means that the worldly "paradise" of "Deux amours" in which Ernest consoled Louisa can no longer exist for Lyonnet and Marguerite. Lyonnet coldly rejects Marguerite's suggestion that they forget their acquired worldliness and return to their old love:

— Oh! grâce! grâce, Lyonnet! Nous partirons, nous irons vivre loin d'ici, vivre dans notre premier amour, oublier tout comme un rêve sanglant. Grâce! grâce!

— Eh! faisais-tu grâce à ceux qui, dans la tour de Nesle, te demandaient la vie sous le poignard de tes assassins? (OJ I, 23–24)

The "paradise" is by no means absent from this work, but it exists now not as a *consolation* for the "enfer" but as the state of innocent love that *preceded* the "enfer," in the days when Marguerite was not yet the "femme adultère" but the "enfant pure et candide."

This vision of an innocent, wholly legitimate love that united the hero with his beloved before they were forced to undertake their "voyage en enfer" is taken up again in "La fiancée et la tombe" and "La grande dame et le joueur de vielle." In "La fiancée" the yearning of the *moine des Chartreux* for the worldly paradise outside his "cage d'un homme" is transformed into the hero's effort to return from his prison to an earlier, preworldly state, to his own *innocent* "souvenirs de jeunesse et d'amour" that are no longer identifiable with the worldly ones of the prior. In setting the paradise *before* the state of worldly alienation, Flaubert demonstrates a clearer insight into the impossibility of making this paradise a truly praxial goal.

CHAPTER IX

PORTRAIT DE LORD BYRON

September 1835–January 1836

Argument. Faites le portrait de Lord Byron d'après ses écrits, et sa vie. (Bruneau, p. 66)

BYRON WAS a man of passion. Believing in nothing but his own genius, patriotism, and the beauty of women, he considered all else mere vanity. He had a hundred mistresses but loved only one; even to her he was cruel.

France was not attractive to Byron; it was neither misty and cold nor sunny and warm. Italy was the country he loved best; there one could always find ardent glances, hearts full of passion, and "quelque sujet de drame ou de roman." He also liked to spend his time in taverns and stables, for he was "chéri du peuple."

Byron was devoted to liberty and braved danger "par plaisir ou par vanité." His heroism in Greece, the country he attempted to lift out of slavery, has immortalized Byron, "le fils du siècle."

THIS BRIEF portrait is another "narration" written for Gourgaud. Flaubert's description of Byron accumulates Romantic clichés and "Byronic" poses without offering any very significant insight into his own attitudes. Byron is idealized as the prototype of the Romantic hero, a living negation of contemporary bourgeois society. The glorification of his role in Greece[1] exhibits the active, "revolutionary" tendencies of Flaubert's Romanticism that will take on a more profound significance in the following work, "San Pietro Ornano."

Conspicuously absent from this portrait is any mention of Byron's literary career. Not only is there no reference to any of his works, as both Cigada and Bruneau have remarked,[2] but there is nowhere even an explicit indication that he was a writer.[3] This is all the more surprising since the "argument" mentioned the "écrits" of the poet. The prestigious word "poète," which Flaubert was to apply so freely to himself in his autobiographical works, is not to be found here; Byron the poet vanishes in the author's eyes before Byron the Romantic hero. Flaubert has not yet come to reject, as he does in the third period of the *œuvres de jeunesse,* the very possibility of a valid worldly praxis; it is only later

---

[1] "Il alla pour relever le char de la Liberté de la fange où l'avaient enfoncé les tyrans" (OJ I, 26).

[2] Sergio Cigada, "Precisazione cronologica su alcuni scritti giovanili di Gustave Flaubert," *Aevum,* March–April 1956, p. 177; Bruneau, *Les débuts littéraires,* p. 67.

[3] The only allusions are to the "puissance de son génie" (OJ I, 25) and to the fact that Italy is said to offer, presumably to Byron himself, "toujours quelque sujet de drame ou de roman" (OJ I, 26).

[46]

that the conception of the "poète," whose *nonworldly* experiences are significant in themselves and are directed to no worldly, praxial goal, makes its appearance.[4]

---

[4] This conception is first outlined in "Main de fer" (February 1837), in the third period.

CHAPTER X

SAN PIETRO ORNANO (HISTOIRE CORSE)

September 1835–January 1836

I. A PROUD frigate enters the port of Genoa; on her deck stands Ornano, a haughty figure dressed half in the Greek fashion, half in the Italian. This man, "naguère paysan de Corse," has only one religion, one thought—"la gloire"; he has come as an ally of France, then at war with Genoa, "faire trembler un doge sur son trône." For the last few days, Ornano has been in a melancholy humor; from his repeated sighs one can see that something out of the ordinary is torturing his soul.

II. Ornano enters the palace and is met by the doge himself. France, he announces, has given him the privilege of setting the conditions for peace; he demands nothing less than the doge's daughter, Vanina, or else he will bombard the city and reduce the doge to slavery. After all, he, no less than a king, is capable of love and passion. But the doge rejects his offer disdainfully and Ornano, after a final threat, leaves the palace.

III. At midnight a group of men scale the castle wall; one of them (Ornano) is masked and heavily armed. "Puis il y a du sang, des cadavres, des cris, et Vanina [est] enlevée." At sea, Vanina weeps for her father, her slaves, her palace, but little by little she grows to love Ornano.

A month later Ornano, true to his promise, attacks the Genoese port, but his ship is trapped in the harbor. Beside himself with anger, he threatens to kill anyone who proposes surrender. A man jumps into the sea on the orders of Vanina; to Ornano's question, Vanina answers that she sent him "d'aller demander grâce à mon père." Ornano tries to shoot the swimmer but he has already disappeared from view. A messenger from the doge soon comes aboard bringing him a note—"ta grâce," says Vanina to Ornano. He looks at her, half-pitying and half-loving; to the messenger he announces, "Ce soir, vous saurez ma réponse!" (Unfinished.)

"SAN PIETRO ORNANO" is the last of the "narrations" written for Gourgaud. Unlike the others, no "argument" precedes it in the manuscript, and I assume with Bruneau that Flaubert chose the subject himself.[1] It is certainly conceivable, however, that it was suggested to him by Gourgaud. The sources (discovered by Bruneau) are an excerpt from d'Aubigné's *Histoire universelle*[2] found in the *Leçons et modèles de littérature française* (Paris, 1835), Vol. I, of P. E. Tissot; and an article, "Sampiero et Vanina, souvenirs de Corse," in the *Revue de Paris*, March 1831, by Rosseeuw Saint-Hilaire. Both of these sources,

---

[1] "Ce serait donc une 'narration' comme les autres, destinée à être lue par Gourgaud, mais dont Flaubert aurait choisi lui-même le sujet" (Bruneau, *Les débuts littéraires*, p. 65).

[2] The passage in question can be found in the *Histoire universelle* (Paris, 1887), II, 291–293.

however, deal chiefly with Ornano's assassination of Vanina; Flaubert's narrative breaks off before reaching this point.

"San Pietro Ornano" is the only story of the period in which the protagonist resolutely seeks and attains a worldly goal. In capturing Vanina from her father, Ornano experiences none of the guilt of the *moine des Chartreux,* nor does he have to justify his deed through the woman's need for consolation as he did in "Deux amours." The "son's" attack on the "father" is now given a frank justification in the former's own desires. The "souvenirs de jeunesse et d'amour" are no longer the father's property, but as seen in "Marguerite de Bourgogne," they have become wholly the son's possession. The relationship of Ornano and Vanina resembles that of Lyonnet and Marguerite not after but before the murder of her father. In the ideal historical atmosphere of this story, Flaubert refuses the guilt of the *moine des Chartreux:* the historical hero, unlike the contemporary one, has no inhibitions to contend with. And because France has given Ornano the right to set his own terms in negotiating with the doge,[3] Ornano's demand for Vanina's hand is a legitimate one. The doge's refusal is motivated only by his aristocratic pride and has no basis in universal morality, for unlike Ernest in "Deux amours" Ornano seeks in his beloved the "enfant pure et candide," not the "femme adultère."

Ornano's freedom as a praxial figure seems to owe a great deal to the "Portrait de Lord Byron" that preceded this story. Much of the idealized descriptive material is borrowed almost textually:

C'était une de ces âmes vigoureusement trempées dans les vertus poussées jusqu'à l'excès;... il ne connaissait d'autre plaisir que de commander ses matelots, de fumer son tabac d'Italie, de regarder l'horizon qui s'enfonce sous les vagues, et de se laisser ballotter par le roulis lorsque la mer est calme, lorsque le vent souffle à peine... (OJ I, 10)

Compare from "Byron":

C'était un de ces hommes à hautes conceptions, à idées généreuses et progressives....

[Il contemplait] la fumée de sa cigarette qui s'envolait au souffle du vent....

A Venise... il... faisait ainsi plusieurs lieues en mer, se laissant ballotter par le roulis. (OJ I, 25–26)

Byron's active position in the world, as well as his hatred of tyrants

---

[3] "Je suis venu, dit San Pietro, pour traiter avec toi [le doge] des conditions de la paix. La France, mon alliée, pour prix de mes services, m'a donné le pouvoir de les faire à mon gré" (OJ I, 10).

and those of high rank ("Il était chéri du peuple et haï de la noblesse" [OJ I, 26]) offered Flaubert a model of an active, "class conscious" hero which may well have influenced his choice of Ornano as the protagonist of his next story. If the idealized Byron could love his mistresses without guilt, why could Flaubert not permit such a love to the hero of a fictional work?

If the story had ended with Ornano's capture of Vanina, Ornano would appear an anomaly indeed, a successful worldly hero standing alone among Flaubert's other protagonists, who are only successful when their actions negate the world (Ernest, Lyonnet). But this does not happen. After having captured Vanina and won her love, Ornano is not content to enjoy the fruits of his conquest; instead he returns to destroy Genoa to make good his threats to the doge. What was to be the outcome of Ornano's attack on the city? Although certainty is impossible, the extract from d'Aubigné used by Flaubert as source material gives a likely indication of the conclusion of the story. In d'Aubigné's historical account, San Pietro killed his wife because she had escaped from him in an attempt at reconciliation with her high-born Corsican relatives (but not the doge of Genoa, to whom she was unrelated).[4] San Pietro himself was killed only later, having been ambushed by Vanina's relatives in the course of a campaign he was leading against Corsica. The hypothesis that naturally suggests itself is that Flaubert intended to bring together San Pietro's "execution" of Vanina with his own death by locating both in the Genoese harbor; only thus can the author's deliberate distortion of history in having Vanina attempt to mollify her father *after* San Pietro had already been ambushed by the father's forces be explained. Undoubtedly Flaubert originally intended to have Ornano kill Vanina for appealing to her father: Ornano had already threatened "qu'il tuerait de sa propre main quiconque parlerait de se rendre" (OJ I, 12). And after killing Vanina there would be nothing left for him to do but to die at the hands of her family, as he does in d'Aubigné.[5]

That Ornano returns to Genoa to attack the doge after he has already gained possession of Vanina demonstrates that his hostility towards the doge goes beyond his love for his bride. This turn of events is of particular significance because it is wholly the result of the author's rearrange-

---

[4] The name "Ornano" which Flaubert gives his hero was that of his wife's family; d'Aubigné refers to him only as "San Petre Corse."

[5] D'Aubigné does not mention Vanina's father in particular: "Enfin il tomba en une embusche dressée par ses ennemis et *principalement par les parens de sa femme*" (D'Aubigné, *Histoire universelle*, p. 293).

ment of his source material; in reality San Pietro's attack on Corsica, the home of Vanina's parents, occurred only *after* she had sought reconciliation with them. What Ornano's attack on the doge demonstrates is the impossibility of basing a worldly praxis on a "legitimate" resolution of the Oedipal conflict; the son cannot be satisfied until he has truly destroyed the position of the father.

Ornano's hostility of the "paternal" doge involved from the first a jealousy of his social position, of his recognized place in the world, that transcends the purely sexual jealousy that was dominant in "Le moine." The stress placed by the author on Ornano's social inferiority to the doge reflects this envy of the father's worldly position:

Mais ce paysan [Ornano], ce corsaire, cet homme aux manières rustiques et sauvages, venait dans Gênes... faire trembler un doge sur son trône. (OJ I, 9–10)

Ornano's tirade to the doge makes his love for Vanina appear as no more than a means of establishing his superiority over his "rival":

Demain j'aurai Vanina; et à toi l'esclavage et le malheur. Ton trône? je le foulerai aux pieds, et ton palais, j'en ferai une prison pour toi. Vous pensiez donc qu'aucun sentiment ne pouvait m'émouvoir, vous croyiez que l'amour ne pouvait surgir de ce coeur de marin; vous croyez que les passions ne remuent pas aussi fort le coeur d'un paysan que celui d'un roi? Et pourtant s'il est ici une tête couronnée et un corsaire, le corsaire est roi et le monarque est esclave. (OJ I, 11)

Thus Ornano's return to Genoa only makes explicit what was already present in his original encounter with the doge. Now the sexual and recognition-oriented elements that had been combined in Ornano's original confrontation with the doge over Vanina are split apart. Ornano already has Vanina, but lacks the worldly being of the doge, which he now seeks *in opposition to* Vanina, who seeks to mediate between the two rivals.

The dichotomy thus set up between the man's sexual aims and his need for recognition becomes one of great importance throughout Flaubert's career. The woman, who exists not in the social world but in her personal love relationships, hopes like Emma Bovary to lose herself in love, to find the ideal lover who will give himself up to her and renounce the world. But the man, like Emma's lovers, always puts aside sexuality when it comes into conflict with the deeper question of social recognition. Ornano cannot be content merely to possess Vanina and to forego, as she herself wishes, his attempt to gain worldly superiority over the doge. In his opening description of Ornano, Flaubert had already indicated in no uncertain terms his hero's appetite for glory: "Il n'avait d'autre pensée que la gloire, d'autre idole que la gloire, d'autre religion que la gloire" (OJ I, 10). For such a man, woman's love can never become an exclusive concern.

My projected conclusion for the story is easily interpreted within this framework. Ornano must kill Vanina for surrendering to the doge because, like the historical San Pietro, he refuses to recognize his wife's family as his superiors, and he prefers death for himself over acceptance of the doge's amnesty.

The question naturally arises as to why Flaubert, apparently so near the end of his story, left it incomplete. This seems doubly strange because "San Pietro Ornano" was a school assignment to be submitted to Gourgaud. One possibility is simply that the author had been unable to complete it by the time it was due. But I prefer to seek an explanation in the development of the story itself.

The following passage, which occurs after Ornano has discovered Vanina's efforts to arrange a truce, seems to indicate his intention to "execute" her:

Ornano était resté pensif, la tête baissée sur sa poitrine; son regard fixé sur Vanina était sinistre; ses lèvres, pâles et tremblantes, semblaient se contracter d'un rire lugubre. (OJ I, 13)

Yet in the very last words of the story, on receiving a message of amnesty from the doge, rather than refusing it outright and killing Vanina on the spot, Ornano reacts as follows:

Il pâlit, *tourna sur elle* [Vanina] *un regard plein de pitié et d'amour,* puis, s'adressant à l'envoyé:
— Ce soir, vous saurez ma réponse! (OJ I, 13)

This "regard de pitié et d'amour" would seem to indicate a change of heart on the hero's (and the author's) part; Ornano no longer unconditionally refuses Vanina's mediation between him and the doge. By renouncing his opposition to the doge, Ornano would be acting more in Vanina's interest than his own; the "regard de pitié et d'amour" is a sign that it was the author's sympathy for his heroine that led him to spare her life by abandoning the story. "La fiancée et la tombe," written later, shows the cruelty of the "son" to his beloved carried out to its unhappy conclusion.

By separating the sexual paradise from the recognition-oriented aspect of the son-father conflict, Flaubert discovers that only the woman is wholly devoted to this paradise. The son-hero must acquire for himself the worldly being of the father; he must obtain recognition in the

world, even if the world is an "enfer." Ornano takes up the "revolutionary" role played in "Voyage en enfer" by the young giant "Liberté"
in combating the aged "Absolutisme," but the essential selfishness of his
aims is not concealed by the libertarian aspect of his opposition to the
doge. And because Ornano seeks "la gloire" for himself he can no longer
enjoy the self-oblivion of the paradise, the "pensée d'amour." Vanina,
in contrast, desires only this self-oblivion in the love relationship; she
seeks her father's mercy because her love for Ornano is stronger than
her worldly pride.[6] The interest that Flaubert shows in the woman
rather than the man in the following works ("La fiancée et la tombe,"
"Deux mains sur une couronne," "La grande dame et le joueur de
vielle," and "Un parfum à sentir") is attributable to this "superiority"
of the woman; because she only passively *awaits* disalienation from her
lovers, her praxis does not involve her in the "enfer" of worldly recognition. "Deux amours" demonstrated that the author felt more secure in
describing the woman's sufferings through the negativity of the world
than in concerning himself with the desires of the son, which are, as we
have seen in "Duc de Guise" and "Le moine," uncomfortably tainted
with this very negativity. In the works that follow, the woman's awaiting
acquires a self-awareness. Flaubert does not merely pity her as he did
in "Deux amours," but identifies with her as a subject in her awaiting
of the ideal, while the son through his avowed need for worldly recognition becomes increasingly a part of the "enfer."

---

[6] This is her own explanation for sending a messenger to the doge against her
husband's orders: "Oh! excuse-moi, pardon, Ornano; *mais je t'aimais* et je lui ai
ordonné d'aller demander grâce à mon père" (OJ I, 12).

CHAPTER XI

LA FIANCEE ET LA TOMBE, CONTE FANTASTIQUE

September 1835–January 1836

ANNETTE, Paul's young fiancée, seems distracted and melancholy. Sighing, begging for pity, she admits to Paul that "le duc Robert est venu en ces lieux et... pour ma honte..."

Near the Seine a lonely young girl climbs the hill to weep for her dead lover. Paul, after hearing of Robert's crime, had gone to his castle to avenge the outrage done to his fiancée. He came upon Robert and fought with him; disarmed by his adversary, Paul still managed to kill him by pushing him into a ditch. But then Paul himself was murdered by the duke's men. Annette found his poor mutilated body the next day and had a tomb erected for him.

A year has passed since his murder, and Annette is at his tomb, when suddenly the stone cracks in two and the ghost of Paul appears to her. If she wants to be united with him, he tells her, she must fetch him the head and dagger of Sir Robert. "Malheur à ma fiancée, si elle ne se dépêche." Annette sets out on her mission but her sword slips from her hand before she can complete the task. Paul's ghost appears to her again, crying "malheur à toi." Now the corpse of Sir Robert comes to life in the form of Satan; demonic dancers surround Annette but she resists seduction. Once again she returns to Paul's tomb and calls to him—but she has failed to bring back the head and dagger. The earth trembles, the gravestone is shattered . . . and the next day instead of one corpse, there are two.

"LA FIANCÉE," like "Deux amours" and "La grande dame et le joueur de vielle," was not included in the Conard edition of the œuvres de jeunesse; it was first published in Le manuscrit autographe (January–February 1929, pp. 1–5), and appears in printed form in Bruneau (pp. 162–165). Handwriting evidence locates this story in the period of the later "narrations," presumably written between September 1835 (the date of "Duc de Guise") and January 1836 (the date of "Deux mains sur une couronne"). Because both "La fiancée" and "La grande dame et le joueur de vielle" have the woman as central figure, I have decided to discuss these stories after "San Pietro Ornano," where a shift of Flaubert's interest from the man to the woman seems to be discernible.

Although Bruneau observes that *"La fiancée et la tombe s'inspire visiblement de la célèbre légende normande de Robert le Diable"* (p. 165), he has found no source for the specific incident recounted in Flaubert's story. The legendary Robert was known for his licentious-

ness, and in one version of the legend[1] he murders his son and the latter's
fiancée; these details may have been sufficient source material for
Flaubert. In any event, the near-hysterical tone of the work suggests
that whatever sources may have been employed were considerably
"improved upon" by Flaubert.

In "La fiancée" the legitimacy of the son's right to his beloved that
was observed in "San Pietro Ornano" is no longer even at issue. Paul
is the fiancé of Annette at the beginning of the story, and he has committed no act of aggression against the "father" in acquiring her. On
the contrary, it is Robert—the father—who, in violating Annette,
commits a crime against Paul and provokes him to a justified revenge.
Thus the son returns to his role of the "Bourreau," but this time without the least question of expiating past guilt. Paul in executing Robert
acts as an agent of God himself:

> l'orsque [sic] tu vins dans la demeure d'Annette que tu as souillée de ton crime
> personne n'y était pour te punir mais dieu te voyait... Personne n'y était pour
> empêcher ton crime mais quelqu'un est là pour t'en donner le chatiment... (Bruneau,
> pp. 163–164)

Yet Paul does not attain as an executioner the impersonal "universal"
status of Lyonnet or Ernest. Instead, upon completing his task he is
immediately killed by Robert's henchmen and cast into a limbo from
which he later emerges before Annette as "un spectre plus livide que
la mort." What does this prompt "punishment" of Paul for his revenge
signify?

If Paul's act has unequivocal moral foundations, Flaubert attaches
to it all the same a certain stigma:

> *Si la vengeance est un crime et une faiblesse de l'humanité,* alors c'était pour un
> bon motif. (Bruneau, p. 163)

> [Annette:] O il y a un an grand Dieu, Paul tu vivais encore,... tu as voulu me
> venger... Non non... *le Christ a dit: malheur à qui se vengera!* (Bruneau, p. 164)

Here the words of Christ are in effect opposed to the will of God which
demanded vengeance. God *the father* upholds the morality of the adult
world, but for Christ *the son* vengeance is an evil act, comparable to
that of Bernardo in stealing the prior's ring. Paul as a worldly adult
figure has every right to his revenge, but his swift dispatch at the hands
of Robert's henchmen demonstrates that the son has no rights in the
world of the father. If in "San Pietro Ornano" the hero was able to

---

[1] *Robert le Diable ou le Château de Molineaux, traditions normandes,* published
by Placide Justin (Paris, 1823); see Bruneau, *Les débuts littéraires,* p. 166.

deal with the doge as an equal, Paul can confront Robert only as an inferior. Significantly enough, Paul loses his dagger in a first futile attempt to kill Robert; he is unable to wound Robert and can only push him into a ditch:

> Paul s'élança sur lui mais hélas Robert sut esquiver le coup et se saisit de lui en lui demandant ce qu'il voulait faire.... Paul alors ne pouvait plus contenir sa colère... *il n'avait plus d'arme* mais il poussa Robert dans les fossés... (Bruneau, pp. 163–164)

This sense of frustration even in victory is in sharp contrast with the effortless assassination of Paul by Robert's bodyguards:

> Paul de suite fut garotté par les gardes et tué à coups de poignard hors des murs du chateau. (Bruneau, p. 164)

The incomplete nature of Paul's execution of Robert is further revealed in the tasks his spirit later assigns to Annette.

The son thus finds it impossible to maintain his paradise against the evil sexuality of the father. The original relationship between Paul and his fiancée is not a truly adult one, like the marriage of Ornano and Vanina, and because it has retained its preadult purity it can be destroyed by the intrusion of adult sexuality. Robert's rape of Annette represents her entry into the adult world. Annette is not depicted as having violently defended her virtue against the assailant Robert. In her present state she does not thirst for revenge; she is described instead as "rêveuse et mélancolique": similar terms are used in "Rêve d'enfer" (March 1837) to describe the adolescent girl Julietta's awakening to sexuality: "un air rêveur, des larmes dans les yeux... la jeune fille est nonchalante et toute mélancolique" (OJ I, 179). The girl has now become a woman, and thereby finds herself outside the preadult world of the son.

This interpretation permits a retrospective insight into the monk Bernardo's ambivalent attitude toward the "souvenirs de jeunesse et d'amour": as *his own* they are part of an irretrievable past; only through the *adult* being of the prior can they be brought into the present as a worldly paradise. In this story, Paul's demand for Annette to bring him Robert's head and dagger is, like Bernardo's theft of the prior's ring, an attempt at acquiring for himself the worldly being of the father which would permit the reestablishment of the preworldly paradise on an adult level.

Seen in this light, "La fiancée" is a clarification of the themes of "Le moine" or of "Marguerite de Bourgogne," but a whole new perspective is created by the central position of Annette. By relinquishing to his fiancée the task of decapitating Robert, Paul also forfeits the son's central role in the story, which is now seen not from his standpoint but from that of the woman.

Why is Annette chosen to take over the son's praxis for herself? We have already witnessed Flaubert's interest in the suffering of his heroines; in "Matteo Falcone" the mother grieves for her dead son, while in "Deux amours" Louisa is shown as cruelly treated by her husband and his mistress. Annette shares the trials of both these earlier heroines: like Albano's mother, she grieves for the son Paul killed by the father Robert, while like Louisa she awaits her lover's avenging of her own sufferings at the hands of the father. This combination of grief and dependency is evident in the following passage:

> O pauvre Annette!... ô pauvre enfant tu souffres bien n'est-ce pas! Si Paul était là il te secourerait [*sic*]... Où vas-tu Annette... tu vas prier sur sa tombe... Sur la tombe de Paul. O s'il était là, ton amant il n'y aurait plus de douleurs. (Bruneau, p. 163)

Significantly enough, Flaubert's anomalous use of a "flashback" technique in "La fiancée" places this passage *before* the account of Paul's ill-fated execution of Robert. Thus Annette's "awaiting" of Paul's return from the grave is assimilated to her earlier dependence on him to avenge her violated innocence.

Paul's appeal to Annette from the grave takes as its basis her desires, not his own:

> Voilà mon ancienne fiancée, *si elle veut m'être unie* il faut qu'elle m'aille chercher la dague et la tete du Sir Robert qui est encore dans les fossés. Va et reviens vite. (Bruneau, p. 164)

Annette is not acting for Paul but for herself in carrying out his commands. It is primarily she, not he, who desires their reunion, for it is she who must experience his absence through her suffering in the world. Paul, however, is in an ambiguously extraworldly position; he desires to repossess Annette through the acquisition of the head and dagger, symbols of Robert's masculinity, but he does not suffer in the world from his lack of them. Paul's "extraworldliness" is not altogether unlike that of the "Bourreaux" Ernest and Lyonnet; he is alienated from the adult world, but he has the advantage of being no longer subject to the negativity of that world—not he but Annette will confront Satan.

Annette's decapitation of Robert is in Freudian terms a symbolic castration; this is apparent from Flaubert's description of the deed: *"Elle avait déjà mutilé son corps de deux coups de son épée..."* (Bruneau, p.

165). Paul's body after his assassination had also been described as
"mutilé";[2] through Annette's action Paul will recover his lost masculinity. But if the significance of this deed for Paul is clear enough, what
does the action mean for Annette? The simplest answer is evidently
that she is acting to enable her lover to take his place beside her in the
world of adult sexuality. This must, however, be further clarified. Annette has already been forced into sexual relations with Robert; she has
become a part of the adult world. But through this entry into adulthood
she did not become a part of a "worldly paradise," but on the contrary
was *alienated* from the preworldly idyll of her engagement to Paul. By
capturing Robert's masculinity she is attempting to bring adult sexuality into the unalienated world of her original union with her fiancé.
Her first sexual experience was enforced upon her from without; now
she seeks to turn the tables and enforce her own ideal upon sexuality.

The structure of this reaction merits a broad interpretation. For the
adolescent in bourgeois society sexuality, and in conjunction with it,
the questions of a worldly career, of finding a "meaning in life," and
the like, are posed from the first in the form of *alienation* from a state
of childhood dependency on his parents. To the rape of Annette corresponds the vision of the worldly hell given to the narrator of "Voyage
en enfer." It is no mere coincidence that in both cases Satan—"Sir
Robert" is only his earthly incarnation—was the initiator. But in the
face of this alienation the adolescent cannot simply refuse the world;
he (or she) seeks in it a *disalienation*, the satisfaction of his new desires.
The appearance of "Une pensée" contemporaneously with "Voyage en
enfer" illustrates this search to forget one's alienation in the world. But
only in "La fiancée" does Flaubert reveal the *regressive* roots of this
desired disalienation. The ideal existence is in the past, before the "fall"
into the world. The praxis of the adolescent, the adult-to-be, is an effort
to return to this preworldly paradise.

Yet this analysis is not complete. Surely Paul, in desiring the head
and the dagger of Robert, is not simply seeking a return to innocence.
Nor does Annette's effort to capture these symbols of masculinity merely
have as its goals the *negation* of her worldliness. In what sense then is
it appropriate to speak of a "return"?

Evidently there is no "return" in the sense of turning back the clock
to an earlier time. The validity of this conception lies rather in the

---

[2] "Le lendemain sa fiancée inquiète se promenant près des fossés trouva le corps
de son amant... ils l'avaient tué! *O les cruels!... Ils l'avaient mutilé!*" (Bruneau,
Les débuts littéraires, p. 164).

wholly negative value it sets on praxis. If the praxis of the adult is experienced as a return to an earlier unalienated state, this means that the
praxis is in itself a mere *negation*, a series of acts whose only value is
in the disalienation they are to effectuate. The conception of praxis as
disalienation is an essentially Romantic one; the Romantic is the first to
experience temporal existence in the form of an alienation that he can
only seek to abolish. "La fiancée" offers us the occasion to delve a bit
more deeply into the structure of this conception. Seeking the "ideal" in
the world is only now felt as a return because only now has Flaubert
come to feel the inconsistency between his vision of the world as an
"enfer" and his hopes of finding a "worldly paradise" through a *for-
ward* movement into this "enfer"—the positive praxis of a hero like
Ornano. The impossibility of such a course is reflected in the frustration
of the son Paul in his attempt on the father Robert's life. For the male
adolescent, worldly and sexual *desire* is opposed to a worldly-sexual
"being," that is, an adult position in the world without which his desire
cannot be realized. Thus in his effort toward disalienation the adolescent
cannot simply *negate* the evil worldliness of the father, as Ernest did in
"Deux amours"; he must take it, and its attendant "Satanic" guilt, for
himself. Paul is also successful as "le Bourreau" in executing Robert,
but this mere negation is inadequate to return him to his original paradise with Annette. It is in "La fiancée" that Flaubert discovers for the
first time the essential impotence of the son as a praxial figure. The man
cannot avoid the curse of "Satanic" worldliness because he can only be
satisfied through the acquisition of a worldly position. Neither his sexual desires nor the need for social recognition that accompanies them
can be satisfied by the passive, essentially *feminine* self-abandonment
that characterized the narrator of "Une pensée."

It is now possible to explain the significance of the woman's praxis
as offering Flaubert an alternative to that of the son, and, in particular,
to interpret the effort of Annette to "return" to her fiancé. The woman,
unlike the man, has no need to acquire on her own a position in society.
This was a simple truth of life in Flaubert's day, when the woman's
social position was wholly dependent on that of her husband. In a
broader sense, the woman in bourgeois society does not seek worldly
recognition for her positive accomplishments but remains an *object*
for male affections.[3] Thus the woman's praxis is essentially an *awaiting*
of the man's desire. For Flaubert, the woman's passivity is now revealed

---

[3] This conception of woman is implicit in the tradition of "Romantic" love that
dates back to the beginning of modern civilization.

as overcoming the fundamental contradictions of the son's praxis between return to a paradisial state and entry into a hellish world. Instead
of seeking worldly being for herself, the woman seeks rather to attract
the man's worldly being and to *remove* it from the world. The ideal
lover awaited by Flaubert's heroines must of necessity renounce his
worldliness in his love, for in giving himself up to this private relationship he loses all need for public recognition. Thus Emma Bovary presses
her lovers to sacrifice their social position for the benefit of their
"Romantic" passion.

With this understanding of the passivity of the woman's praxis, it
is not difficult to see that despite the active nature of Annette's attempted decapitation of Robert, it falls within the same framework
as, for example, the wholly passive awaiting of an ideal lover that characterizes the courtesan Marie in "Novembre."[4] Annette's act is not an
attempt to establish herself as Robert's superior; its goal is to remove
Robert's masculinity and bring it back into Annette's ideal, unworldly
relationship with Paul.

At the same time, Annette's failure makes visible the fundamentally
illusory nature of the woman's praxis for Flaubert. Just as Emma
cannot turn Rodolphe or Léon into "ideal" lovers, Annette is unable
to obtain for the "ideal" Paul the masculinity of Robert—the difference
being, of course, that in *Madame Bovary* the very possibility of such
an ideal love is revealed to be an illusion. The specific obstacle to
Annette's success is the unalterably Satanic nature of the worldly being
that Annette has set out to capture. This is revealed by Robert's return
to "life":

le cadavre de Robert se ranima et se mit à danser autour d'elle, or c'était Satan sous
la figure de Robert. Bientôt elle fut entourée de démons qui dansaient comme leur
maître... Ils tâchèrent de la séduire mais Annette secourue par le Ciel résista au
démon. (Bruneau, p. 165)

The woman can "capture" masculinity only in the form of *desire,* not
as a concrete object transferable, like the prior's ring, to a third party.
Annette's confrontation with Robert must remain wholly within the
Satanic world. She can resist his evil worldliness, but this resistance
is of no use in reestablishing her unworldly relationship with Paul:
the head and dagger remain permanently in Satan's possession.

---

[4] This image of the courtesan is prefigured in the first period in "La grande dame
et le joueur de vielle" (q.v.).

Annette's praxis, like Emma's, fails in its aims, but these two failures have very different structures. The impossibility of returning to the ideal that is here enforced upon her from without by Satan-Robert is in *Madame Bovary* revealed exclusively within the worldly experience of the heroine herself. But the internal sources of such failures as Annette's cannot be uncovered before the author renounces his characteristically Romantic identification with his protagonist.

CHAPTER XII

LA GRANDE DAME ET LE JOUEUR DE VIEILLE [*SIC*] OU LA MÈRE ET LE CERCUEIL

September 1835–January 1836

IT IS A WARM, clear day; two young lovers lie under a beautiful oak tree, bidding each other a melancholy farewell. Ernest has tears in his eyes; from time to time a sigh is heard from Henriette. "Oh Henriette t'en ressouviens-tu... il y a aujourd'hui un mois sous ce même arbre à pareille heure, il fesait [*sic*] beau aussi..." After reassuring one another their love will endure, they kiss and leave.

One month later Henriette is married in an impressive ceremony to M. de la Prevobine, "un des plus importants capitalistes du royaume," and after only seven months the young wife gives birth to a son, Paul.

Two years have passed. A poor itinerant musician stands before the home of the Prevobine family; from the second story window Henriette's little son Paul throws him a coin. Henriette too looks out, but she does not recognize her old lover. When the child comes downstairs to see the "joueur de vielle," Ernest embraces him like a father.

"Pourtant s'avançait l'avalenche [*sic*] terrible,... c'était la gigantesque et formidable révolution de 89." Plunging M. de la Prevobine into destitution, the Revolution not only restores Ernest to his former position but permits him to acquire a fortune equal to that of his old rival. Henriette, soon left a widow, goes to get her young son back from the *nourrice*, but she learns that "un monsieur" has taken away the little boy. She weeps, thinking of the old days with Ernest under the oak tree, and of her husband and child. "A vingt-ans les larmes rendent belle": the young widow is sought in marriage by a variety of suitors, but she rejects them all. Finally an old woman approaches her and proposes "une chose... horrible"; at first Henriette runs away but "elle a faim" and consents to become a prostitute.

Many years later, when Henriette is already forty years old, a young man enters "ce lieu-là." Never had she experienced such pleasure, never had the kisses been so sweet as with him. After paying, the young man leaves. Soon after, Henriette hears shouts, the sound of knives, and then a final gasp of life; she hurries to the scene, examines the dead body, and suddenly falls on it, kissing it, begging for pardon, cursing fate and God. "Cent fois elle appela son fils cent fois elle retomba épuisée sur cette tête ensanglantée..." When Henriette rises, it is with a Satanic laugh: she is mad.

Two days later a wagon passes by in the street, carrying Paul to his final resting place, when a crazed woman rushes over to it; she wants to say goodbye to her son, she will not move. "Puis l'on entendit un bruit semblable à celui d'une pierre que l'on broie. La folle était écrasée!"

"LA GRANDE DAME" is, like "La fiancée," an undated story published by

Bruneau.[1] The manuscripts of the two stories resemble each other[2] and were thus probably written at about the same time. I have decided to treat this story after "La fiancée" because of its numerous points of similarity with the posterior "Un parfum à sentir" (April 1836), notably in the introduction of social distinctions within modern society as obstacles to the protagonists' success, and in the final suicide of the heroines of both works. If my chronology is correct, the transformation of Henriette from the girl loved by Ernest at the beginning of the story to a forty-year-old prostitute at the end would link the youthful Annette of "La fiancée" with the *baladine* Marguerite of "Un parfum à sentir" who is also forty years of age.

The detailed nature of the plot of "La grande dame" strongly suggests that Flaubert made use of source material; it is scarcely imaginable that he invented details like Ernest's reappearance as a "joueur de vielle" on his own. Unfortunately no likely sources have been discovered.

It is not difficult to draw connections between this story and several of the preceding works; in particular, the lover's name Ernest recalls "Deux amours," while that of his son Paul is shared by the hero of "La fiancée." Nor do these resemblances stop at mere names. Ernest is, like the hero of "Deux amours," a successful son figure who defeats the father (here, M. de la Prevobine,[3] who dies ruined in the Revolution that enriches Ernest) and goes free of any punishment; Paul, like his namesake in "La fiancée," is guilty in his love relationship and must suffer death as the consequence. Thus, again on the assumption that "La grande dame" and "La fiancée" are in their proper order, "La grande dame" appears to combine the two possibilities of the son's praxis that were treated separately in these two earlier works.

The original love relationship of Ernest and Henriette is an amplification of Paul and Annette's engagement in "La fiancée" to include an overt sexual relationship. The legitimacy of this relationship is unquestioned—it distinguishes this Ernest from that of "Deux amours" —and it is destroyed, as in "La fiancée," by an external force, the "paternal" social pressures that force Henriette into her marriage with Prevobine. Thus the original paradise is now made to include overtly sexual elements. This inclusion should not be taken as controverting

[1] The text is found in Bruneau, *Les débuts littéraires*, pp. 124–127.
[2] See *ibid.*, p. 162.
[3] Note that "Prevobine" is the first in the celebrated series of Flaubert's "bovine" names: Bovary, Bouvigny, Bouvard, etc.

the irreconcilability of worldly and ideal love that was revealed in "La fiancée." The relationship of Ernest and Henriette is not a worldly one in our sense of the term. It is not sexuality per se that is worldly, but *oedipal* sexuality that has as its precondition the adolescent's entry into the world. In both "La fiancée" and "San Pietro Ornano" the son's possession of the woman was not a problem in itself but only in its connection with his attack on the father. This connection also appears in "La grande dame," but it is not present from the beginning; it must reveal itself through the actions of the characters. For it to exist a priori the author would have had to conceive consciously of sexuality as "Satanic" per se; such a conception is indeed expressed later in this period in "Un parfum à sentir."

The "father's" obstacle to Ernest and Henriette's union is now given a *social* basis rather than remaining on the purely symbolic ground of "La fiancée." This socialization of the obstacle is indeed what permits the overtness of the couple's premarital sexual relationship. The concept of the world as the "enfer" in which the alienated protagonist finds himself is now given a concrete social significance; it is no longer the undefined "monde" of "Voyage en enfer" where all men lived, but has become limited to the social order of the adult world—the domain of the father—outside which Ernest and Henriette as unmarried adolescents are able to subsist as lovers.

Ernest is, like Paul in "La fiancée," replaced as his beloved's consort by a wordly father figure, M. de la Prevobine. Stretching my interpretation, we may say that as a beneficiary of the Revolution Ernest is indirectly responsible for the death of Prevobine, just as Paul was for that of Robert. But here the resemblance ends, for Ernest is not guilty, as Paul was, and he is not made to suffer for the "murder." The death of Prevobine is wholly a matter of worldly, "paternal" justice—the justice of the God, not the Christ, of "La fiancée." This is demonstrated not only in its being attributed to the impersonal agency of the Revolution, but by the fact that after Prevobine is dead, Ernest does not return to possess Henriette. What went wrong with Paul's revenge in "La fiancée" was that instead of taking the father's place as a result of his deed, he remained the son throughout, still hoping to return to the ideal love of Annette. Ernest, like his namesake in "Deux amours," becomes an agent of justice, but, instead of situating himself above the world as a "Bourreau," he benefits from the social circumstances of the "execution" to become himself a "father," a successful worldly figure. His loss of interest in Henriette is a consequence of this newly acquired worldliness. But now Ernest, having become a "father," has essentially no more problems; thus he vanishes from the story, leaving the stage to Henriette and their son Paul. In the course of Flaubert's development from "Deux amours" to "La grande dame," Ernest, the successful son, has been transformed from "le Bourreau" into a mere *repetition* of the father. The negative features of this transformation are not visible here, but they are evident in the son-father figure of Pedrillo in "Un parfum à sentir."[4]

In Paul's "return" to his mother the Oedipal roots of the adolescent's sexual desire become manifest. This does not, of course, imply that Flaubert at any time experienced a conscious desire to possess his mother sexually. But by replacing the "legitimate" lover Ernest with the son Paul, Flaubert expresses the *forbidden* nature of the son's search for disalienation through worldly sexuality. Ernest could possess Henriette in the original preworldly idyll, but once the desire for the ideal must pursue its aim in the world, it is no longer a legitimate but an *incestuous* passion. The man's search for the ideal is shown as leading to the ultimate guilt of the Oedipal situation.

But again in "La grande dame" as in "La fiancée," it is not the man's action but the woman's that is of greatest importance. The subtitle, "La mère et le cercueil," like "La fiancée et la tombe," serves to emphasize the heroine's primary position in the final catastrophe. Paul's death is an artificially contrived "execution" for his act of incest; it is Henriette alone who articulates her suffering and expiates her crime by suicide. Paul never develops an existence of his own; he exists only as the "lover" of Henriette. The scene of their encounter in the brothel is described wholly from Henriette's point of view:

Un jour entra dans ce lieu-là un jeune homme de vingt ans... Le jeune homme avait bonne tournure de noble manière [*sic*] et une figure, oh une figure à séduire toutes les femmes. Henriette ne ressentit jamais tant de plaisir qu'avec celui-là, jamais les baisers n'avaient si suaves [*sic*], les propos de tendresses si doux et si bien choisis. (Bruneau, p. 126)

It is Henriette's pleasure, not Paul's, that is here described. Flaubert does not identify with the son having intercourse with his mother; he is concerned rather to show how much pleasure the mother derives from

---

[4] The next character to whom Flaubert gives the name Ernest is a thoroughly contemptible figure, the faithless lover of Mazza in "Passion et vertu" (December 1837).

the act. Henriette's career of prostitution now takes on a new significance; it is an *awaiting* of the son as her only hope for returning to the
lost paradise of her relationship with Ernest:

> *Elle se ressouvint de sa jeunesse de son amour de ses beaux jours qui s'était envolés*
> *comme un songe* de sa grandeur passée elle se ressouvint du vieux chêne des champs,
> d'Ernest, de son mari, de son enfant, et la pauvre femme pleurait pleurait et pleurait
> toujours. A vingt-ans les larmes rendent belle et on vint lui faire la cour. D'abord
> ce fut un tribun puis un général puis un officier puis un soldat enfin le bourreau vint
> lui proposer de se marier avec elle. Elle recula d'horreur.
>
>   Cette fois elle ne pleura pas, la douleur la suffoquait. Enfin une vieille femme vint
> s'approcher d'elle, et lui proposa une chose... horrible, elle s'enfuit d'abord mais
> elle avait faim. Elle y consentit ensuite. (Bruneau, p. 126)

Henriette had been obsessed by "des souvenirs de jeunesse et d'amour"
which could not be recaptured through marriage to any of the worldly
dignitaries who offered themselves to her. The return of her son demonstrates that Henriette's seemingly irrational choice of a "career" was
her only means of returning to the ideal through the world. This does
not simply mean that prostitution offered the only "realistic" possibility
for Henriette to be possessed by her son. For Flaubert the prostitute
is the archetype of the woman in her position of passive awaiting. The
fallen "grande dame" of this story already resembles the courtesan
Marie of "Novembre"—herself formerly a "grande dame"—awaiting
her ideal lover:

> Moi qui après des bains de fraises au lait, je suis venue ici, m'étendre sur le grabat
> commun où la foule passe; au lieu d'être la maîtresse d'un seul, je me suis faite la
> servante de tous. ... Mais ma dernière pensée, mon dernier espoir, le sais-tu? Oh,
> j'y comptais, c'était de trouver un jour l'homme qui m'a toujours fui... chimère qui
> n'est que dans mon coeur, et que je veux tenir dans mes mains... (OJ II, 226)[5]

Henriette's praxis, that of the courtesan, does not differ essentially
from Annette's: it is the woman's effort to re-establish the ideal in the
world, to achieve a final disalienation. But Henriette's passivity brings
out more than Annette's assault on Robert the specifically feminine
nature of this praxis. Henriette's life becomes wholly an awaiting of
Paul; rather than seeking, like Annette, actively to make the son into
the father, she simply lets him come to her in an adult sexual role.

The suicide of the "grande dame" is more than an expiation of the
incestuous act that led to the death of her son. It is a voluntary re-

---

[5] A few pages earlier, Marie had indeed described herself in her earlier existence
as a "grande dame": "Grande dame, je me levais à midi, j'avais une livrée qui me
suivait partout" (OJ II, 223).

nouncement of life based on a conscious recognition that all hope of disalienation has been lost. The heroine herself comes to realize the impossibility of returning to the ideal in the world, because this return has been revealed as forbidden, incestuous. Thus Henriette's experience expresses in a more absolute form than Annette's the necessary inadequacy of the woman's praxis; its object is by its very nature a forbidden one. But this work still belongs to a Romantic, aprioristic stage in the author's development. The ideal is shown as impossible of attainment, but this is discovered only through a symbolic revelation of its incestuous origins. The worldly experience of awaiting that is Henriette's does not itself demonstrate its own hopelessness, as is the case with Emma Bovary.

In identifying with the woman's passive awaiting of the ideal, Flaubert has uncovered the essentially regressive nature of the Romantic praxis that models itself on an impossible return to the paradisial state of childhood. The "grande dame" discovers in the incestuous nature of her ideal the impossibility of returning to a state now cut off by the very fact of adulthood. But this impossibility is revealed only through her encounter with the incarnate ideal itself in the person of Paul. The invalidity of worldly praxis is revealed from without by the unworldly ideal itself. For this revelation to become a truly *aesthetic* discovery and to result in a transcendence of Romantic literary forms, it must install itself wholly within the world of everyday, unideal experience.

CHAPTER XIII

DEUX MAINS SUR UNE COURONNE, OU PENDANT LE QUINZIEME SIECLE (EPISODES DU REGNE DE CHARLES VI)

January 1836

I. *La Reine à Paris:* It is towards evening when King Charles VI appears at the gates of Paris; his lovely queen riding behind him casts meaningful glances at the duke of Orléans and receives the wild acclamations of the flower-throwing crowds. That evening there is a ball at the court such as was never seen before—a royal orgy. "Le roi avait quitté son diadème, la reine sa pudeur, la femme sa vertu!" Isabeau, dancing in the arms of Orléans, returns his smiles and his words of love; in the duke she has found a kindred soul, a heart worthy of her own.

II. *Le duc mort!* One day, long afterwards, Isabeau returns, weeping with anger, from the Parlement. Vowing to seek vengeance for this outrage, she tells Orléans what has happened: the Parlement has accused her of being the cause of the king's madness and of the nation's woes, and has taken away her regency to give it to Jean sans Peur. Orléans swears that the Burgundian will die. Yes, his mistress continues in her rage, and when he is dead then the two of them will reign; all alone they shall wield power in the kingdom and govern the people, "masse aveugle et stupide!"

Eleven o'clock strikes and the duke departs; Isabeau feels uneasy at his being without bodyguards. Suddenly she hears the noise of fighting from the street and a voice crying, "C'est le coup de Bourgogne." Orléans, mortally wounded, is brought back to his mistress' house, where he dies.

III. *Le roi fou:* News of the assassination spreads through Paris the next day, and reactions to the crime are diverse: some want to declare open war on Jean sans Peur; others want to assassinate him secretly. When the Parlement convenes, the King in a rare moment of lucidity rises to denounce the felony of Jean sans Peur and the treachery of the Parlement for having admitted him to their ranks. But here the King falters and, falling back into idiocy, he cries "Au feu!... roi, ne vas pas plus loin, tu es trahi!" Pale and trembling, he rushes from the Parlement.

IV. *A vendre:* A long time has passed since the death of Orléans. Tanneguy Duchâtel is exhorting a group of nobles at the Club des Armagnacs: "Quoi! vous laissez ainsi blanchir les os de Bocherville [the duke of Orléans] sans les venger?" Shamed into action by his insistence, they agree to draw Jean sans Peur into a trap. And to make sure he falls into it, they decide to bribe his mistress, Henriette de Giac.

V. *Plus de mains! plus de couronnes!* Henriette, won over by Tanneguy Duchâtel, is alone with Jean sans Peur, trying to persuade him to go to the fatal meeting with the Dauphin. "Allez-y donc," she urges him, "vous perdriez votre nom de Jean sans Peur." Her lover is tortured by premonitions of his approaching death, but he gloomily resigns himself to his fate and departs. Five minutes later Henriette has a change of heart; she quickly summons a page to ride after the Burgundian and warn him of the trap. But, once more changing her mind, she instructs the page only to say "qu'il prenne bien garde à sa loyale personne." Jean sans Peur rides unwarned into the ambush; he is murdered and his body exhibited in the streets.

Isabeau dies in shame and poverty soon after. "Le tombeau n'a pas été pour elle un lit de repos, son siècle l'a maudite et les historiens l'ont flétrie."

"DEUX MAINS," dated by Flaubert January 1836,[1] is the longest and most ambitious of the *contes historiques* of the first period; to judge from its chaotic construction one might well say that it is too long and too ambitious. Like "Duc de Guise" it is composed of independent scenes, but while the scenes of "Duc de Guise," following Chateaubriand's narrative, form a coherent whole, those of "Deux mains," taken from a variety of unrelated sources, are correspondingly uncoordinated. Flaubert's narrative attempts to bring together historical events in fact unconnected and occurring many years apart. The queen's entry into Paris took place in 1389; Orléans's murder, which directly follows it in Flaubert's story, occurred in 1407, and the assassination of Jean sans Peur, which Flaubert attempts to depict as a revenge for that of Orléans, was only carried out a full thirteen years later in 1420. The product of Flaubert's efforts is chaotic indeed; evidently the fitting together of disparate historical elements spread over a thirty-year period was a task beyond his powers at this early stage in his career.

Bruneau mentions a number of well-established sources for "Deux mains":[2] extracts by Juvenal des Ursins (for I) and Alain Chartier (for II) found in Tissot's *Leçons et modèles de littérature française* (an anthology Flaubert had already utilized in "San Pietro Ornano"), Barante's *Histoire des ducs de Bourgogne* (for the description of Jean's murder in V), and Dumas's novel, *Isabel de Bavière,* which deals with the heroine of Flaubert's story. It seems likely that still other sources were used, notably for III (the King's speech to the Parlement).

"Deux mains," in sharp contrast to the guilt laden "La fiancée" and "La grande dame," illustrates the positive, self-assertive side of Flaubert's Romanticism, the taste for orgy and sadism that found expression in his maturity in *Salammbô* and *Hérodias.* Here historical idealization has abolished the separation between world and ideal which is at the heart of the "contemporary" stories, and the adolescent's frustrated desires for sexual pleasure and worldly recognition are released in defiance of the taboos of bourgeois morality:

[1] From this point on all the stories save "Une leçon d'histoire naturelle, genre commis" are dated by the author himself.

[2] See Bruneau, *Les débuts littéraires,* pp. 83–85.

Le soir, il y eut fête à la Cour, mais une fête comme jamais aucun Français n'en avait vu, une fête avec le luxe effréné d'une imagination jeune, exaltée; une fête, mais une fête à la Isabeau, une fête où la passion était jusque dans la danse, où la musique respirait la volupté; une fête où, pour la première fois, il y eut des fanfares, des danses impudiques; une fête où le vin ruisselait à flots, où la mollesse avait été chercher ce qu'il y a de plus raffiné, la richesse ce qu'il y a de plus resplendissant; une fête! non, une orgie royale. Le roi avait quitté son diadème, la reine sa pudeur, la femme sa vertu! Et se dépouillant de toute parure comme d'un manteau, le roi en se montrant semblait dire: "Voilà votre roi qui se vautre dans l'orgie, la reine qui donne des leçons de volupté, les femmes qui sont à vendre." (OJ I, 42)

This fête is, like the ball witnessed by the *moine des Chartreux*, a "frenetic" version of the dance of "Une pensée"; its orgiastic nature reflects, however, not a removal of the author's sexual inhibitions but the reverse. Only in orgiastic violence can the inhibited soul lose itself and so permit itself pleasure. The portrayal of the king and queen "giving lessons" in voluptuousness involves a renouncement of authority by the rulers who would normally be expected to maintain the standards of "parental" morality. Thus is worldly sexuality legitimized. And in Isabeau's love relationship with Orléans, Flaubert represents the worldly paradise he only glimpsed in "Une pensée":

Elle avait trouvé dans le comte d'Armagnac [Orléans] une âme qui pût se répandre entière dans son âme, un coeur qui pût s'épancher dans son coeur, une bouche qui pouvait dire: "je t'adore" à sa bouche qui disait: "je t'aime!" (OJ I, 42–43)

Orléans's perfect suitability as Isabeau's lover is reminiscent of the perfection the "grande dame" found in her son Paul. But now there is no question of revealing the intrinsic impossibility of this perfect union. It too is destroyed, through Orléans's murder, but the cause of destruction is wholly external, "accidental."

In the second part of the story, the union of Isabeau and Orléans reveals another characteristically Flaubertian dimension. Isabeau seeks to gain power over the Burgundian faction led by Jean sans Peur, but she cannot act directly. Instead, she is dependent on Orléans to murder Jean and restore her to power:

— Oh! duc d'Orléans! je ne me contiens plus de colère! Quelque chose que je le broie, que je le déchire; je me meurs de soif! C'est du vin qu'il me faut, mais du rouge, duc d'Orléans!
— Isabeau, soit! oui, le Bourguignon mourra, je vous le jure. (OJ I, 44)

Throughout her speech is visible an impotent envy that reappears in "Un parfum à sentir" and in the "worldly" stories of the next period:

Sais-tu ce que c'est que l'envie? L'envie, c'est quelque chose qui est là, bouillonnant et rude; c'est un serpent qui vous dévore, qui est là dans votre lit, dans vos rêves, qui vous poursuit comme un remords; c'est comme une goutte de poison qui mange et qui tache le marbre le plus poli. (OJ I, 44)

These passages reflect the frustration of the imprisoned adolescent that is the author. Why is it given to a *woman* to express it? Here again, as in "La grande dame," it is not so much the man's active quest for worldly goals but the woman's passive awaiting of them that attracts the author. The passivity of Isabeau is a translation into "external," worldly terms of the "internal" passivity of Henriette. The latter awaited her son because only by giving herself up to him could she return to the preworldly paradise; Isabeau "awaits" the action of Orléans simply because as a woman she wields no worldly power. Henriette represents Flaubert's guilty, inhibited side which regards worldly action as evil, while Isabeau reflects that part of him which would like to act, and feels itself constrained *from without* by his inferior adolescent position. Indeed, the "awaiting" fails here as well; the externally imposed destruction of Isabeau's hopes through Orléans's murder is consistent with the "external" pattern of their relationship.

The most important development of the remainder of the story, the murder of Jean sans Peur, is the third variation of the historical assassination theme that first appeared in "Duc de Guise" and was repeated in the death of Orléans earlier in this story. What is the source of Flaubert's obsession with this theme? In "Duc de Guise" the murder was interpreted as the killing of the father by the jealous son. But the "father" that Guise represented was not a villain opposing the son's rightful interests, like Robert in "La fiancée," but an inhabitant of a historically idealized worldly paradise; his death involved the destruction of this paradise by the son Henri. The murder of Orléans, which is dealt with only briefly, is similar to that of Guise in the indifference of the victim to his dangerous situation; each protagonist, secure in his paradise, goes to his death with utter unconcern, as though not believing in his own mortality. But in Jean sans Peur Flaubert represents the idealized historical hero as filled with dread of his own impending doom. Jean has no loyal friends or sweetheart like Guise; even his mistress is an agent of his assassins. He subsists in the idealized paradise only in the sense that he is a "monumental" historical figure, whose greatness lies within himself and need not be sought in the world. But his ideal existence has lost the serenity of Guise's or Orléans's; instead he feels an intense anxiety at its prospective dissolution:

— Ce jour-là, si j'en réchappe, aura été pour moi un jour bien cruel; j'ai assisté à bien des batailles, Henriette, j'ai vu bien des sièges, reçu bien des blessures, entendu siffler bien des balles, eh bien, j'aime mieux la plus sanglante bataille, le siège le plus acharné, les plus larges blessures que ce que j'éprouve maintenant....

— Oh! non, ne craignez rien, allez-y donc; vous perdriez votre nom de Jean sans Peur.

— Oh! Jean sans Peur, c'était jadis; maintenant il est mort.

— Mort! que voulez-vous dire?

— Je veux dire qu'il le sera bientôt. (OJ I, 51–52)

The historical hero has thus internalized the necessity of his own destruction, a necessity that had been experienced by Guise purely as an *external* force. What does this signify? The historical "worldly paradise" had never been depicted as a permanent state, but always as something about to be destroyed. Guise's serenity corresponded not to the ultimate truth of his life as it actually turned out, but to his vision of it "as it should have been." The nostalgic falseness of Guise's attitude corresponded closely with the superworldly poses of the "executioners" of the works contemporaneous with it: "Deux amours" and "Marguerite de Bourgogne." In each story the incompatibility of the ideal with the worldly is recognized but at the same time refused. But, just as the "Bourreau" Ernest of "Deux amours" evolved into the guilty spirit Paul in "La fiancée," the serene Guise is transformed into the trembling Jean who experiences within himself the necessary dissolution of the worldly ideal.

Thus in "Deux mains" historical idealization loses its privilege of permitting a legitimate expression of worldly desires. In the person of Jean, the historical hero has now been made to experience like the contemporary protagonist his own *falling* into the unideal world in which praxis must be paid for with guilt. In the second period, the historical heroes experience the guilt of their praxial existence with great intensity; in them the "internal" and "external" elements hitherto found separately are united.

In comparison with works like "La fiancée" and "La grande dame," "Deux mains" appears superficial and relatively impersonal, telling the reader apparently little about the author. But this impersonality is largely deceptive. The external, worldly oriented side of Flaubert's character cannot be neglected in order to concentrate exclusively on his self-critical, inhibited "interior." If it is this "interior" that presents the problems of existence in Flaubert's works, it will be the "exterior" that is given the task of solving them. The intuitions that in "La fiancée" and "La grande dame" seemed to preclude all possibilities of worldly praxis cannot remain internal; they must be worked out *through* the world, through the uncovering of the protagonist's illusions about the world. This *Madame Bovary* shows us. But we cannot understand how Flaubert ever "forced himself" to write *Madame Bovary* unless we recognize that contemporaneous with the pessimistic intuition of "La grande dame" was the passionate desire for worldly pleasures expressed in "Deux mains." The pessimism of "La grande dame" cannot be wholly "true" if the author still yearns for the joys of the world despite their negative, dissolving nature. It is the lesson of the mature works to demonstrate the truth of "La grande dame" *through* the dissolution of worldly desire itself.

CHAPTER XIV

UN PARFUM A SENTIR, OU LES BALADINS: CONTE PHILOSOPHIQUE, MORAL, IMMORAL *AD LIBITUM*

April 1, 1836

THE "TROUPE acrobatique du sieur Pedrillo," consisting of Pedrillo himself—a poor *baladin*—and his three young sons, is giving a performance when an ugly woman dressed in rags forces her way into the tent. She is Pedrillo's wife Marguerite, just returned from the hospital. Pedrillo insists that she join in the performance, but, as Marguerite had feared, the audience breaks into a derisive laugh at the sight of her.

Once the family is alone, Marguerite complains that she is not well, she still suffers as a result of her broken leg. "Si tu m'aimais comme je t'aime!" she says plaintively to her husband. But Pedrillo is tired of her whining, and he treats her roughly, as he does the children. The real question is what Marguerite can do to earn her keep—unfortunately she still limps. Tomorrow, Pedrillo orders, she and the children are to perform in the street to provide the family with food.

Marguerite sets out with the children the next day, but no one stops to give money to the unattractive *baladine*. Desperate at the idea of returning home penniless, for a moment she considers prostituting herself, but then thinks, "Oh! non! non! qui voudrait de moi?" When she gets home, she is beaten by Pedrillo.

Driven to despair by an unfeeling and callous society, Pedrillo goes to a gambling den to try his luck. His ten francs grow miraculously to ten thousand—but bad fortune follows and once again reduces him to nothing. He goes out into the night and, while walking home, is assailed by visions of all kinds: heaps of money, a corpse, a lion roaring.

The next morning the family folds up their tent and sets out in a cart when suddenly Pedrillo recognizes the owner of a menagerie traveling in the opposite direction—it is his old friend Isambart, and with him is his young and beautiful sister Isabellada. The two families decide to join forces, to the great joy of Pedrillo.

For two years now the two families have been performing together; the collaboration has had great success. But Marguerite is even more wretched than before: Pedrillo has taken Isabellada as his mistress and they now have a young child. Marguerite is humiliated by the daily comparisons between her and her rival; ugly, awkward, forty years old, she is forced to dance beside Isabellada, who at twenty is seductive and full of grace. And at a masked ball Marguerite, dressed in a *domino noir*, is pursued by the jeers and taunts of Isambart, dressed as "un pierrot avec une tête de boeuf." With sadistic relish, he enumerates her inferiorities to the beautiful Isabellada. Marguerite, stunned by Isambart's unprovoked outburst of hatred, turns against God and man; "à cette société qui n'avait voulu lui donner ni pain, ni amour, ni pitié, elle voua la haine et la jalousie."

Early the next morning Marguerite is awakened by the voice of one of her sons arguing with Isabellada. The latter had taken the boy's cover to give it to her own child. Enraged at this new provocation, Marguerite grabs the blanket from her hated rival. "N'est-ce pas assez, fille de Satan, de nous insulter en public par ta beauté... sans que tu viennes encore arracher les linges qui cachent le sang de nos plaies!" Pedrillo, who enters the tent at this moment, will listen only to Isabellada's protestations of innocence, and Marguerite, writhing in anger, tells her husband to throw her to the lion on the day when she can bear her torment no longer.

One day in June the menagerie is once again on the move, and Marguerite and Pedrillo are walking beside the moving wagons. Suddenly she turns to him with a final reproachful tirade. Interrupting her threats of violence against Isabellada, Pedrillo warns her to be silent and finally, exasperated, he opens the door of the lion's cage and throws her in. The proud beast has already grabbed her when Isambart rushes in and saves Marguerite.

A madwoman, unsteady in her gait and dressed in rags, leaves the hospital; street urchins jeer at her strange appearance. It is Marguerite. Suddenly she sees a carriage pass by and she recognizes the beautiful face of Isabellada, now the "dame de compagnie" of a rich nobleman. "C'est toi, Isabellada! Oh! va, je te reconnais bien, c'est toujours cet air de courtisane, cette taille impudique." But Isabellada pretends not to know Marguerite and has the coachman chase her off with his whip. "La mort!" laughs Marguerite. And she runs off toward the Seine.

Marguerite's corpse is recovered from the water. Exposed at the morgue, it attracts the attention of two young medical students, but they are forced to interrupt their examination of the cadaver to make way for a passing coach. It is carrying Isabellada to the Opera.

MORALITE

"C'est de bonne foi que sont écrites ces pages, et même je les ai composées avec feu et enthousiasme." Flaubert claims that his intention in this story is to rail against prejudices. As for the title, it refers to Marguerite; Isabellada is "une fleur à voir," because for her, beauty is everything.

CE QUE VOUS VOUDREZ

What a pleasure it is to create, cries the author. "Ecrire, oh! écrire, c'est s'emparer du monde..." Flaubert gives the timetable of composition of his story, and engages the reader to seek for himself its bitter philosophical message.

"UN PARFUM à sentir," a full forty pages in length, is more than twice as long as any other work of the period; it is the longest piece of narrative fiction that Flaubert was to write before the first *Education sentimentale* (1843–1845). No significant sources have been found for it, although Bruneau (pp. 120–121) has shown the influence of Balzac's *Peau de chagrin* on the concluding "Moralité"[1] and on the gambling

---

[1] This suggestion was first made by Algernon P. Coleman in *Flaubert's Literary Development in the Light of his "Mémoires d'un fou," "Novembre," and "Education sentimentale" (Version of 1845)* (Baltimore, 1914), p. 69, n. 2.

scene in chapter iv. Bruneau also suggests that Flaubert's heroine Marguerite was modeled on "la célèbre équilibriste Mme. Saqui" who had visited Rouen at about the time this story was written; this ingenious hypothesis is founded on a curious similarity between Flaubert's description of his heroine and a journalist's portrait of the entertainer.[2] But this source is experiential, not literary; and to judge from the concreteness of Flaubert's description of the *baladins'* performances in chapter vi (OJ I, 91–93), "Un parfum à sentir," despite the literary reminiscences it may very well contain, is the first of Flaubert's fictions to be inspired directly by his own personal experiences.

The first half of the story, comprising the first five chapters, follows the familiar Romantic pattern of the "social" novel. Both Marguerite and Pedrillo are pitted in their misfortunes as unfree victims of the evils of society. Numerous "philosophical" observations generalize the author's sympathy for his characters, who are seen not as individuals but as examples of a social type:

> Pour moi, rien ne m'attriste tant que la misère cachée sous les haillons de la richesse, que le galon d'un laquais autour des cheveux nus de la pauvreté, qu'un chant qui couvre des sanglots, qu'une larme sous une goutte de miel; aussi je plains d'un amour bien sincère les baladins et les filles de joie. (OJ I, 78)

> Vous frémissez peut-être, aimable lectrice, à la peinture de cette moitié de la société, la maison de jeu? L'autre, c'est l'hôpital, c'est la guillotine. Ah! voyez-vous, jeune enfant, c'est que faussée par une éducation vicieuse, vous n'êtes pas descendue jusque dans la misère, vous n'avez pas vu son délire, vous n'avez pas entendu ses hurlements de rage, vous n'avez pas sondé ses plaies, vous n'avez pas compris ses douleurs amères, son désespoir, et ses crimes! (OJ I, 82)

We have already seen elements of social concern in "La grande dame," where the misfortunes of both Ernest and Henriette are given an economic significance:

> un joueur de vieille [*sic*] vint devant l'hôtel du chevalier.... *Oh le pauvre homme, il avait l'air bien triste, ses pieds étaient nus.* Son habit pourtant était de drap très fin et tout en lui annonçait que c'était un revers de la fortune qui l'avait poussé dans cette extrême misère. (Bruneau, p. 125)

> Enfin une vieille femme vint s'approcher [de Henriette], et lui proposa une chose... horrible, elle s'enfuit d'abord *mais elle avait faim.* Elle y consentit ensuite. (Bruneau, p. 126)

This "social" content in "La grande dame" is a means of externalizing in the world the personal relations of the characters. The wealth of M.

---

[2] Bruneau, *Les débuts littéraires,* p. 128.

de la Prevobine is an external indication of the worldly superiority of the "father" over the "son" Ernest as a husband for Henriette; the Revolution is a manifestation of social justice that rewards the son and punishes the father *in the world*. Can a similar relationship be sought in "Un parfum à sentir" between the "external" poverty of Marguerite and Pedrillo and their "internal" significance within the universe of the author?

To answer this question we must first understand what is meant by externalization. This does not simply involve an arbitrary symbolism in which feelings of guilt, justification, and the like, are translated into elements of a worldly situation. The character's position in the world is what he is given, independently of his wishes, to react against or to accept as the condition of his existence. Through the "external" poverty of Marguerite and Pedrillo is made visible on a concrete level the negativity that bourgeois society represents for Flaubert. Here the author is not merely a follower of the "social" Romantics, but an adolescent painfully conscious of his own lack of recognition within the adult world. It is Flaubert's own personal experience of the "enfer" that is externalized in the poverty of Marguerite and Pedrillo.

The poverty of the *baladins* is more radically a part of their nature than that of Henriette; it exists a priori and cannot be construed as a punishment for a crime. Nor is the injustice of the world presented in this story as the act of a villain destroying an original ideal state; it is simply a necessary fact of life. This a priori representation of the negativity of the world coincides with the absence of any "paradise." Unlike Annette or Henriette, Marguerite never shared an ideal happiness with her beloved. The "external" career of the *baladins* as a family and the "internal" one of Marguerite alone have the same structure: they desire not return but advancement to a *new* status. This is as true of Marguerite's unsuccessful "awaiting" of the affection of her husband, which she had never possessed, as of their common efforts to lift themselves out of poverty. This development is of profound significance: it marks Flaubert's recognition of the inevitability of the unideal world as the only possible scene of action for his protagonists. The conception of the "return" expressed in "La fiancée" and "La grande dame" has not vanished forever from Flaubert's works, but he never again represents the original paradise as a concrete worldly possibility.

If Pedrillo, like Marguerite, is a victim of society, a *baladin* far closer to the "joueur de vielle" Ernest than the wealthy M. de la Prevobine, he is far from feeling any ideal affection for Marguerite. On the contrary, his poverty is presented as an excuse for his cruelty to her and the children:

> Oh! plaignez-le, ce joueur, ce baladin, cet homme de mauvaise vie, cet homme qui n'aime pas ses enfants, qui bat sa femme. Oh! plaignez-le, parce que c'est un infâme, un baladin, un homme de mauvaise vie, un homme qui bat sa femme et qui n'aime pas ses enfants.
> C'est que la misère a voulu qu'il soit baladin, la faim lui a tellement aiguisé les dents qu'elle l'a poussé dans une maison de jeu, son éducation l'a fait un homme de mauvaise vie, sa femme est laide, rouge, édentée. Oh! une femme rouge! et ses enfants lui déplaisent parce qu'ils lui disent: "J'ai faim!" et ce cri-là lui fait mal, car il n'a rien à leur donner. (OJ I, 83)

The poverty of Pedrillo makes him, in his worldly position, rather a "son" than a "father," and in the first half of "Un parfum à sentir" it is this aspect and not his personal relationship to Marguerite that is predominant.[3] Flaubert, however, creates no ideal son-lover for Marguerite that could be opposed to Pedrillo. Pedrillo thus plays the parts of son and father at once: this was already hinted at in Ernest's development in "La grande dame." By combining the two roles in a single character, Flaubert affirms the son's identity with the father in his rejection of the "ideal" love of Marguerite. The all-important sexual basis of this identification is still only implicit in the passage quoted above, where Pedrillo's rejection of Marguerite is excused in part by her unattractiveness ("sa femme est laide, rouge, édentée"); it becomes overt in the second half of the story with the introduction of Marguerite's beautiful rival, Isabellada. At this point it is not so much the specifically sexual element that is in question as the negativity of Pedrillo's social condition in general; his wife's ugliness is only one more aspect of the misery that surrounds him and whose degrading influence he cannot escape.

Flaubert's solidarity with both Marguerite and Pedrillo depends upon the situation of both as victims of bourgeois society. In his hostility to this "paternal" force Flaubert is able temporarily to reconcile the active, pleasure-seeking side of his personality with the passive side that renounces action as guilty—the external with the internal. The gambling scene exemplifies this reconciliation particularly well. Pedrillo enters a gambling den, a place of prostitution and violence:

> une maison de jeu avec toute sa prostitution hideuse, un de ces taudis où parfois, le lendemain, on trouve quelque cadavre mutilé entre des verres brisés et des haillons

---

[3] It is noteworthy that the children, before whom Pedrillo acts with assurance in his role of father, play a very minor part throughout all but the first pages of the story.

tout rouges de sang.... Quelque femmes à moitié nues se promenaient paisiblement...
et plus loin, dans un coin, deux hommes armés, debout devant une jeune fille couchée
sur le pavé et liée avec des cordes, tiraient à la courte paille. (OJ I, 82)

Yet Pedrillo's "orgy" has none of the voluptuousness of the "fête à la
Isabeau" of "Deux mains." After winning a large fortune, he promptly
loses it all; his temporary pleasure is justified by the agony of his
defeat:

Et il découvrit sa poitrine, elle était toute sanglante, et ses mains avaient de la
chair humaine au bout des ongles. (OJ I, 86)

But this reconciliation of exterior and interior cannot be permanent.
At the end of the fifth chapter, the introduction of Isabellada (which,
as Flaubert's preface indicates, had been planned from the beginning)[4]
gives Pedrillo a satisfactory sexual object and thereby destroys the basis
for the author's sympathy with him. Because he is no longer cut off
from adult sexuality, he has obtained a "place in the world" and has
become an unambiguous father; thus in Flaubert's scheme of things he
is no longer a victim of society. And thus Marguerite in her final jealous
attack on Pedrillo denounces him as a "riche" although he is still only
a *baladin* as before:

Tu es heureux, toi, je hais les heureux; *vous êtes riches* et je hais les riches, parce
qu'on ne m'aime pas, parce que je suis malheureuse et misérable. (OJ I, 103)

The split between the two halves of the author's personality can no
longer be covered over. Although Flaubert himself as a worldly individual has not had the success of Pedrillo, this is a secondary matter;
the question here is not one of success but of tendency. To the extent
that Flaubert must admit to sharing the unideal desires of Pedrillo,
he must resign himself to being not merely a victim but a participant in
the worldly "enfer." The guilty nature of his participation in Pedrillo's
sexual attraction to Isabellada is given a most explicit expression:

Isabella [*sic*], en robe blanche, une écharpe rose autour du cou, sautait, dansait,
tourbillonnait sur le vieux tapis de Perse.... C'était sa valse, *sa danse tourbillon-
nante comme des pensées d'amour* qui bondissent dans le coeur d'un poète. Et sa
gorge si blanche, blanche comme du marbre le plus blanc, sa gorge si pure, si
fraîche, si suave, et sa tête, et ses yeux, et son sourire! Oh! la gorge d'une femme,
quand elle est jeune et jolie, quand on la sent comme une rose à travers la mous-

---

[4] In the preface he states his intention to:
Mettre en présence et en contact la saltimbanque laide, méprisée, édentée,
battue par son mari, la saltimbanque jolie, couronnée de fleurs, de parfums
et d'amour, les réunir sous le même toit, les faire déchirer par la jalousie
jusqu'au dénouement qui doit être bizarre et amer. (OJ I, 69)

seline sautillante au mouvement de sa danse; oh! la gorge d'une femme! n'est-ce pas que c'est là, *dans vos rêves d'amour,* dans vos nuits d'insomnie, *dans ces nuits que l'on passe à pleurer et à maudire sa mère,* n'est-ce pas que c'est sur sa gorge que vous avez posé votre tête toute chaude et toute bouillante? c'est sur sa gorge que vous avez tressailli d'amour, que toutes les fibres de votre âme ont vibré, comme la lyre touchée par le doigt d'une jeune fille, et se sont raidies de volupté comme les muscles d'un athlète. (OJ I, 91)

Here Flaubert's "pensée d'amour" reappears once more, but the dance no longer represents an unproblematic worldly paradise; along with the narrator's pleasurable self-absorption in Isabellada's beauty goes a confession of guilt: "vos nuits d'amour... *ces nuits que l'on passe à pleurer et à maudire sa mère.*" Quite evidently Flaubert is here confessing his adolescent autoerotic experiences, but what concerns us above all is not the particular nature of his sexual activity but the guilt he expresses for it. And it cannot be a coincidence that this guilt is directed specifically to the mother. This does not mean that the son "desires his mother" in a simplistically Oedipal sense. Rather it involves a recognition of the lost prepubertal basis of the original paradise, in which the child loves his mother without guilt; the worldly paradise is inaccessible because it is modeled on the paradise of child and mother and not on that of husband and wife. "La grande dame" revealed the maternal component of this ideal relationship, but from the mother's, not the son's point of view. Marguerite is the same age in this story as Henriette when she was visited by her son: "Marguerite était laide, *elle avait quarante ans*" (OJ I, 90). Compare "La grande dame": "Un jour entra dans ce lieu-là un jeune homme de vingt-ans. Il y avait bien long-temps qu'elle était là Henriette. *Car elle en avait 40 alors*" (Bruneau, p. 126). And even in the earlier story there was never any mention of Henriette's attractiveness for her son. What is recognized now in "maudire sa mère" is that adult sexuality represents a negation of the child's preworldly relationship to his mother. The mother, and with her the original paradise, has become unattractive not merely for Pedrillo but for the author himself.

Thus far I have discussed the effect of Isabellada's entry into the story only in its effect on Pedrillo. But since Marguerite, not her husband, is the real protagonist of "Un parfum à sentir," it is her reaction that will ultimately prove of deeper significance. There is indeed a considerable transformation in Marguerite's character after Isabellada makes her appearance. If earlier Marguerite was a purely passive victim of Pedrillo's hatred, her jealousy of Isabellada, although never manifesting itself in action, is an active, violent emotion; there is no longer any unprotesting acceptance of suffering. The violence of Marguerite's feelings is first made known at the *bal masqué* in chapter vii:

Un seul masque [Marguerite] reste pensif sur sa banquette, il est triste, et les applaudissements de la salle le font pleurer, la grâce d'Isabellada lui est à charge. C'est qu'aussi là, comme autre part, il est venu apporter sous son masque sa jalousie amère et sa haine furieuse et ses peines et ses plaies saignantes et ses blessures profondes. (OJ I, 94–95)[5]

This is an accent hitherto unheard in Flaubert's works. Earlier protagonists had experienced feelings of rivalry, and in "La fiancée" Paul had expressed an intense hatred for Robert, but never before had any of Flaubert's characters been rejected by his (or her) beloved in favor of a rival. Previously the ideal relationship of the hero and heroine had always been destroyed from without by the evil act of a villain like Robert, but now the ideal has broken up from within and Marguerite is forced to view herself as unsuitable per se as a love object.

Later in the same scene her unattractiveness is brought home to her with singular intensity in the insulting tirade of Isambart. In a strictly literary sense this encounter adds nothing to the story, since Marguerite's ugliness has already been emphasized, an emphasis that only serves to make the scene more significant. Through the intermediary of a secondary character the author is evidently expressing the opinion that his worldly self holds of Marguerite and of the "internal" side of his personality, which she represents. The conclusion of Isambart's speech is particularly revelatory:

—[Marguerite]: Oh! Isambart, que t'ai-je fait?
—Rien, mais tu me déplais; tantôt, quand je te voyais faire tes tours, que j'aurais eu de plaisir à jeter de la boue sur ta robe bleue, à tirer tes cheveux, à meurtrir tes seins! Je sais bien, tu ne m'as jamais rien fait, tu es peut-être meilleure qu'une autre, mais enfin tu me déplais, je te souhaite du mal, c'est un caprice. D'abord, pourquoi pleurer toujours? avoir un air si sombre, une démarche si déplaisante, une tournure qui me fait bisquer enfin? Et puis, toujours, geindre et se lamenter! Eh bien, morbleu! pourquoi ne t'en vas-tu pas d'avec nous? (OJ I, 196–197)

The sympathy for Marguerite expressed so copiously throughout the first half of the story is no more; Marguerite may perhaps be "meilleure qu'une autre" but she is simply repulsive and there is no longer any question of redeeming her by emphasizing her superior moral qualities.

In what sense does Isambart's tirade express the feelings of the

---

[5] Note that Flaubert refers to his heroine by the masculine "le masque" and "il"; the change of gender evidently reinforces his identification with her torments.

author? In "La fiancée" and "La grande dame" Flaubert manifests a tendency to dwell on the sufferings of his heroines which can be interpreted as reflecting a certain sadistic enjoyment, an identification with the Satanic forces of the "enfer." Yet these heroines' difficulties are ultimately a punishment for their worldly infidelity to their original "ideal" lovers; Paul's own attitude to Annette in "La fiancée" is overtly punitive ("malheur à ma fiancée, si elle ne se dépêche"). In "Un parfum à sentir" there is no longer any question of justified punishment: Marguerite's only crime is her ugliness. In attacking Marguerite, Isambart-Flaubert is supporting the evil against the good; he is taking an overtly Satanic position. The worldly is given precedence over the ideal because it is more pleasurable, but in particular the "ideal" is shown to be not paradisial at all, but of only *moral* value. Marguerite is "better" than Isabellada, but this is no longer of any consequence because, from the standpoint of one alienated in the world, only the satisfaction of worldly desire can offer a possibility of disalienation. Isambart's violent outburst expresses the author's own chagrin at finding himself cut off from any legitimate possibility of worldly pleasure, left with a sense of his own virtuous superiority as his only compensation. By insulting this useless virtue the Flaubertian hero stands ready to take the truly praxial step of accepting for himself the guilt inherent in entering the world; and this must involve the renouncement of the facile Romantic superiority of the narrator of "Voyage en enfer," and the admission of his own need for recognition not above the world but within it .

But all is not so simple. If Flaubert's development were reducible to a simple case of "growing up" it would not concern us here. In spite of the hedonistic tendencies of Pedrillo and the "Satanic" ones of Isambart, Marguerite remains the central figure of the Flaubertian universe. What is of the greatest significance in Pedrillo's abandonment and Isambart's insults is the manner in which Marguerite must transform herself in order to deal with them. We have already seen a brief exhibition of Marguerite's jealousy. What are the consequences of this new emotion on her attitudes toward life in general? The answer is given in the following passage:

Elle demanda de l'amour à la société, on lui rit à la face; de l'humanité? on lui montra le chemin de l'hôpital; de la pitié? c'est une baladine. Ah! de la pitié à une baladine, à une voleuse d'enfants, à une coureuse des rues! Eh bien, *à cette société qui n'avait voulu lui donner ni pain, ni amour, ni pitié, elle voua la haine et la jalousie;...* à Dieu qui n'écouta pas ses prières, elle donna l'impiété; à la nature qui l'avait maltraitée, le mépris.

Aussi, quand elle voyait des gens riches, heureux, estimés, dont on prenait soin, elle leur souhaitait les calamités les plus grandes; elle riait des prières des pauvres, de leurs voeux, de leurs reliques, et en passant elle crachait sur le seuil des églises. (OJ I, 98–99)

This hatred for society is not at all equivalent to the mere observation, "le monde, c'est l'enfer," that made up the theme of "Voyage en enfer." Nor can it be reduced to the *ressentiment* against society that Marguerite's poverty would justify. The world is not simply unparadisial in the abstract, nor does it merely offer specific obstacles to the individual who seeks disalienation; world and ideal are utterly irreconcilable. Marguerite expresses the author's disillusionment with the very conception of awaiting the ideal in the world, the essence of the woman's praxis that has dominated the period. Henriette, for all her sufferings, never expressed any such opposition to the world nor was her awaiting altogether in vain, for she was able to enjoy, if only for a moment, the forbidden embraces of her son. For Marguerite, no such possibility remains; her only recourse is suicide.

Thus Marguerite in her new disillusioned outlook has come to agree with the author's own equation of the world with "l'enfer" as expressed in "Voyage en enfer." There is nothing fortuitous about this agreement. Because she has renounced the woman's position of awaiting disalienation from without, she has become *the first of Flaubert's protagonists to share his own basic insights about existence.* How far such a sharing was from Pedrillo, Marguerite's companion in poverty in the first half of the story, is demonstrated in the following passage:

Mais il ne comprenait pas, par exemple, pourquoi sa famille était malheureuse, non, il ne le comprenait pas; et, se raidissant contre le ciel, s'il l'avait pu, il aurait détruit la création, il aurait anéanti Dieu. (OJ I, 85)

Flaubert had just employed a page and a half, from which I have already quoted a lengthy passage,[6] in uncovering the roots of Pedrillo's and Marguerite's poverty in the necessary negativity of bourgeois society. But he showed Pedrillo as being able only to experience this negativity, not to understand it; if he had, "il aurait anéanti Dieu." This phrase is most revealing: because Pedrillo is a man, a realization such as Marguerite has arrived at would lead him to *act* against his fate by attempting to destroy God and his creation. Such indeed is the reaction of the heroes of the next period. But Marguerite, as a woman, does not have this possibility of action; and that is in effect why it is she and not Pedrillo—the woman and not the man—who is the first Flau-

---

[6] See above, p. 78.

bertian character to share the world view of the author. The male heroes of these works have always had the opportunity to act; when they lost it, as in "La fiancée," they relinquished the stage to the woman. But this active masculine experience of the world is a mode of existence foreign to the author himself. We should recall that the vision of "Voyage en enfer" was a wholly passive one, obtained through observation rather than action. Like the author, the woman has stood outside the world of action, not observing it, but waiting, like Henriette in "La grande dame," for the ideal to come out of it. Once this awaiting has revealed itself to her as illusory, the woman's extraworldly stance permits her to grasp, as if from without, the truth of worldly experience.

Beyond the question of whether it is the man's or the woman's praxis that permits a "correct" insight into worldly existence lies the nature of the author's identification with his characters which makes such an insight possible. If his very first work contained the conception of the world as an "enfer," why did Flaubert wait until the end of the period to share his conception with his heroes? How was he previously able to identify with protagonists that were in his own view deluding themselves about the true nature of the world?

The answer is that the source of Flaubert's identification came not from "Voyage en enfer" but from "Une pensée." Flaubert stands outside the world only in that he does not act in it, but as an adolescent he is aware of his own worldly desires. Although he cannot himself implement these desires, he is able to identify with heroes who as a consequence of their adult situation already possess a legitimate right to the "paradise." But this is only possible so long as the worldly evil that obstructs their legitimate pursuit of disalienation remains an external, contingent factor in their experience. The duality of Flaubert's position depends upon a separation of worldly desire into the rightful desire of the son and the evil one of the father, between the Paul and Robert of "La fiancée"; as long as this remains the case, even if the son's praxis becomes invalid, as it did in "La fiancée," the woman can still await his legitimate desire as *her* ideal. But in "Un parfum à sentir" the son and the father have merged into one figure, and there is no legitimate desire for Marguerite to await. Now that the son's "pensées d'amour" have become those of one whose nights are spent "à maudire sa mère," Marguerite's only course is to throw off her status as an *object* for these "pensées." In his identification with Marguerite, Flaubert shows himself to be in the process of casting off the illusory "adulthood" of his earlier protagonists and accepting the validity of his own preworldly adolescent position, with its external vision of the adult world as an "enfer." The author has been forced to recognize the *validity* of the inhibitions and frustrations that keep him from adulthood. Thus the succeeding works will have as protagonists not youthful, independent lovers like Paul or Ernest, but adolescents explicitly dependent on their family situation.

But this identification of Marguerite's position with that of the fourteen-year-old author, despite the similarity of their "philosophical" views, has still not been wholly clarified. It is easy to understand how Marguerite as a love object rejected by the worldly Pedrillo can remain an *object* of sympathy for the author. But in what way can he identify with this rejected love object when she becomes a *subject?* Or to turn the question around, in what way does Flaubert experience his own existence as that of a rejected object? The second-period story "La peste à Florence" offers a clue. In this work, the protagonist is engaged in a violent and unsuccessful rivalry with his elder brother for recognition by their father; the position of this hero has much in common with that of Marguerite.[7] Now the brother rivalry has evident roots in Flaubert's own family situation; his elder brother Achille was at this time preparing to follow their father into the medical profession, and, in the words of Thibaudet,

Achille, qui réussissait alors brillament dans ses études de médecine, était sans doute l'exemple proposé constamment et aigrement par leurs parents à Gustave le mauvais sujet.[8]

Marguerite's jealousy of the preferred Isabellada may well reflect in large measure Gustave's jealousy of the preferred Achille. Yet this is still only a superficial explanation. Why does the need for paternal recognition become explicit only now in his works? Because once Flaubert has come to experience his dependent adolescent position as a necessity, he must admit his own similarity with his heroines in *awaiting* recognition from his father rather than seeking to acquire it directly through "masculine" worldly activity.

After "Un parfum à sentir" the female protagonists that dominated the last half of the first period go into a long eclipse; only in "Rêve

[7] There are numerous textual resemblances as well: the description of Marguerite in the ball scene is later used in describing the hero of "La peste à Florence," who delivers to his brother a tirade quite similar to Marguerite's final harangue to Pedrillo. These passages are quoted in the discussion of the later work (q.v.).

[8] Albert Thibaudet, *Gustave Flaubert, 1821–1880: Sa vie, ses romans, son style,* 4th ed. (Paris, 1935). p. 18.

d'enfer" in the third period does a woman again play any but a minor role in Flaubert's stories. Because the "worldly paradise" has lost its validity, the woman's awaiting of the man's ideal love is no longer possible. The woman's passivity is simply reduced to its source in Flaubert's own experience: the passivity of the male adolescent before the paternal world. This does not by any means signify that passivity is for Flaubert nothing more than a temporary, adolescent phenomenon. The woman regains her predominant position later in the early works and dominates the first masterpiece of his maturity, *Madame Bovary*. But first Flaubert must examine the possibilities for worldly existence that remain open to the adolescent who no longer accepts the validity of an adult praxis. He returns to a female protagonist only when, having exhausted the possibilities of the *self*, the hero that shares the author's own consciousness of the negativity of the world, he is thrown back upon the praxis of the *other*, the woman who still retains her illusions of finding happiness in the "enfer."

CHAPTER XV

CHRONIQUE NORMANDE DU DIXIEME SIECLE

May 1836

"CONNAISSEZ-VOUS la Normandie, cette vieille terre classique du moyen âge, où chaque champ a eu sa bataille, chaque pierre garde son nom...?" On August 28, 952, King Louis IV enters triumphantly into Rouen, where he is hailed with enthusiasm by the assembled crowds. With him is the twelve year old Richard, son of the recently assassinated duke of Normandy; he is a beautiful child "aux cheveux blonds, aux yeux tendres." The king assumes a protective air towards the orphan, and promises publicly to avenge his father's murder.

At midnight in the palace Richard is asleep, and Louis looks out from his balcony at the peaceful calm of the night. The king's reveries are interrupted by the arrival of Arnould, a tall, sinister-looking individual. What news? Louis asks of his henchman. The people's discontent over the assassination of the duke of Normandy has been silenced, Arnould answers, by a "distribution de blé aux pauvres." Now the question is how to deal with the duke's young son. Arnould advises the king to give out news that Richard is ill, and then to have the boy secretly killed. Louis, pleased with this advice, promises to make Arnould his prime minister.

The next day Osmond, the young duke's tutor, comes to the palace to ask for his pupil; in so doing, he explains to the king, he is carrying out the last wishes of Richard's father, who made him promise to care for the boy after his death. The king retorts haughtily that Richard is in perfectly good hands at the palace; but the next morning when Osmond returns to ask about Richard's "illness" the king throws off his mask:

"Il est temps de cesser cet inutile carnaval; dans une heure huit mille hommes sont aux portes de Rouen, j'ai envoyé Arnould vers Bernard, général des troupes de Normandie."

Osmond, wounded by the king's insults, hurries from the palace to spread the news of Louis's treachery. He quickly gives orders to a group of loyal noblemen: "Va, dis [au peuple] qu'on lui a pris son duc, son enfant bien-aimé, excite-le, mets-lui les armes dans les mains." Within two hours a maddened crowd is besieging the palace, threatening to break down the doors if the king does not appear. "And yet these same crowds had welcomed him with flowers and cries of adoration!"

Louis sits alone and frightened in his room, waiting for Arnould; the latter arrives bringing bad news: Bernard has refused, in the most insulting terms, to lend his support to the king. With no other course left open to him, the king appears at the palace window, holding the young duke in his arms. At this sight the people drop their weapons and shout "Noël! vive le roi! vive le duc!" And this great shout resounded through the street of the city and found an echo in every heart.

"CHRONIQUE NORMANDE" is anomalous among Flaubert's early works; it is the only one of them to have a "happy ending," to reconcile the world with the ideal.

The chief historical source, as discovered by Bruneau, seems to be the

Histoire de Normandie by Théodore Licquet (Rouen, 1834); but this work could have provided Flaubert only with Louis's sequestration of the young duke and the popular uprising, which the king appeases by appearing before the people with the duke in his arms. The other elements of Flaubert's story—the king's plotting with Arnould, his conversations with Duke Richard's tutor Osmond,[1] and Bernard's particularly historic-appearing refusal to support Louis against the duke—were no doubt taken from a missing source.

"Chronique normande" describes a reconcilation of the "son" Richard with the "father" Louis; it is the only work of the period to do so, although the last page of the unfinished "San Pietro Ornano" reveals that such a reconciliation was earlier a temptation for the author. But the duke Richard is precisely the opposite of the active, worldly Ornano. Ornano was tempted to accept the doge's pardon, but only after he had established himself in the adult world by capturing his bride Vanina. Richard, however, remains a helpless child; in two of his three appearances he is shown asleep, and he never displays the least knowledge of his dangerous situation. His only action in the story is to demonstrate his unqualified respect for Louis's superior position:

Le jeune Richard, fils du duc Guillaume assassiné en Flandre, alla au-devant de lui [Louis]. Il était âgé de 12 ans, et c'était un bel enfant aux cheveux blonds, aux yeux tendres, au teint pâle; pourtant il montait habilement sa jument noire, et sa main portait fort bien une grande épée, *qu'il abaissa devant le roi, comme vassal et sujet.* (OJ II, 257–258)

The reconcilation between father and son is thus effected only by reducing the latter to a wholly passive position. With the elimination of the woman as protagonist, the male hero takes over her passive role, but even his "awaiting" takes place outside the consciousness of the sleeping duke, who never experiences the alienation that was the lot of Henriette or Marguerite.

Since the duke is entirely inactive, the worldly praxis that brings about the reconciliation of the pair can only be that of the king. What finally forces him to renounce his hostility to Richard? At the opening of the story, Louis and Richard make a triumphant entry into Rouen; here Louis makes a hypocritical display of affection to the young duke which prefigures the protective attitude forced upon him at the end:

—Pauvre enfant! dit Louis IV en l'embrassant et en versant une larme que chacun vit couler sur sa joue... (OJ II, 259)

---

[1] In Licquet, Bernard is the duke's guardian, and Osmond a noble later associated with an abduction of Richard from a prison where Louis had confined him. (See Théodore Licquet, *Histoire de Normandie* [Rouen, 1834], pp. 124 ff.)

It is in the difference between Louis's situation in this scene and in the final one, where he appears holding Richard in his arms, that we can see the result of his experiences in the story. And the sole factor that has changed is the attitude of the people toward Louis. In the opening scene the populace greets the king enthusiastically, with no apparent interest in Richard:

Le roi arriva à la porte Beauvoisine à huit heures du soir, on l'attendait depuis le matin. Dès qu'il parut, ce furent des trépignements, des bravos, des cris de joie, des hurlements d'enthousiasme, et l'on vit même des mains qui laissaient tomber des lis et des roses à travers les meurtrières des tours.

Le peuple sautait de joie, il bondissait, il dansait, et ses bras tatoués jetaient des couronnes qui tombaient sur le casque du monarque. N'est-ce pas que tout ce peuple, suspendu à chaque proéminence d'église, de rue, de muraille, n'est-ce pas que *toute cette multitude enfin, bénissant un seul homme,* avait quelque chose d'auguste et de solennel? (OJ II, 257–258)

This popular enthusiasm for Louis reflects his position in the historical "worldly paradise"; the whole opening scene is in large measure reproduced from Isabeau's entry into Paris in "Deux mains."[2] The people here, as in "Deux mains," grant unquestioned, absolute recognition to the privileged status of the historical hero. But the hero's attitude toward this recognition is noticeably different in the two works. For Isabeau the people are slaves to be governed at will; their recognition is taken for granted as a simple sign of power:

[Isabeau to Orléans:] Oh! le trône! être seule et maîtresse! Y songes-tu? Seule gouverner tout un peuple, le voir, là, frémir à vos paroles, plier sous votre regard, s'abaisser au niveau de vos pieds pour en essuyer la poussière de vos sandales sur sa tête! *Ah! le peuple! mot ridicule et vide de sens, masse aveugle et stupide!* On le gouverne facilement, c'est un troupeau comme un autre, qui porte le nom d'hommes. *Le peuple! Ah! c'est l'amusement des rois, leur plaisir, leur hochet...* (OJ I, 45)

The people here are merely an *object*, a plaything of the ruler; what frustrates Isabeau is that Jean sans Peur and not she is in command. King Louis, however, already holds power; he enjoys the enthusiasm of

---

[2] Cf. with the above the following passage from "Deux mains":
La reine! oh! dès qu'on la vit dans les rues, ce furent des cris d'allégresse, des trépignements de pieds, des hourras sans fin, des pluies de fleurs... En effet, il y avait dans toute cette foule qui trépignait et qui hurlait de joie, dans tout ce cortège si rempli de luxe et de magnificence, dans ce couple noble du roi et de la reine, dans le piétinement de tous ces chevaux qui faisait jaillir les fleurs avec les étincelles du pavé, oui, dans tout cela enfin il y avait quelque chose de grand et de majestueux, d'indéfinissable et d'exquis. (OJ I, 41)

the populace but, what is more, he is preoccupied with their opinion of
his actions:

[Louis:] Ah!... c'est toi, Arnould. Quelles nouvelles de Flandre?
—Vous savez *la grande* [italics Flaubert's] d'abord? [i.e., the murder of Richard's
father, Guillaume]—Oui, et *qu'a dit le peuple?* (OJ II, 259)

[After the conspiracy to kill Richard is settled:] En ce moment le vent devint
plus fort, et son souffle dans l'air souleva quelques fleurs que le soleil avait fanées
et qui vinrent voltiger devant la fenêtre du roi. *"Les fleurs du peuple,"* se dit-il en
riant amèrement, *et un remords lui tortura l'âme.* (OJ II, 260)

[Louis to Osmond:] Tenez, je vais vous le dire, je veux garder le duc auprès de
moi, je l'aurai. Il est temps de cesser cet inutile carnaval; dans une heure huit mille
hommes sont aux portes de Rouen, j'ai envoyé Arnould vers Bernard, général des
troupes de Normandie... Allez maintenant, le masque est jeté, *montrez-le au peuple.*
(OJ II, 261)

The last of these passages is of particular interest. Louis has no rational
motive whatever for disclosing his plans to Osmond or for daring him
to inform the people of them. Louis throws off his mask because his
power, to be of any value for him, must be absolute, unquestioned; if he
must fear the hostility of the population, then he is not really a ruler
at all, and his place in the historical "paradise" has been lost. For Louis,
power is wholly the equivalent of recognition.

But the king cannot rule absolutely: the people are the ultimate
source of his power and once they turn against him he becomes impotent:

C'était pourtant le même peuple qui était venu avec des fleurs et des cris d'amour!
Maintenant il trépignait d'impatience et de rage, comme un homme en délire, il
demandait à grands cris: le roi! le roi! et mille bras agitaient dans l'air des piques,
des haches, des hallebardes, des poignards, des lances et des poings fermés.
Le roi était resté dans sa chambre, seul, assis sur son lit; il attendait Arnould
avec impatience, et les hurlements effrénés du peuple, qui allaient toujours croissant,
étaient pour lui l'heure qui précède le moment où la tête du condamné doit rouler
sur l'échafaud. Un instant il eut le courage de s'approcher du balcon et de regarder
par la fenêtre; mais lorsqu'il vit toute cette mer de têtes qui s'agitait dans les
rues tortueuses et qui montait vers le palais comme la tempête, il trembla, il faillit
s'évanouir, ses jambes pliaient sous lui, ses dents claquaient, et ses mains humides
d'une sueur moite et maladive touchaient instinctivement un crucifix de bois qu'il
avait sur la poitrine. (OJ II, 263)

Louis's fear resembles that of Jean sans Peur cast out of his niche in
paradise, but now the fear has been given a specific *raison d'être.* Absolute recognition is impossible, the original nonalienated state of the
historical father-hero cannot be maintained. But at the same time, be-

cause the obstacle to Louis's remaining in the paradise is a concrete one—popular loyalty to the duke—the king can overcome this obstacle without renouncing his power by simply consenting not to infringe upon the rights of his young vassal. Once this is done Louis returns to the ideal state :

En ce moment-là le peuple avait brisé les portes, il était dans les escaliers, ses pas retentissaient sous les voûtes.
   —Le roi! le roi! criait-il.
   La fenêtre s'ouvrit et laissa voir Louis IV, portant dans ses bras le duc de Normandie.
   Les piques et les armes tombèrent des mains.
   —Noël! Noël! vive le roi! vive le duc! criait le peuple.
   Et cette immense acclamation se répandait dans toutes les rues, et trouvait un écho dans tous les coeurs. (OJ II, 264)

Worldly recognition in this historically idealized universe can only be maintained by remaining within the bounds of one's authority. Like the Roman populace in *Bérénice,* the people of Rouen have become the enforcers of universal order.

   The development of Louis from conspirator to protector marks a transition between the villainous father figures of the first period (the duke Henri d'Harmans, the doge, Robert, Pedrillo) and the figure of the *real* father as enforcer of the laws of bourgeois morality that appears in the second period, in particular in "La peste à Florence." Louis is is not Richard's real father, but his relationship to him is overtly paternal. I have already described the "renouncement of adulthood" implicit in Flaubert's identification with Marguerite in "Un parfum à sentir"; here in "Chronique normande" this renouncement has become explicit, and accordingly the adult, worldly figure who had hitherto played the role of obstacle to the son must now reassume his paternal obligations as protector. Because the son has renounced the Oedipal conflict, the father's hostility becomes superfluous. And when it reappears in the second period, it is conceived as the hatred of a father for his son, not—as in "La fiancée"—the opposition of two adult rivals.

   The world of "Chronique normande" has returned to the paradisial state; everything is now in its proper place. For this to occur, all worldly desire has had to be overcome. The king's hostility toward the duke has been grounded on ambitions of conquest; in his assumption of a paternal role these ambitions have had to be put aside. Existence in the ideal world is founded on *being,* not becoming. For Louis the conclusion of "Chronique normande" involves an accession to the stable being of the father; for Flaubert it is a realization that such stability can validly exist in the world, that the adult can occupy *without alienation* his place in society. The father need not steal the son's possessions as did Robert in "La fiancée," but neither are his own vulnerable to the other's attack, as was the case with Guise or the prior of "Le moine."

In "Chronique normande" the son as well as the father occupies his worldly position in perfect serenity—but only so long as he remains asleep. The "awakened" adolescents of the second period find that what they lack is precisely this stable, legitimate place in the world that the adult already possesses. The legitimacy of the first-period hero's desires is exposed as illusory. But the stability of the adult, the father, is a permanent acquisition. Throughout the rest of Flaubert's career, the "bourgeois" inhabits his social niche in wholly unalienated complacency. In this sense King Louis IV of France is for Flaubert but a remote, idealized ancestor of Homais.

Chapter XVI

LA FEMME DU MONDE

June 1–2, 1836

" 'Tu ne me connais pas, frêle et chétive créature; eh bien, écoute.' My name is accursed on earth, and yet its rulers—envy and despair—often call upon me, the daughter of Satan, for help. I take the sheep from the fold, the bird in its flight, the king on his throne; avidly I grind into dust whole empires, centuries filled with glory. I like to slip into the bed of a young girl, suck her blood, wither her cheeks, ravish her from her lover, her parents; and I contemplate joyfully the worms that crawl over her body.

"And when I see children laughing and adorning themselves with flowers, I like to adorn myself and laugh like them; but when they hear the hollow and ghostly sound of my laugh, they realize that I am but a phantom. Yet this phantom is the truest truth of all—'et contre [cette vérité] venait se briser tout, tout, et le fils de Dieu lui-même.'

"I was there in the Coliseum, roaring with the lions and tigers; I sat at the councils of the monarchy—'j'étais alors, par exemple, la Saint-Barthélemy.' To the arrogant century of Voltaire, I sent the Terror. And this century has not escaped me either: 'à lui, si content de ses colonies d'Afrique, de ses chemins, de ses voitures à vapeur, je lui ai envoyé un fléau... le hideux choléra.'

"And when I pass by in a funeral procession, I shiver in ecstasy at the curious spectacle of man's futile vanity. The dear departed was rich and liberal; praise him for his generosity to the poor... and for the gluttony with which he devoured his daily portion.

"Now do you recognize me? I am Death." Her shroud tore open to show a serpent sucking at her decaying entrails.

In "La femme du monde," Flaubert returns to the "mystère" form of "Voyage en enfer," concluding the first year of his literary career with the same genre in which he began it. As with "Voyage en enfer," the style of this work is borrowed largely from the *Paroles d'un croyant*, but again no bona fide source material has been found. Although it is not impossible, as Degoumois claims,[1] that the "femme du monde" was inspired by the Death-figure Mob in *Ahasvérus* by Edgar Quinet, no textual similarities lend support to this contention. "La femme du monde" is not a laborious reworking of source material as is "Deux mains"; according to the author's own indication on the manuscript the work was "fait en moins d'une demi-heure" (OJ I, 109). Even if we do not take this statement literally—it would seem impossible even to copy the approximately 110 lines of printed text in half an hour—we can be as-

---

[1] Léon Degoumois, *Flaubert à l'école de Gœthe* (Geneva, 1925), p. 20.

sured from it that "La femme du monde" was composed in a moment of inspiration, and that its content was not premeditated but derived *currente calamo* from an original intuition.

What is this intuition? Throughout the year, death has been one of Flaubert's chief preoccupations; the words "mort," "tombe," or "cercueil" have appeared in the title or subtitle of six of the sixteen works. A number of them end with the description of a corpse; of these "Un parfum à sentir," where Marguerite's body is described with a great deal of gruesome detail, is the most notable.[2] But until now death has always been a consequence of human action; the old prior of "Le moine" dies the only natural death of any character in the period. The appearance of "La femme du monde" serves to unmask the real essence of death as something inhuman over which man has no control. Death mocks man's impotent search for disalienation in a world where, as a mortal, he is *ipso facto* alienated from any possibility of accession to the unchanging "being" of the ideal. The "femme du monde" thus offers the *antithesis* of the conception of death presented in the earlier works. By treating death not as a natural but a human, praxial phenomenon, these works depict the world as in itself a paradise for man which becomes an "enfer" only through his own crimes; this is an essentially moralistic interpretation of the "fall of man." In "La femme du monde," man's crimes have as litle importance as his virtues. The mere fact of his mortality denies any permanent value to his existence.

If "La femme du monde" can be opposed to the other first-period pieces in a general sense, it is the precise contrary of the preceding work, "Chronique normande." Its protagonist is the female figure that had been absent from "Chronique normande," and its message exactly the opposite: for Louis and Richard, reconciliation in a timeless ideal; for "La femme du monde," the destruction by time of all human values:

"Car cite-moi une vague de l'Océan, une parole de haine et d'amour, un souffle dans l'air, un vol dans les cieux, un sourire sur les lèvres qui ne soit effacé." (OJ I, 111)

A more specific opposition to the reconciliation of "Chronique normande" is to be found in the following passage, the penultimate section of the work:

Je bondis de volupté quand je me vautre à mon aise dans un beau char de parade, quand les hommes déploient la vanité jusqu'au bout; c'est un curieux spectacle.

---

[2] Ce corps couvert de balafres, de marques de griffes, gonflé, verdâtre, déposé ainsi sur la dalle humide, était hideux et faisait mal à voir. L'odeur nauséabonde qui s'exhalait de ce cadavre en lambeaux... faisait éloigner tous les passants oisifs. (OJ I, 106)

Allons donc, chien, rends des honneurs au chien qui pourrit sur la borne!

Allons donc, société, rends donc des honneurs au riche qui passe dans un corbillard; les chevaux, tout couverts d'argent, font étinceler le pavé; les dais, reluisants d'or et de pierreries, sont magnifiques; on fait des discours sur les vertus du défunt, il était libéral sans doute, et magnifique: les pauvres ont deux sous, un pain et un cierge; il dépensait splendidement son argent.

Allons donc, chien, fais le panégyrique du chien que dévorent les corbeaux; dis qu'il mangeait avec gloutonnerie son morceau de cheval qu'on lui jetait chaque soir. (OJ I, 113)

Here the social being of the "bourgeois," precisely what was sanctified in "Chronique normande," is savagely attacked as worthless and illusory. The funeral, where man seeks to eternalize this social being beyond the reach of death, where the honors given the dead man purport to allow him to continue in his worldly role beyond the grave, is Death's *bête noire*. For her the funeral ceremony is only a "vanité," but her transcendent viewpoint is not shared by its mortal participants; among mortals only the narrator—the "frêle et chétive créature" to whom Death reveals herself—is aware of this truth. The still implicit identification of the worldly "being" of Louis IV with that of Homais which was made in the analysis of "Chronique normande" is now realized; the celebrants subsist in an *inauthentically* paradisial state, unconscious of their own alienation from true, permanent being. The narrator here may be a "frêle et chétive créature" like the young duke of "Chronique normande," but now it is he who is awake, while the "bourgeois" remain asleep in their own self-satisfaction.

At the beginning of the period, "Voyage en enfer" proclaimed the superiority of the narrator over the inhabitants of the "enfer" on a *moral* basis; he alone stood aloof from the crimes of the worldly. But the sexual confession of "Un parfum à sentir" showed the unworldly "son" to be no more virtuous than the worldly "father"; both could be merged in the figure of Pedrillo because both were equally guilty of the crime of worldly desire. In the revelations of "Chronique normande" and "La femme du monde," the son-father split returns once more, but this time it is grounded not on desire but on *being*. The adolescent alone can grasp the negative truth of worldly existence because unlike the "bourgeois" adult he does not yet have a place in the world, a falsely permanent social being that shields him from awareness of temporality.

This worldly negativity was apparent to Marguerite of "Un parfum à sentir," who as a woman also lacked worldly being and could only *await* it. Now the mortal woman's unsuccessful awaiting has been transformed into that of Death who can never be disappointed: all things will come to her in time. The "femme du monde" is the vindication of Marguerite; she destroys at will the worldly success of Isabellada:

J'aime à m'introduire dans le lit d'une jeune fille, à creuser lentement ses joues, à lui sucer le sang, à la saisir peu à peu et à la ravir à son amant, à ses parents qui pleurent et sanglotent sur cette pauvre rose si vite fanée.

Alors je me réjouis sur son front encore blanc, je contemple ses lèvres ridées par la fièvre, j'entends avec plaisir le bourdonnement des mouches qui viennent autour de sa tête, comme signes de putréfaction.

Et je ris avidement en voyant les vers qui rampent sur son corps. (OJ I, 110)

By identifying with the "femme du monde," the adolescent Gustave avenges himself on the sexual object that has led him to "pleurer et maudire sa mère."

The first-period protagonist knew the world to be an "enfer," but he felt justified in seeking within this hell a worldly paradise where sexual and other pleasures were legitimate. Death was only a final *sign* of the protagonist's estrangement from this ideal; the source of this estrangement had always been some concrete obstacle that blocked the path to the ideal. Now the very temporality of mortal existence itself has destroyed the stability of the hero's worldly paradise; only the self-deluding bourgeois remains unshaken in his social position. Precisely what has impressed upon Flaubert the negative significance of temporality? It is the discovery of the temporality of *his own* existence; the realization, already anticipated in "Un parfum à sentir," that his own life cannot subsist on an eternal mountaintop like that of the narrator of "Voyage en enfer," but is subject to the same alienation that his worldly protagonists have been forced to suffer. Even in "Un parfum à sentir," where the identification of author and protagonist reached the level of a shared conciousness of the world's negativity, Flaubert was able to separate himself from his heroine in the epilogue, to sing the praise of the writer's freedom:

Vous ne savez peut-être pas quel plaisir c'est: composer! Ecrire, oh! écrire, c'est s'emparer du monde, de ses préjugés, de ses vertus et le résumer dans un livre; c'est sentir sa pensée naître, grandir, vivre, se dresser debout sur son piédestal, et y rester toujours. (OJ I, 107)

In the following work, "Chronique normande," the author's choice of an *unconscious* hero was as if a confession of his reluctance to face the truth of his own existence. But from Death's self-revelation to the "frêle et chétive créature" there is no escape. The suddenness of this revelation, written down in one brief sitting, testifies to its profound personal significance. The concern shown in the first works of the next period with the frustrating inferior status of the adolescent protagonists betoken the author's awakening to his own particular position in the temporal, unideal world. And from this awakening springs a consciousness of the need to find a praxial means of overcoming temporality. The heroes of the first period act without reflection; those of the second consciously seek to affirm through their actions their own significance in the face of death. In the sense in which praxis is not mere automatic activity but the individual's chosen answer to the question posed by his temporal finitude, only the works that follow "La femme du monde" depict a genuine praxis.

Thus the first period ends on a note of anticipation. In "La femme du monde" Flaubert can still identify with the universal figure of Death, but henceforth he and his heroes are forced to avow themselves her subjects.

PART TWO

September 1836–November 1836

The works of the second and third periods are, in keeping with the author's greater age and literary experience, longer and less dependent on their sources than those of the first period. None of the works of the second or third period is a school assignment as were the "narrations" of the first period. Because the later works are fewer and more personal, and because their exact chronology is known (with the sole exception of "Une leçon d'histoire naturelle, genre commis" which can, however, be located with a high degree of probability), it is a far less problematic task than in the first period to trace Flaubert's development continuously from work to work.

In terms of chronology, the second and third periods could be considered as a unit. Nevertheless, a particularly evident reorientation in Flaubert's approach between "Bibliomanie" (November 1836) and "Rage et impuissance" (December 1836) has led me to divide the unit at this point into periods II and III. The works of the second period have as their common theme a rivalry that has an evident personal origin in Gustave's own rivalry with his brother Achille. Those of the third period share the world-renouncing theme of *René*. The heroes of this latter group of stories have as their praxis not a concrete goal-directed activity but the disillusioning discovery that no such activity is possible. I shall in the course of my analyses refer to their career as the "null-praxis"; the negativity of this expression reflects the wholly negative nature of these protagonists' experience of the world.

CHAPTER XVII

UN SECRET DE PHILIPPE LE PRUDENT, ROI D'ESPAGNE (CONTE HISTORIQUE)

September 1836

A GRAVE, elderly gentleman is seated by the fire; two other men stand beside him, silent and respectful. The younger of the two is dressed entirely in black; on his neck is a medallion containing a piece of the true cross. This slight, melancholy figure is Philippe II, king of Spain and Navarre. Seated at the fire is Don Olivarès, Grand Inquisitor, wielder of all power in the kingdom. Philippe obeys him in all matters, both religious and worldly; "mais il arrivait souvent que le chien se révoltait contre son maître et le faisait trembler."

The king is the first to break the long silence. "What news?" he asks the Inquisitor. Don Olivarès hands a portfolio of letters to Philippe, who gives it to his attendant, Don Ruy Gomès, to read. The first important piece of news is that Don Juan, bastard son of Charles-Quint and Philippe's half-brother, has escaped from the convent where he was being held; he has set out for England and intends to "faire la guerre au roi d'Espagne." This infuriates the king, who first threatens to have his brother killed; but Olivarès dictates the king's official response: "Cherchez don Juan... éloignez-le de son père."

It is of the latter, Charles-Quint (now called Father Arsène since his abdication of the throne), that the next letter speaks. The ex-emperor has learned that his son Don Juan is being pursued by Philippe, and he is threatening to take back the crown. A letter from Charles to Don Juan has also been intercepted. Philippe grabs it from Gomès, although the thought of his father makes him tremble.

"Mon cher Juano," the letter reads, "je suis un cadavre vivant qui passe la vie à compter l'heure qui coule." Happiness, confides Father Arsène, exists only in his past memories; he ofen feels the desire to return to his former active life, but then the weakness of old age overcomes him. Only one thought gives him pleasure, that of his son Juan, "toute ma vie et mon amour." "Si le fils légitime était celui de la femme aimée," he adds, Juan would be the king of Spain and Philippe the hated bastard. In closing, he has no course of action to recommend to his beloved son, "ayant beaucoup vu et n'ayant jamais eu dans mon existence un seul jour de bonheur."

Philippe is stricken with terror upon finishing the letter. His guilt for having spied on Charles overcomes him, and he throws the letter on the fire. When the Inquisitor questions him about its contents, Philippe nonchalantly answers that it contained "des choses insignifiantes... je suis désolé de l'avoir machinalement brûlée."

Now, says Philippe, what should we do with my son Don Carlos? The same thing we do with all the heretics, answers Gomès. Philippe presses a secret button and the wall recedes to show the chamber of the young prince. The room is dark and shabby, the walls covered with various types of weapons. Carlos appears; although only twenty years old, "ses joues creuses... ce front chargé de rides" give him an aged appearance. Despite a limp in his left leg, his bearing is gracious:

cette figure triste et douce [indiquait] une de ces âmes si pleines de passion...
qu'elles se dilatent, se crèvent, et s'abîment, ne pouvant contenir tout ce qu'elles
recèlent.

The young man contemplates his fine Toledo sword and thinks of suicide. Suddenly
he hears a suspicious sound. Realizing that it is his father who is spying on him,
Carlos flies into a range: "Toujours là,... me ravissant ma femme, m'ôtant la
liberté"—but it is his father, the king, and nothing can be done! Breaking his dagger ("puis-je te briser ainsi, homme sans coeur!"), he vows that he will see his
beloved again, "dût-il m'égorger entre ses bras," and strides purposefully from the
room. (Unfinished.)

"Un secret de Philippe" is a "conte historique" like many stories of the
first period, although it differs greatly in structure from even the last
of the preceding works. As to source material, the interrelated careers
of John of Austria and of "Don Carlos" (the latter made famous by
Schiller's drama) which form the basis for this work were too popular
during the Romantic period for any specific source to be isolable.
Delavigne's *Don Juan d'Autriche*—mentioned by Bruneau (*Les débuts
littéraires,* p. 89) as "la source principale"—was certainly employed,
but at least one other source must have been used for the episode
dealing with Carlos, since it is not found in Delavigne's play.

The story as a whole is unfinished. To judge from the author's strong
identification with Carlos in the final pages, his intention seems to have
been to make him the central figure, but the first part of the story,
which is concerned with Philippe's opposition to his illegitimate brother
Juan, takes up nine of the twelve completed pages of text. This first
section and that dealing with Carlos are, as the story stands, related to
each other only through Philippe's presence in both. But Carlos's historical connection with Juan in their joint conspiracy against Philippe
was of course known to Flaubert, who may have intended to use it to
bring the two rebels together later in the story.

The description of Philippe and his entourage in the very first lines
of the story indicates a major transformation in Flaubert's method
from that of the first period:

Le personnage le plus grave [the Inquisitor] se tenait au milieu, assis dans un large
fauteuil à bras.... A ses deux côtés étaient debout et la tête nue deux autres hommes
qui paraissaient ses confidents ou du moins ses valets car à leur air respectueux et
soumis on les aurait pris pour tels.

Le plus jeune des deux [Philippe] était vêtu de noir de la tête aux pieds,... il
était grand, maigre, avait le front pâle, les cheveux blonds, les joues creuses....
Quelque chose de sombre, de doux et de mélancolique à la fois, annonçait une âme
qui avait souffert, un corps qui s'était usé dans les jeûnes, et un esprit qui s'était
rapetissé dans les croyances. (OJ I, 55)

The historical stories of the earlier period had all begun with an immediate emphasis on the universal public recognition of the principals (thus the fête of "Deux mains sur une couronne," the king's triumphant entry into Rouen in "Chronique normande," the historical-descriptive introduction of "Marguerite de Bourgogne," or the club scene in "Duc de Guise"); this recognition located the hero from the outset within an idealized historical paradise. But in "Un secret de Philippe" the emphasis is placed on the interpersonal rather than the public element. This change of perspective reflects the author's new orientation toward the concrete realities of his own family situation. Flaubert no longer merely presents his characters; he reveals them in their intimate relationships:

Cet homme, si petit devant cet autre homme assis devant lui et se chauffant à son feu n'était rien moins que Philippe II, roi d'Espagne et de Navarre. Quant au vieillard, c'était don Olivarès, le Grand Inquisiteur d'Espagne, celui qui avait toute puissance, toute liberté, tout pouvoir. (OJ I, 56)

Here the public importance of Philippe, "roi d'Espagne et de Navarre," is contrasted with his personal inferiority to the Inquisitor: "si petit devant cet autre homme assis devant lui."

What do these interpersonal relations signify for Flaubert? In familial terms, we can in the first section roughly identify Philippe with Gustave's older brother Achille, and Philippe's illegitimate brother Juan (who does not himself appear in the story) with the author himself. The conflict between the honored and the outcast brother is taken up again in "La peste à Florence"; in its essentials it was already present in the Marguerite-Isabellada rivalry of "Un parfum à sentir." But here the outwardly favored Philippe plays much the sorrier role, humiliated by his father Charles who demonstrates in his letter an open preface for Juan:

Je contemple le ciel avec extase en pensant à cette belle tête noire si pleine de feu et d'énergie, à cette figure rosée, à ces deux grands yeux bleus qui sont toute ma vie et mon amour... je pense à don Juan, et je maudis le sort qui fait que je ne l'embrasse pas. Car toi, Juano, je t'aime autant qu'un coeur d'homme flétri par la royauté peut encore conserver de tendresse et d'amour. (OJ I, 62)

Within the family itself Philippe has been defeated by his absent brother; this is evident from his reaction upon reading the intercepted letter:

Le roi pâlit, et, chiffonnant dans ses doigts la lettre volée, il s'assit sur une table placée près de la fenêtre, car ses jambes pliaient et une singulière frayeur vint le saisir tout à coup. Alors il pensa à son père, à son vieux père dont il avait surpris les secrets, dont il avait espionné les actions... (OJ I, 62)

Philippe realizes now that his persecution of Juan involves the violation of his father's desires; his only defense is to escape the evidence of these desires by burning the letter.

Yet Juan is unable to reap any worldly advantage from his father's preference. Charles may love his bastard son, but since his abdication from the throne he has renounced all paternal worldly authority. The unreal, wish-fulfillment nature of this father-son relationship is further demonstrated by the significant fact that neither Charles nor Juan actually appears in the story. The father expresses his love only in a letter that the son never receives. Nor does Juan ever himself confront Philippe with the evidence of Charles's preference. Apparently the author can only conceive of himself as the preferred son by imagining his father's feelings; he cannot identify subjectively with Juan as the recipient of this paternal affection.[1]

There is another "father" in the story: the Inquisitor who unlike Charles holds worldly authority and accordingly favors the legitimate brother. Don Olivarès can thus be said to represent the "real" father (as opposed to the "ideal" Charles). But even he is anything but permissive to Philippe, and at one point rebukes him for blasphemy when he uses abusive language in referring to Juan:

—Ah! messire don Juan d'Autriche, dit [Philippe] avec un accent de colère concentrée... vous avez des chevaux pour vous conduire ainsi, vous sautez par-dessus les murs de votre couvent, nous aurons pour vous une prison désormais; s'il vous prenait fantaisie d'en sortir, le bourreau en ouvrirait la porte. Oh! par la mort-dieu! ajouta-t-il en trépignant, non, il n'en sera pas ainsi, ou la couronne de Charles-Quint tomberait de notre tête royale.

— *Sire, dit le Grand Inquisiteur, sire, écoutez ceci: Tu ne blasphémeras point le nom de mon père, a dit le Christ.* Sire, qu'avez-vous fait? Pour cela vous donnerez à l'église del Pilar un calice d'or avec trois flambeaux d'argent.

— *Pardon, mon père, dit le monarque,* et il s'inclina. (OJ I, 58)

Later Don Olivarès openly protects Juan from Philippe's hatred by refusing to approve his decision to have Juan put to death:

[Philippe:] Vous [Juan], le pauvre, l'obscur, l'impie, le mécréant, le bâtard, vous voulez attenter à notre couronne sacrée; mais l'on saura bien se débarrasser de vos mains en faisant tomber la tête.

---

[1] In contrast, Carlos, who plays the "maudit" role in the second part of the story but who is hated by his father, appears *as a subject* in his undisguised and uncompensated adolescent frustrations.

— Don Ruy, interrompit Olivarès, écrivez ceci de la part du roi: Cherchez don Juan, emparez-vous de sa personne; éloignez-le de son père. (OJ I, 59)

Thus even the "real" father defends the outcast son from his brother's excessive wrath.

The element of wish fulfillment in Juan's relationship to his father is evident; in it Flaubert continues the vision of reconciliation expressed in "Chronique normande." But this reconciliation remains wholly unreal. The brother-rival Philippe is humiliated, true, but Juan himself gains nothing thereby, for he has no place of his own in the world of the story. At least in "Chronique normande" the sleeping duke was permitted to be present in person at the reconciliation with his "father." But the duke had his own worldly position to assert; Juan has no rightful place in the world.

Thus Juan cannot truly be spoken of as a "protagonist." His success in obtaining the affection of his father involves no action on his part, nor is the father's protective role imposed upon him by the son's allies, as it was in "Chronique normande." Flaubert's identification with Juan shows that he is aware of his father's esteem as a value for him, a desire object. But from the adolescent's wholly dependent position, this paternal affection can only be accepted as a *gift;* the son has no way of grasping it through action in the fashion of Bernardo stealing the prior's ring.

With the revelation of his father's preference in the letter scene the story of Juan is finished, and our attention shifts to Philippe's son Carlos. For Carlos, who in contrast to Juan, possesses a subjectivity with which the author can identify and a worldly situation that symbolizes his own, the reconciliation with his father which Juan achieved is impossible. Philippe has stolen away his son's fiancée, just as Robert did to Paul in "La fiancée et la tombe." But unlike this first-period hero, Carlos has no way of retrieving his beloved. Paul was able to kill the father figure Robert, but Carlos cannot attack his real father Philippe:

Toujours là comme un mauvais génie, s'opposant à mon bonheur, me ravissant ma femme, m'ôtant la liberté... je ne pourrai pas pleurer et maudire, me venger! *Non! c'est mon père! et c'est le roi! Il faut supporter ses coups, recevoir tous ces* [sic] *affronts, accepter tous ces outrages.* (OJ I, 65–66)

Carlos is the first of Flaubert's protagonists to experience explicitly adolescent frustrations. He is confined not *within* the world, like Paul in "La fiancée," but *from* the world, like the *moine des Chartreux*. For it is his real father that is keeping Carlos imprisoned, and there is no longer a symbolic ring to hold out promises of liberation. In grasping the father-son relationship as the essential obstacle to his hero, Flaubert reveals this hero's situation to be explicitly unadult.

But once the father has himself become the obstacle to the protagonist, no action is possible; there is no praxis through which Carlos can express his opposition. Philippe does not even appear before his son; he merely spies on him in the fashion of an inhibiting superego. Here, as in the relationship between Juan and Charles, the nonpresence of the father to the son signifies the absence of any concrete confrontation. In the one case there is freely given love, in the other persecution, but in neither does the son's position contain any possibility for action, any basis for a praxial totality. And just as the story of Juan was never really begun, that of Carlos cannot be continued. Flaubert must break off "Un secret de Philippe" because his chief protagonist, Carlos, is unable to act; his declaration of revolt in the last words of the story expresses only the need for action, not its possibility:

Je la [his fiancée] verrai encore, dût-il m'égorger entre ses bras, dit-il en ôtant les verrous de la porte, et il sortit précipitamment. (OJ I, 66)

The historical situation of Carlos did of course involve such action, but this historical situation must be abandoned by the author when it comes into conflict with his own fundamental attitudes.

Yet the Juan-Philippe relationship had shown that the father-brother Philippe could be opposed *qua* brother if not *qua* father. In the following work, "La peste à Florence," Flaubert takes as his subject the overt conflict between the protagonist and his brother. There is no longer any question of either reconciliation with the father (Juan) or recapture from him of the lost fiancée (Carlos); in confronting his brother alone, the protagonist leaves untouched his father's hostile worldly authority. The adolescent comes to admit his utter inability to modify the essentials of his dependent position within the world.

CHAPTER XVIII

LA PESTE A FLORENCE

September 1836

"C'est que je te hais
d'une haine de frère."
—A. Dumas, *Don Juan de Marana*

I. THERE ONCE lived in Florence an old hag named Beatricia who made her living by fortunetelling. One day she is accosted by two young gentlemen who order her to conduct them to her home. En route, the younger of the two, Garcia, reproaches his brother François: "Quelle singulière idée as-tu... de vouloir aller chez cette femme?" To go through the most wretched neighborhood with their rich swords and garments! "Quel lâche tu fais," retorts his brother. But, asks Garcia, do you even know this woman? "Oui, c'est Beatricia." At this name, the young man shudders but repressing his fear, he draws nearer to his brother. Finally they arrive at her apartment, a dingy room strewn with skulls and "de longs cheveux encore tout sanglants."

First Beatricia tells François's fortune: all his plans will succeed, but he will die "par la trahison d'un de [ses] proches." Next she examines the palm of Garcia: "Ta vie sera entremêlée de biens et de maux, mais le cancer de l'envie et de la haine te rongera le coeur." His humiliations will finally be expiated in the blood of his victim.

II. Having returned home, the younger brother finds himself obsessed with Beatricia's prediction. Ugly, awkward, lacking in both energy and wit, Garcia de Médicis is filled with envy of his brother, "le chéri de la famille." Certainly Garcia is bitter and hateful, but it is not hard to see how his torment grew out of "toutes les tracasseries qu'il eut à endurer." What he finds especially hard to bear is the thought that François is soon to become a cardinal, while he remains "toujours pauvre et obscur, comme le valet d'un bourgeois!" In his hatred, Garcia understands the joys of vengeance and he wishes for his brother's death.

III. It is an August night in Florence; people everywhere are dancing, laughing— yet the plague has already struck down many of the city's inhabitants. At the ball given by Cosme de Médicis in honor of his son François, a plague of a different kind is ravaging the heart of Garcia.

Few words have been addressed to him since the ball has begun. Finally François comes over to ask what is the matter. Garcia retorts proudly, "Oh! je n'ai rien, monseigneur." Shrugging his shoulders, François walks away. His brother continues to suffer the pangs of hatred and jealousy; finally, no longer able to bear his torments, he collapses, and a valet carries him unnoticed from the room.

IV. Cosme de Médicis together with his sons and a group of friends prepares to set out for the hunt. As the company passes through the castle gate, François's horse shies—"mauvais présage," grumbles his father. The company then splits up; Garcia is paired off with François.

The forest becomes denser and soon the two brothers are able to advance no farther; they dismount and sit down on the grass. "Te voilà donc cardinal," exclaims

Garcia, who until then had remained silent. Laughing cruelly, he proceeds to give vent to his hatred and envy. "Do you remember the words of Beatricia?" he asks menacingly. She was right—"tes projets ont réussi"—but is François forgetting her predictions concerning Garcia, that a bloody crime of jealousy would be his only joy?

François draws back in fear at these mad words. "Ecoute," pursues Garcia, "tu m'as supplicié toute ma vie, je t'égorge maintenant." And ignoring his victim's frantic pleas, Garcia stabs him, then mounts his horse and gallops off.

At midnight the citizens of Florence are awakened by the duke returning from the hunt; he walks beside four valets carrying a litter. When the procession reaches the castle, Cosme's wife rushes out asking for François. What is in that litter? she inquires of her husband. Glancing coldly at Garcia, the duke replies: "Un cadavre."

V. Cosme is walking up and down in his cold, humid room. Suddenly he stops and cries out, "Oui, oui, que justice se fasse!" Garcia, summoned by his father's servant, enters the room; Cosme observes sarcastically that he is no longer wearing the clothes he had on the day before—"les taches se font bien voir sur un vêtement noir, n'est-ce pas, Garcia?" Taking his sword, Cosme leads his son to the back of the room and draws open a large black curtain. The corpse of François is revealed stretched out on a bed.

"Le cadavre était nu, et le sang suintait encore de ses blessures." At this sight Garcia mutely falls to his knees. Cosme's sword whistles through the air and a frightful cry is heard.

VI. "Florence était en deuil, ses enfants mouraient par la peste." The death of the two sons of Cosme de Médicis, publicly attributed to the plague, serves as a distraction to the people in their misery and despair.

The funeral procession moves along slowly to the sound of prayers and church bells. "Is it possible," someone asks of Dr. Roderigo, Cosme's physician, "that a man who died of the plague should have such large scars?" "Oui,... quelquefois,..." comes the answer, "ce sont des ventouses."

"LA PESTE à Florence" is the best written and most significant work of the second period. Like "Un secret de Philippe," it is based on historical sources.[1] Flaubert, however, has readapted his source material to his own purposes, notably by combining in the character of François the figures of Francesco, the eldest son of Cosimo de' Medici, and Giovanni, the one actually killed by Garcia. This could scarcely have been the result of mere carelessness on Flaubert's part; it involves a conscious or unconscious assimilation of the source material to the author's own family situation, in which there are only two brothers.[2]

---

[1] *"La peste à Florence* raconte un épisode, d'ailleurs peu sûr, qui se trouve dans toutes les histoires d'Italie" (Bruneau, *les débuts littéraires*, p. 88; see also n. 40 of this page, where Guingené's *Histoire littéraire d'Italie* is cited as the probable source).

[2] We should not of course overlook the possibility that this fusion of the two brothers was suggested by an earlier but unknown fictionalization of the episode.

In "La peste à Florence," full use is made of the brother-rival theme that was implicit in the first part of "Un secret de Philippe." The reflection of the relative status of the brothers in Flaubert's own family (Garcia = Gustave, François = Achille) is quite transparent:

C'était [François]... l'aîné, le chéri de la famille: à lui tous les honneurs, les gloires, les titres et les dignités; au pauvre Garcia, l'obscurité et le mépris. (OJ I, 119)

This correspondence is almost entirely uncomplicated by the shifts of identification that were found in "Un secret de Philippe." Yet the author's identification with Garcia is not altogether complete; he is forced to condemn his hero's more antisocial aspects:

En effet, c'était un homme méchant, traître et haineux que Garcia de Médicis, mais qui dit que cette méchanceté maligne, cette sombre et ambitieuse jalousie qui tourmentèrent ses jours, ne prirent pas naissance dans toutes les tracasseries qu'il eut à endurer? (OJ I, 118)

Flaubert, while excusing Garcia's criminal propensities, is not prepared to identify fully with them. But his very need to question his hero's merits demonstrates a newly problematic aspect of historical fiction for Flaubert. The hero's praxis, which consists wholly in his crime, is no longer, as in the first period, naïvely participated in by the author. Flaubert's own law-abiding inaction thus comes into conflict with the criminal action of Garcia, which must be justified on the grounds of its historical authenticity.

Whatever the contribution of historical factors, Garcia's situation of resentful inferiority to a favored rival is not new in Flaubert's works. We have already seen a quite similar situation in the first period: that of the persecuted Marguerite in "Un parfum à sentir." This similarity extends to the very language Flaubert uses to describe these protagonists. In the ball scene of "La peste à Florence" the description of Garcia is borrowed directly from a similar scene in the earlier work:

Il était venu là... apporter au milieu des rires et de la joie, sa blessure saignante et son profond chagrin... (OJ I, 122)

Compare from "Un parfum à sentir":

Il [le masque Marguerite] est venu apporter sous son masque sa jalousie amère et sa haine furieuse et ses peines et ses plaies saignantes et ses blessures profondes. (OJ I, 95)

And Garcia's speech to his brother before killing him is essentially identical in content to Marguerite's tirade to Pedrillo:

Tu [François] es cardinal, j'insulte ta dignité de cardinal; tu es beau, fort et puissant, j'insulte ta force, ta beauté et ta puissance... (OJ I, 126–127)

Compare:

Elle [Isabellada] est belle, je hais les belles parce que je suis laide;... tu es heureux, toi, je hais les heureux; vous êtes riches et je hais les riches... (OJ I, 102–103)

But "La peste à Florence" also reflects the transformation in Flaubert's outlook since the first period. Garcia, unlike the inactive Marguerite, willfully affirms through his crime the necessity of self-assertive action even in the absence of any ideal goal. The jealousy that in "Un parfum à sentir" was expressed in the form of an appeal to the "father" (Pedrillo) who favored the rival is now embodied in an act of revenge against the rival himself.[3] Marguerite still hoped to convince Pedrillo of her superior worth, and thereby to supplant her rival in his affections. Garcia, however, has renounced all hope of convincing his father to rectify his inferior status. If Marguerite was after all the legitimate spouse of Pedrillo, Garcia, like Gustave in his own family or Juan in "Un secret de Philippe," has no legitimate basis for seeking to alter his situation. In terms of the worldly morality incarnated in the father, the present state of affairs is fully justified; Gustave-Garcia's only possible response to his situation is to attack it by illegitimate means.

Here, as in "Un secret de Philippe," the protagonist is explicitly portrayed within a family situation; his relations are no longer with a father figure but with the father himself. And again, as in the preceding work, the explicitness of the son-father relationship guarantees the invulnerability of the father and of the social order he upholds in the face of any possible challenge by the son. Garcia cannot hope to modify his status; the murder of his brother cannot become more than the praxial expression of his *ressentiment*. Not only can he not attack his father directly, but even his indirect attack on him through the intermediary of the brother cannot go unpunished. Neither the author nor Garcia himself denies the justice of Cosme's execution of the murderer; the legitimacy of "father morality" is scrupulously respected.

Yet the ultimate preservation of the worldly order does not destroy the significance of Garcia's revolt against it. For the first time a Flaubertian protagonist must choose a course of action as a means of self-assertion against the world. Garcia does not seek any form of "paradise." The paradise can only be either that of the child ("Chronique

---

[3] Garcia's outburst to François just before the murder is not an appeal, but an element of his revenge.

normande") or of the adult ("Deux mains sur une couronne")—a
secure position either in the world or outside it. But Garcia is a truly
adolescent hero; he has been thrown out of childhood into the world, yet
lacks any recognized place in it. And thus his crime is not an "oedipal"
grasping of adulthood like Ornano's abduction of Vanina, but a reaffir-
mation of his *adolescent* status in the only way open to him: by the
annihilation of his successful brother who is making without difficulty
the transition from youth to adulthood.

Garcia's action is essentially negative. His jealousy of his brother does
not result from a frustrated effort to achieve comparable honors and
recognition. In effect, these goals have no concrete existence for Garcia;
they cannot be actively sought after but are entirely dependent upon
the will of his father. François's superiority has already been settled,
just as in Gustave's own family situation Achille is unalterably Dr.
Flaubert's favorite son and the future successor to his professional
position. The question of whether Garcia—or Gustave—would be happy
in his brother's situation has no meaning, for this possibility never
existed. Had Gustave been born in Achille's place, he would no doubt
have been a "bourgeois" youth like him, but once having become a
Romantic he could not accept his brother's success as an authentic one.
And in the same way, Garcia has no real desire to become a cardinal;
he simply envies his brother for *being* a cardinal when he himself is
nothing. But Garcia is not sustained, like his creator, by a Romantic
faith in his ultimate superiority to his bourgeois brother; that is precisely why he must assert his adolescent status in *action* by killing
François. As becomes evident in the third period, the adolescent who
is fully aware of his superiority to the adult world can have no praxis
at all.

The morbid atmosphere of the plague that runs through the story
serves to unite Garcia's sufferings with those of mankind in general
and to emphasize the universal significance of his revolt against the
mortal condition:

Partout c'était des danses, des rires et du bruit, et pourtant la peste avait exercé ses
ravages sur Florence et avait décimé ses habitants.

Au palais aussi c'était des danses, des rires et du bruit, mais non de joie, car la
peste, là aussi, avait fait ses ravages dans le coeur d'un homme... mais une autre
peste que la contagion; le malheur qui étreignait Garcia dans ses serres cruelles le
serra si fort qu'il le broya comme le verre du festin entre les mains d'un homme ivre.
(OJ I, 120)

The negative vision of the world that is here presented is essentially that of "La femme du monde," but now the protagonist is not a spectator but a victim of Death's power.

The necessity of Garcia's act is revealed to him on a personal level in the striking predictions of the old fortuneteller Beatricia with which the work opens:

Ta vie sera entremêlée de biens et de maux, mais le cancer de l'envie et de la haine te rongera le coeur, le glaive du meurtre sera dans ta main et tu trouveras dans le sang de ta victime l'expiation des humiliations de ta vie. (OJ I, 117)

Beatricia also predicts François's death: "Tu mourras par la trahison d'un de tes proches..." (OJ I, 117). These predictions cast the shadow of Garcia's personal fatality over the rest of the story. The mysterious Beatricia herself is described in considerable detail; she is a human incarnation of the "femme du monde," raised by her knowledge of the future above the temporal limitations of mortal men. Her prediction of Garcia's crime is a "blessing" of the deed by the forces of death themselves; to this extent, Death confides in Garcia just as she confided in the narrator of "La femme du monde."

Because Garcia has no positive worldly goals, his revolt remains a pure negation, an expression of adolescent *ressentiment* against the father-world. In his next work, "Bibliomanie," Flaubert gives a genuine worldly object to his hero's rivalry, in a somewhat artificial attempt to extend the adolescent praxis of Garcia into an adult career. But rather than asserting like "La peste à Florence" the value of its hero's deeds, "Bibliomanie" demonstrates in its disillusioning conclusion the invalidity of all worldly action.

CHAPTER XIX

BIBLIOMANIE

November 1836

GIACOMO, a bookseller of Barcelona, is a man of satanic appearance whose sole passion is collecting rare books and manuscripts. Although he can scarcely read, he loves to spend his nights looking over his treasures, sniffing their dusty covers, admiring their strange illustrations, their illegible dates.

One day a young noble, a student from Salamanca, enters his shop. "N'avez-vous point ici, maître, des manuscrits?" In particular, the young man wishes to buy the *Chronique de Turquie*. Giacomo first denies having the manuscript but then admits that he possesses it—to the envy of his archrival, the bookseller Baptisto! The student finally prevails upon Giacomo to accept 600 pistoles for it. In return he informs the poor *bibliomane*, who already regrets having sold his precious manuscript, of the whereabouts of the *Mystère de Saint Michel*, a rare book Giacomo has always coveted.

The latter immediately sets off to buy the *Mystère* but is informed that the book was sold the day before to the curé of Oviedo. Giacomo returns home, crushed.

A week later, there is an auction of the first book ever published in Spain, a Latin Bible. Giacomo dreads the thought that it may fall into the hands of his rival Baptisto. At the auction his worst fears are realized: Baptisto outbids him and carries off the book in triumph. Dazed by his defeat, Giacomo starts for home; in the street he catches fragments of conversations: "Tiens... as-tu entendu parler de l'histoire de ce pauvre curé d'Oviedo qui fut trouvé étranglé dans son lit?" "On m'a dit ce matin à l'église que [le jeune homme de Salamanque] était mort." All these "souvenirs" bring a fierce grin to the bookseller's face.

That night Giacomo is awakened by cries of "fire!" When he hears that it is Baptisto's house that is burning, he joins the crowd that is gathering around it. With the aid of a ladder, he climbs in through the window and, braving flames, searches frantically for the *Mystère de Saint Michel*.[1] Suddenly he spies it—he snatches it up and escapes.

A few months pass. Spain is in turmoil; each day brings news of terrible crimes, and the police are totally baffled. One day Giacomo is brought into court: the poor *bibliomane* is accused of having set fire to Baptisto's house and stolen his Bible; "il était chargé encore de mille autres accusations."

The prosecutor maintains that the Bible now in Giacomo's possession must have been stolen from Baptisto, since it is the only copy in Spain. Giacomo's lawyer rises to defend his client; at the end of a long speech he dramatically produces . . . another copy of the Bible!

At this sight Giacomo utters a shriek, and collapses. Asked if it is he who set fire to Baptisto's house, he replies: "Non, hélas!" But he begs them to condemn him anyway: "La vie m'est à charge." He then admits to a whole series of crimes, including the murder of the curé of Oviedo and the student from Salamanca. The

---

[1]This is evidently an error; it is not the *Mystère* but the Bible that Giacomo is later accused of taking from Baptisto's house.

bibliomane listens impassively as he is condemned to death. After the sentencing he asks his lawyer for the second copy of the Bible. He gazes at it lovingly, then tears it to shreds. Throwing the pieces in his lawyer's face, Giacomo exclaims: "Je vous disais bien que c'était le seul [exemplaire] en Espagne!"

"BIBLIOMANIE" is, with "Une leçon d'histoire naturelle, genre commis," the only early work known to have been written for publication; it appeared in the *Colibri* (Rouen) on February 12, 1837. Like the historical stories that preceded it, it is highly dependent on source material. Only a single source seems to have been employed: the narrative "Le Bibliomane," published in the *Gazette des Tribunaux* of October 23, 1836;[2] from it Flaubert took virtually the entire structure of his plot. But the strictly literary aspects of Flaubert's story (style, characterization, description) are almost entirely his own, the account of the *Gazette* having been written in a dry, cursory language quite foreign to Flaubert. The essentially anecdotal form of the original relation is transformed in his narrative into a character study, and there is a corresponding de-emphasis of the crimes that were the chief subject matter of the *Gazette* story; at the end of his narrative, Flaubert even denies— with evident inconsistency—that his hero has committed them.

The protagonist of "Bibliomanie" is an adult whose interests are wholly absorbed in his professional activity of book collecting. This unproblematic concentration on a positive goal is in sharp distinction to the careers of the adolescent protagonists of the two preceding works. The praxis of "La peste à Florence" was after all a wholly negative act, a momentary rejection by Garcia of his necessarily subordinate existence. Unlike Garcia's conflict with his brother, Giacomo's rivalry with Baptisto is situated within the framework of an established worldly career.

In describing this rivalry Flaubert makes use of material familiar from both "La peste à Florence" and "Un parfum à sentir." It is notable that, while in the original *Gazette* account there had been no particular hostility between the two booksellers before the auction,[3] Flaubert

---

[2] Pp. 1149–1150 (see Bruneau, *Les débuts littéraires,* pp. 168–171). Camille Pitollet, in "Une mystification littéraire: le Bibliomane assassin; contribution à l'histoire des œuvres de Flaubert," *Mercure de Flandre,* November 1930, pp. 26–47, suggests (p. 46) as an alternative source the *Voleur* of October 31, 1836, where the account printed in the *Gazette* was published in an abridged version.

Pitollet reproduces the *Gazette* story in full in his article (pp. 28–38). This account was itself a fiction, which Pitollet speculates (without offering any positive evidence) to have been the work of Nodier or Mérimée.

[3] Paxtot, the rival in the original version, had become the leader of a pool of book-dealers jealous of Vincente's (Giacomo's) success (Pitollet, "Une mystification littéraire," pp. 31–32).

assimilates their relationship to the rivalry pattern of "La peste à Florence":

Oh! que de fois le pauvre moine, dans ses rêves d'ambition et d'orgueil... vit venir à lui la longue main de Baptisto... lui enlever un trésor qu'il avait rêvé si longtemps, qu'il avait convoité avec tant d'amour et d'égoisme! Que de fois aussi il fut tenté de finir avec un crime ce que ni l'argent ni la patience n'avait pu faire; mais il refoulait cette idée dans son coeur, tâchait de s'étourdir sur la haine qu'il portait à cet homme, et s'endormait sur ses livres. (OJ I, 139–140)

The indication that Giacomo had already thought of robbing Baptisto presumably sets the stage for the crimes that, in the original, follow the latter's disappointment at the auction. But Flaubert employs a curious device for avoiding the direct representation of these acts. Returning home from the auction in a half-crazed state, Giacomo overhears groups of people discussing the crimes that in the *Gazette* version were attributed to and confessed to by Giacomo himself:

Sa pensée n'était plus à lui, elle errait comme son corps... sa tête lui pesait comme du plomb, son front le brûlait comme un brasier....

Ce jour-là... le peuple se promenait dans les rues en causant et en chantant. Le pauvre moine écouta leurs causeries et leurs chants; *il ramassa dans la route quelques bribes de phrases,* quelques mots, quelques cris, mais il lui semblait que c'était toujours le même son, la même voix, c'était un brouhaha vague, confus, une musique bizarre et bruyante qui bourdonnait dans son cerveau et l'accablait.

— Tiens, disait un homme à son voisin, as-tu entendu parler de l'histoire de ce pauvre curé d'Oviedo qui fut trouvé étranglé dans son lit?...

[A group of women recount the murder of the young nobleman from Salamanca.]

Giacomo en entendit encore d'autres; *tous ces souvenirs le firent trembler,* et un sourire de férocité vint errer sur sa bouche. (OJ I, 142)

The word "souvenirs" near the end of the passage makes Giacomo appear responsible for the murders, although it can also be conceived of as referring to the memories of his just-overheard conversations. It seems more probable, however, that at this point Flaubert had not yet decided (if indeed he ever did) whether to disculpate Giacomo of the crimes.[4] In any case, the fire at Baptisto's is definitely not to be blamed on Giacomo who was at home when it broke out, even if he does take advantage of it to steal the Bible and to indulge in some *Schadenfreude*

---

[4] Lest Flaubert's apparent inconsistency in this matter appear surprising, we should note that this story has at least two other inconsistencies that point to a considerable carelessness in reviewing the manuscript: (1) at the auction Giacomo finds himself unable to bid over 500 pistoles, while we know he has just received 600 pistoles from the Salamancan student; (2) Flaubert has (in error) Giacomo steal the *Mystère de Saint Michel* from Baptisto's house, instead of the Bible actually involved.

at his rival's expense.[5] Following the fire Flaubert describes a whole
series of murders and other crimes not attributable to Giacomo and
unrelated to those mentioned in the *Gazette* narrative; without regard
for consistency, the author creates from these crimes an atmosphere
of universal fatality and evil such as the plague supplied in "La peste
à Florence":

> Un mauvais génie semblait peser sur [l'Espagne]; chaque jour, de nouveaux
> meurtres et de nouveaux crimes... on ne savait à qui attribuer cet horrible fléau, car
> il faut attribuer le malheur à quelqu'un d'étranger, mais le bonheur à soi. En effet,
> il est des jours si néfastes dans la vie, des époques si funestes pour les hommes, que,
> ne sachant qui accabler de ses malédictions, on crie vers le ciel; c'est dans ces époques
> malheureuses pour les peuples que l'on croit à la fatalité. (OJ I, 144)

This development prepares the final trial scene, where Giacomo is
depicted simply as an innocent martyr to the popular desire to find
a culprit for the murders. He confesses to the crimes on learning that
his copy of the Bible is not unique; but presumably this admission,
although it parallels the far more limited confession of the original
version, is only made out of his despairing wish for death.

The relationship of Giacomo to the crimes is thus made highly equivo-
cal. When Flaubert writes,

> il était donc là, assis sur les bancs des meurtriers et des brigands, lui, l'honnête
> bibliophile; le pauvre Giacomo, qui ne pensait qu'à ses livres, était donc compromis
> dans les mystères de meurtre et d'échafaud (OJ I, 145),

evidently the author wants to blame the arbitrary injustice of society
for the destruction of Giacomo's career rather than, as in the spirit
of the original, to illustrate how this career itself has led Giacomo to
perdition through its refusal to be bound by moral limitations. But
he is identifying with Giacomo as a martyr rather than as a criminal;
Flaubert is defeated by the very subject matter of the story he has
chosen: the theft of the Bible from Baptisto, the only crime of real
significance for the *bibliomane,* cannot be attributed to anyone but
Giacomo himself. It would seem that in the course of composing the
story Flaubert became unwilling to identify with the violation of
worldly morality involved in the crimes and sought to transfer Giacomo's guilt to the hostile "father"-world. This inconsistency only
became possible because ostensibly in "Bibliomanie" guilt is not as in
"La peste à Florence" a necessary component of the hero's activities;

---

[5] "Le moine contemplait son [Baptisto's] désespoir et ses cris avec calme et
bonheur, avec ce rire féroce de l'enfant riant des tortures du papillon dont il a
arraché les ailes" (OJ I, 143).

whereas the adolescent Garcia could only act as a criminal, the adult Giacomo can assert himself within a legitimate worldly career.

But the refusal of the guilt involved in Giacomo's rivalry destroys the basis for the Flaubertian hero's praxis. Without his crimes this rivalry would never have been written about, either by the author of the *Gazette* account or by Flaubert himself. That our author now shows a reluctance to accept this guilt is a sign of the coming transition to the "null-praxial" heroes, who accept their adolescent position guilt-lessly because they lack any desire to engage in a worldly praxis.

There is in the course of the story a transformation in Giacomo's career. Originally, his bibliomania is given as essentially *infinite* in nature, involving no final goal in which his activities would culminate. Regardless of the size of his collection, Giacomo would presumably never lose interest in book hunting but would eternally seek after new rarities. But such a career would be merely *picturesque;* its lack of finality would make it not a form of becoming but of static being, not a praxis but a function. Thus in fact the original vision of Giacomo as interested in an unlimited number of different books only provides the backdrop for the real action of the story.

With the appearance of the rivalry with Baptisto over the Bible, this single volume becomes Giacomo's exclusive goal. One might at first wish to conceive of this as a temporary phenomenon, an understandable con-centration of interest on the book presently at issue, but Flaubert is careful to point out that this is not the case:

Jamais... il n'avait tant désiré. Oh! qu'il eût voulu alors, même au prix de tout ce qu'il avait, de ses livres, de ses manuscrits... avoir ce livre! Vendre tout, tout pour avoir ce livre; n'avoir que lui, mais l'avoir à lui; pouvoir le montrer à toute l'Espagne, avec un rire d'insulte et de pitié pour le roi, pour les princes, pour les savants, pour Baptisto, et dire: A moi, à moi ce livre! (OJ I, 140)

Thus the Bible has become the sole object of value for Giocomo; beside it his whole collection is as nothing. By associating the possession of this book with a sense of superiority to the king, and in particular to Bap-tisto, Giacomo like Garcia in "La peste à Florence" enters into compe-tition with his rival for public recognition.

This rivalry becomes the very substance of Giacomo's existence; once Baptisto is defeated, the goal of the *bibliomane* has been reached, and he engages in no further action until the concluding trial scene. Thus it is as a symbolic object of rivalry that the Bible becomes of exclusive importance for Giacomo. The theft of this book from Baptisto involves the complete annihilation of the rival just as much as Garcia's murder of François in "La peste à Florence."[6] Both the theft and Giacomo's subsequent punishment thus parallel the preceding work: Giacomo's positive desire for the Bible is merely a more worldly version of Garcia's envy of his brother's honors.

But the concluding scene of the story, where Giacomo discovers to his dismay that his Bible is not unique, puts his positive desire in a different light and foreshadows the renouncement of the rivalry theme in the third period. In "La peste à Florence" there is no such disillusioning discovery for Garcia to make: he has no possibility of gaining his brother's privileges for himself, and the issue of the value he attaches to these paternally awarded honors is consequently avoided. But in "Bibliomanie" the explicit positive value placed on the Bible by Giacomo allows for its *devaluation*. The existence of the second copy of the Bible destroys the very meaning of Giacomo's praxis, which had come to be directed exclusively toward possession of this one work:

> Son avocat... souleva sa robe et en tira... un autre exemplaire de cette Bible.
> Giacomo poussa un cri et tomba sur un banc et s'arrachant les cheveux....
> On lui demanda s'il était coupable d'avoir mis le feu chez Baptisto.
> — Non, hélas! répondit-il.
> — Non?
> — Mais allez-vous me condamner? Oh! condamnez-moi, je vous en prie! la vie m'est à charge... Messeigneurs, tuez-moi, je suis un misérable. (OJ I, 146)

One should not interpret Giacomo's sudden despair as revealing to him in any explicit fashion the vanity of his career as a whole, or the futility of worldly action in general. There is merely a loss of all meaning from a life that had made the possession of the "unique" Bible into its exclusive goal. But in the light of the following story, "Rage et impuissance," where such an explicit disillusionment does occur, Giacomo's abrupt "depraxialization" would appear to reflect the author's comprehension of the essential falseness, within his own system of values, of his hero's unproblematic concern for a single goal. Giacomo's loss of interest in life places him, if only momentarily, in the same suicidal situation as the hero of the "null-praxial" "La dernière heure." The *bibliomane* is not, like Marguerite of "Un parfum à sentir," driven to suicide through being deprived of the object of his desires. His situation is more radically "unworldly" than hers; he no longer has any such desire object. Giacomo has been thrown from his goal-directed innocence into an

---

[6] In this connection it is curious that Flaubert does not depict Baptisto as having been killed in the fire, as happened to the rival (Paxtot) in the original. Evidently he wished to make the possession of the Bible the sole decisive issue between Giacomo and Baptisto.

awareness of the nonexistence of valid worldly goals. Like Garcia in "La peste à Florence," he is condemned to death for the destruction of his rival, but unlike him he survives long enough to experience for an instant the valueless existence that is the lot of the heroes of the succeeding works.

PART THREE

December 1836–March 1837

CHAPTER XX

RAGE ET IMPUISSANCE: CONTE MALSAIN POUR LES NERFS SENSIBLES ET LES AMES DEVOTES

December 15, 1836

ON A COLD night in the town of Mussen, an old woman sits by the fire waiting for the return of Dr. Ohmlin, the well-loved doctor of this Alpine town. Berthe "avait vu naître M. Ohmlin, elle avait été sa nourrice, plus tard sa servante." Shortly after midnight Ohmlin appears, drenched and shivering from the cold; he draws close to the fire to warm himself. Ohmlin complains that he has been unable to sleep for the past four nights; this night he will take some opium. Finally he retires, "avala son opium et s'endormit dans des rêves d'or."

In the morning when Berthe gets up she is surprised to find that the doctor is still in his bedroom. Soon maître Bernardo, a neighboring physician, arrives and asks for his colleague. He enters the room of the sleeping doctor, calling out "Allons! levez-vous donc! il est tard." But Ohmlin does not budge. Aghast, Bernardo realizes that the prone figure is dead, and he rushes out of the room.

A few hours later a dozen physicians are surveying the body of their colleague, "et un seul mot errait sur leurs lèvres: il est mort!" One doctor hesitatingly suggests that Ohmlin is perhaps only asleep, but lacking proof he soon accedes to the majority opinion.

The day of Ohmlin's funeral is gloomy and damp; and the villagers too are sad, for their benefactor is dead. Ohmlin's coffin is carried slowly to the cemetery; "les prêtres chantaient tout bas, car les larmes couvraient leurs voix." After the funeral, everyone leaves but one devoted friend—Fox, Ohmlin's favorite dog, who remains howling at his grave. But in the tomb, "M. Ohmlin dormait toujours;... il rêvait et c'étaient des songes beaux d'illusions, voluptueux d'amour et d'enchantments." He was dreaming of the seductions of the Orient; "mais le réveil allait venir, morne, impitoyable, comme la réalité qu'il apporte."

When Ohmlin finally opens his eyes, the horror of his situation dawns on him: buried alive! Enraged, he tears his hair, rips his shroud. Suddenly he hears a sound above him and, transformed with hope, he prays devoutly to God, thanking him for this early delivery. But it is only the gravedigger who has come to get a spade that he had left out in the rain. Ohmlin, again reduced to despair, begins to curse and blaspheme, daring God to come and deliver him if he exists. Finally, in a supreme effort, he succeeds in breaking open the top of his coffin. "Mais la terre était là, haute de six pieds, la terre qui allait l'écraser s'il faisait le moindre mouvement." In his frustrated rage, Ohmlin attempts to break out of the coffin, but the lid falls and crushes him.

Attracted by the howling of Fox, the gravedigger digs up Ohmlin's coffin, thinking to find some buried valuable. When he opens it, he finds the corpse turned over on its stomach, the shroud torn, and the face distorted in a horrid grimace.

MORALITÉ (CYNIQUE) POUR INDIQUER LA CONDUITE
QUE L'ON DOIT TENIR À SON HEURE DERNIÈRE

Maître Michel de Montaigne was wont to say: "que sais-je?" Likewise, maître
François Rabelais used to say: "peut-être." And if the good doctor had been asked
his opinion on Providence, he probably would have replied: "J'en doute ou je la nie."
Hence the moral of this story: "J'engage... les hommes (à jeter) leur existence à
la face de Dieu lorsqu'elle est amère."

"RAGE ET IMPUISSANCE" opens the third period. Since nearly all of
Flaubert's preceding works were in some way dependent on source
material, we can reasonably assume that at least the seemingly arbitrary Swiss locale of the story is derived from an as yet undiscovered
source. Both Bruneau[1] and Shanks[2] wish to attach the vision of death
in "Rage et impuissance" to the author's childhood memories of the
Rouen hospital where he was raised, but the physical aspect of death
is in fact scarcely touched on in this story. Certainly there is no reason
to suppose that Flaubert knew of any cases of premature burial from
his own experience; a literary source is far more likely.[3]

This story marks a transition from the problematic worldly orientation of the second period to the null-praxis of the third period. Dr.
Ohmlin's "career" in the tomb can hardly be called a praxis in the
normal sense. It is a self-contained experience in which the protagonist's
aim (i.e., escape from the tomb) is meaningful only in his immediate
situation and stands in no relation to any goal in the normal world.
But within this situation his praxis is perfectly adequate, fully absorb-
ing his concern. This is quite unlike the utter indifference of the hero
toward his existential possibilities that we find in "La dernière heure."

Yet life outside the tomb only has so great a value for Ohmlin because
it has come to represent an ideal, paradisial freedom in contrast with
the adolescent frustration symbolized by the burial; the life he longs
for is not the everyday one he has left behind, but the lost paradise of
childhood.

---

[1] "Ainsi *Rage et impuissance*... se rattacherait aux impressions si fortes et si
durables que la vie à l'Hôtel-Dieu de Rouen a laissées dans l'âme de Flaubert"
(Bruneau, *Les débuts littéraires*, pp. 172–173).

[2] Lewis Piaget Shanks, *Flauberts' Youth; 1821–1845* (Baltimore, 1927): "I prefer
to think that Flaubert's violence in *Rage et impuissance* is not entirely imitative
(*sc.* of literary sources). For the frightful dreams he relates in *Mémoires d'un fou*
(Chapter IV) show clearly the brand left upon his imagination by the dissecting-
room of the hospital" (p. 23). Shanks is, however, aware of the relationship of Dr.
Ohmlin's intense frustration to the author's "crisis of puberty" (p. 24).

[3] Bruneau (*Les débuts littéraires*, p. 171) mentions the popularity of the *mort
vivant* theme in Romantic literature, citing the opera *Guido et Ginevra* of Scribe
and Halévy (1838).

Ohmlin's worldly situation before his awakening in the tomb offers a striking contrast to that of the heroes of the preceding works. The problematic and frustrated worldly ambitions of Garcia or Giacomo have been transmuted into unquestioned success. Ohmlin is an esteemed doctor and the chief benefactor of his village; at his premature funeral he is sincerely mourned by the population:

Ce jour-là il était triste... le village! son père, son bienfaiteur était mort! Les maisons étaient fermées, on ne se parlait pas, les enfants ne riaient plus sur la place, les hommes étaient attendris et l'on pleurait. (OJ I, 152)

Thus Ohmlin has achieved success and recognition in Dr. Flaubert's own profession—a success far beyond the accomplishments Gustave so bitterly envied in his brother Achille. Ohmlin's career fully satisfies the author's need for worldly recognition; this hero is not forced to suffer the frustrations of Carlos or Garcia. But in endowing his protagonist with such good fortune, Flaubert also demonstrates, even before he depicts the awakening in the tomb, the ultimate valuelessness of such worldly achievements. Ohmlin is never shown as deriving any satisfaction from his status; it is, in fact, only after his burial that we learn of the extent of his success. His sole source of pleasure while he is still in the world is to escape from it in his exotic, sensual dreams from which he finally awakens in the tomb.

These dreams are the first overt expression of the author's sexuality since "Un parfum à sentir"; never before had Flaubert so explicitly expressed his own sexual life in his works:

Il rêvait l'Orient! l'Orient, avec son soleil brûlant, son ciel bleu, ses minarets dorés,... avec ses parfums,... ses caravanes dans les sables; l'Orient! avec ses sérails, séjour des fraîches voluptés.... Il rêvait de grands yeux noirs qui n'avaient d'amour que pour lui, il rêvait cette peau brune et olivâtre des femmes de l'Asie... (OJ I, 153–154)[4]

The desires that lay submerged throughout the second period emerge into the open now that Flaubert has come to deny any ultimate significance to worldly accomplishments. But this is not to say that he now makes the sexual desires of his protagonist the basis for a praxis that would substitute for the worldly crime of a Garcia. On the con-

---

[4] Compare Ohmlin's visions with Flaubert's own dreams as expressed in "Mémoires d'un fou":

Je voyais l'Orient et ses sables immenses, ses palais que foulent les chameaux... l'horizon rougi par le soleil;... un ciel pur, un sable d'argent; je sentais le parfum de ces océans tièdes du Midi; et puis, près de moi... quelque femme à la peau brune, au regard ardent, qui m'entourait de ses deux bras. (OJ I, 491)

trary, the unreal, purely cerebral nature of Ohmlin's sexuality is entirely faithful to the "underground" character of the author's own sexual life and does not involve the least attempt to elevate it into a praxis. The guilt that led to the repression of sexuality in the second period retains its full force. The expression of sexual desire is only possible in Ohmlin's dreams because they occur outside his normal in-the-world consciousness; the opium that puts him to sleep removes him from the domain of paternal morality.

But, despite his lack of positive satisfaction in his career and the unreality of his erotic dreams, Ohmlin's worldly existence is far from unbearable. His career, even if it fails to satisfy his deepest needs, gives him a worldly occupation worthy of Dr. Flaubert himself, while his sexual desires find a guiltless outlet in his dreams. Thus a double existence allows Ohmlin both worldly success and, what is more important, guiltless sexual satisfaction. Evidently the author himself, in his present situation, could hope for nothing better.

But with the awakening in the tomb the wish fulfillment ends abruptly. The duality of Ohmlin's position is abolished. In the tomb he no longer has either a worldly career or an erotic dream life; he has become a prisoner, like Bernardo in "Le moine des Chartreux"— like Flaubert himself.

The moment of awakening represents the confrontation of Flaubert's protagonist with what for the adolescent author is the real significance of life in the world. The falseness of Ohmlin's dream world gives way to an unpleasantly authentic consciousness of his true situation:

Et il voulut se rendormir... effacer de sa pensée cette masse de plomb qui pesait sur sa tête et se bercer dans d'autres rêves.

Non! il avait trop rêvé. Ah! d'autres rêves maintenant? rêve l'éternité si tu veux. Eh bien, l'Orient? maintenant rêve donc l'Orient dans ta tombe, dans une pensée de volupté et dans des rêves dorés! Non! non! l'agonie et les rêves d'enfer,[5] l'agonie qui s'arrache les cheveux, se tord de désespoir, appelle Satan et maudit Dieu! (OJ I, 154–155)

There is a strong element of self-mockery in this passage. Flaubert too has dreamed of the Orient and its seductions, participated in a guiltless, cerebral version of adult sexuality, and now he too shares the "agonie" of awakening from his dreams, not to the worldly preoccupations of Ohmlin's career as a doctor (which too is only a "dream" for Flaubert),

---

[5] "Agonies" and "Rêve d'enfer" are the titles of two of Flaubert's future works.

but to the frustrating, guilt-ridden reality of adolescence. Specifically the scene suggests an awakening from a nocturnal sexual experience[6]— the "nuits que l'on passe à pleurer et à maudire sa mère" of "Un parfum à sentir." Thus a definite element of sexual guilt manifests itself in this awakening. As soon as the separation between dream and reality is abolished, the paternal morality of the real world comes to apply to Ohmlin's fantasies, and the guilty, unideal nature of his "adolescent" sexuality must be recognized. At the same time, Ohmlin's successful career no longer exists to occupy his time and to protect him from the frustrated emptiness of worldly existence. The bringing together of the two halves of the protagonist's life destroys the inauthentic modus vivendi he had established within each half separately.

But with his awakening, Ohmlin's desires do not simply disappear. They are transformed instead into the urgent will to live that becomes the basis for his "praxis" in the tomb, his effort to escape. In this transformation the desires lose their specifically sexual character and, along with it, their guilty, clandestine nature; "life" in general becomes Ohmlin's goal. This life appears to him as an idyllic relationship to nature from which he has only now been cut off:

mourir! ne plus rien voir de tout ce qui se passe sur cette terre; la nature, les champs, le ciel, les montagnes, tout cela... je les ai quittés pour toujours! (OJ I, 155)

---

[6] For example:

Il avait froid, il se sentait nu, et l'humidité du sépulcre humectait sa peau; il tremblait, ses dents claquaient, la fièvre battait dans ses artères; il se sentit piqué au doigt, le porta à ses yeux, il ne vit rien, il faisait si noir! à ses lèvres, il sentit l'odeur du sang; il s'était écorché à un clou de sa tombe. (OJ I, 155)

The indications of nakedness, perspiration and feverishness speak for themselves. As for the bleeding, a similarly symbolic experience can be found in a dream recounted in "Mémoires d'un fou":

Ma porte s'ouvrit d'elle-même, on entra. Ils étaient beaucoup, peut-être sept à huit... tous avaient une lame d'acier entre les dents...

Ils écartèrent mes rideaux blancs, et chaque doigt laissait une trace de sang... Ils soulevèrent tous mes vêtements, et tous avaient du sang...

Puis, quand ils n'y furent plus, tout ce qu'ils avaient touché, les lambris, l'escalier, le plancher, tout cela était rougi par eux.

J'avais un goût d'amertume dans le coeur, il me sembla que j'avais mangé de la chair. (OJ I, 493–494)

Reik (*Flaubert und seine "Versuchung des Heiligen Antonius"*) associates this dream with Gustave's fears of castration by his father which (although Reik does not specifically mention it) evidently must involve a strong element of guilt for his autoerotic activities.

This is essentially the vision of the lost childhood paradise, expressed in terms of the child's unity with nature, that reappears throughout the third period.[7] In "Le moine des Chartreux" the imprisoned monk's desire for life was directed toward future pleasures, the not yet experienced joys of the *adult* world, although these too, it may be recalled, were connected with "des souvenirs de jeunesse." But now "life" in the positive sense, the life that Ohmlin longs for, is envisioned explicitly as a *past* existence that cannot be recaptured. The desire for the pleasures of this life is devoid of sexual guilt, because the childhood paradise, when it existed for Ohmlin-Flaubert, was innocent of any such guilt.

Ohmlin's desire for an ideal, guiltless existence profoundly transforms the sense of the worldly revolt that dominated the second period. Unlike Garcia or Giacomo, Ohmlin has no worldly goals. His desire is not for some specific improvement in his situation, but for an absolute, ideal existence altogether different from his present imprisonment in the tomb. While Garcia too was "imprisoned" in his worldly situation, he sought only to act within its limits, to take advantage of the small leeway left him for action. In Ohmlin's entombment, Flaubert has come to terms with the utter unfreedom of his own worldly situation and of the "fallen" human condition in general, irrevocably cut off from the freedom of the childhood paradise. Ohmlin cannot, as Garcia does, act *within* his prison; he must react against it altogether, renouncing his adult worldly and sexual interest to take as his goal the childhood ideal itself, the child's unconscious unity with nature. Because this ideal is essentially unattainable in Ohmlin's present situation, the praxial aspect of his revolt is only secondary; it is primarily an internal, spiritual rebellion against the horror of the human condition. Ohmlin rebels against the very meaning of existence, against Providence, against God himself:

Bah! se disait-il en riant d'un rire forcé, où est-il le créateur des misères? où est-il? qu'il vienne me délivrer s'il existe!... Je te nie, mot inventé par les heureux; je te nie, tu n'es qu'une puissance fatale et stupide, comme la foudre qui tombe et qui brûle. (OJ I, 161)

The metaphysical nature of Ohmlin's revolt is of the deepest significance, for it permits him to share the "philosophical" conceptions of

---

[7] Cf. "Rêve d'enfer": "... au milieu des champs... elle y avait passé son enfance, se jouant dans les bois" (OJ I, 170), and "La main de fer": "Enfant, il aimait à cueillir des roses, à écouter la mer qui se brise sur les rochers" (OJ II, 272).

the author.[8] Flaubert has rejected the orientation of his hero's praxis toward a particular goal, with which the author-narrator as a "universal" consciousness could identify only from a distance. Now for the first time the protagonist is placed on the author's own level. Flaubert has renounced his identification with the adult lovers of the first period and the youthful but already worldly rebels that followed them; his hero now puts into symbolic action his own adolescent rejection of the adult world. Because Flaubert has not yet become a part of this world he is able to renounce his hopes of worldly success in order to hold fast to the childhood ideal, which he has now come to recognize as the only truly disalienated existence. The null-praxial works that follow "Rage et impuissance" uncover the specific childhood content of this ideal, which Ohmlin still conceives only as a harmonious relationship with nature.

"Rage et impuissance" represents a key point in Flaubert's early development in that it permits us to witness for the first time the total, "adolescent" separation between the real world and the ideal which becomes the cornerstone of his future transcendence of Romanticism. Such a separation is by no means foreign to the Romantic world view. But the Romantic, in the course of his experience of the world, is never entirely cut off from the hope of disalienation. For René, life is a *process* of disillusionment in which the worthlessness of worldly possibilities is revealed through his experience of them. But Flaubert, unlike René, has not rejected worldly experience a posteriori on empirical grounds; as part of a generation that accepted from childhood the truth of René's disillusionment, he has learned to renounce all hope of worldly satisfaction at a point prior to any adult experience.

But if this is true, how can worldly experience, thus cut off from the ideal, ever again be depicted in Flaubert's works? In "Rage et impuissance" this question presents no problem since Ohmlin's awakening in the tomb eliminates any further possibility of life in the world. But in the works that follow, the necessity of reintroducing such experience despite its a priori separation from the ideal forces Flaubert to modify profoundly the terms of his identification with his heroes.

---

[8] This is made clear in the "Moralité" at the end of the story where the author offers Ohmlin's denial of Providence as exemplary:

J'engage donc, ayant trouvé la conduite du sus-écrit docteur louable et bonne... les mourants [à jeter] leurs âmes quand ils crèvent, et les hommes leur existence à la face de Dieu lorsqu'elle est amère. (OJ I, 161)

Chapter XXI

LA DERNIERE HEURE
(CONTE PHILOSOPHIQUE)

January 1837

THE NARRATOR is seated in his small, narrow room; he has turned up his stove and is waiting for the gas to take its effect. He has only one hour left to live, just enough time to retrace his memories.

I. A man is usually considered happy if he is rich and healthy. The narrator has all the outward trappings of happiness—"et je suis si heureux qu'aujourd'hui, à 19 ans, je me suicide!"

II. One day, when he was ten years old, he suddenly missed his sister, Lélia. But when he went to fetch her, he found her dead, wrapped in a white sheet. "On m'a souvent demandé depuis pourquoi j'étais triste."

III. The two women who were watching over his sister's body told him to pray for her. He obeyed, in the naïve hope that it would bring her back to life. But he soon saw that prayers were to no avail, and he bitterly accused the women of having deceived him. They tried to explain that the prayers were for her soul. But what did he know about her soul? He wanted his living sister, Lélia who used to play with him in the woods and on the lawn. He cursed the two women, but "cette malédiction est retournée sur moi, philosophe imbécile, qui ne sais pas... croire à une âme sans la sentir, et craindre un Dieu... que je méprise trop pour blasphémer."

IV. Often, when he sees man's mad race for glory, he thinks, "où tend tout cela?" The sight of the trees, the stars, the ocean fills him with despair, and he thinks to himself, "pourquoi tout cela existe-t-il?"

V. Only one "remords" still troubles him—"j'aurais dû vivre comme je meurs, gai et tranquille"; he should have laughed at God instead of cursing him, and since he was unable to find "l'amour, prendre la volupté!"

VI. The narrator states that very early in life he conceived a profound disgust for mankind. When he was twelve years old he was put in a *collège;* there he observed in miniature all the vices and stupidities of the adult world. (Unfinished.)

THE UNFINISHED "La dernière heure," Flaubert's only first-person work of narrative fiction,[1] is the most characteristically "null-praxial" work of the third period. No source material has been found for this story, and in the absence of descriptive material or complications of plot I have no reason to suppose that any was specifically employed. But neither the protagonist's intense relationship with his sister, despite its roots in Flaubert's own family life, nor his worldly disillusionment in general can be thought of without reference to *René.*[2]

---

[1] "Agonies," "Mémoires d'un fou," and "Novembre," also written in the first person, like "Voyage en enfer" and the fragment "Une pensée" in the first period, all consist essentially of either autobiographical material or "philosophical" content.

[2] See below, pp. 132–133.

In "La dernière heure" the separation between worldly existence and ideal that was represented symbolically in Ohmlin's burial in "Rage et impuissance" is brought back into everyday reality. The expulsion from paradise expressed in the earlier work by Ohmlin's awakening within the tomb is now placed within a childhood setting that permits a more detailed articulation of the experience. At the same time, because the hero of "La dernière heure" has been brought out of the tomb and placed in the real world, the ideal life that for Ohmlin existed in the inaccessible outside world no longer has any *present* existence; its equivalent is the irretrievable *past* paradise of the hero's life with his sister. As a result no counterpart is possible here to Ohmlin's active effort to escape the tomb and enter this ideal life. The anonymous hero of "La dernière heure" cannot attempt to escape his present condition for something better; his only possibility for praxis lies in suicide, in the flight from his unideal life in the world into a tomb of his own making.[3]

The central experience of this work is the death of the hero's sister Lélia, the original cause of his expulsion from the childhood paradise. The idyllic relationship between the hero and his sister which is terminated by her death is highly reminiscent of the idylls of the first period —the significant difference being that now there is no question of extending the brother-sister relationship into an overtly sexual one.[4] The hero's desire to bring his sister back to life is, like Ohmlin's yearning for the earthly paradise outside, a fully justified, guiltless desire; indeed it is his sister's death that symbolized his fall from innocence into the guilty world of adult sexuality which only her return to life could annul. And again like Ohmlin this hero places the blame for his loss not on the concrete familial or social order but on the evil of man's mortal condition itself:

Souvent, en regardant le soleil, je me suis dit: "Pourquoi viens-tu chaque jour éclairer tant de souffrances, découvrir tant de douleurs, présider à tant de sottes misères?" (OJ II, 269)

But the reality of this condition is not, as in "Rage et impuissance," brought home to the protagonist by the imminence of his own death; his awakening to his fallen state is placed instead in the past. Ohmlin, by means of his erotic dreams, had been able to cover over his separation

---

[3] "Ma chambre est basse et étroite, mes fenêtres sont bien fermées, j'ai eu soin de boucher la serrure avec de la mie de pain" (OJ II, 265).

[4] Compare "La dernière heure": "Lélia qui jouait avec moi sur le gazon, dans les bois" (OJ II, 268) with "La grande dame": "Dans les bois un couple gracieux était étendu sur le gazon" (Bruneau, *Les débuts littéraires*, p. 124).

from the paradise of childhood until long after he had already entered the adult world, and only in the face of death did he become aware of this separation. For the hero of "La dernière heure," such an awareness is prior to all worldly experience; his expulsion from "paradise" as the commencement of his fallen existence is a concrete fact from which he cannot possibly hide.

Yet for the author no such concrete fact ever existed. Lélia's death, like the destruction of the preworldly paradise by the father figures of the first period (the rape of Annette in "La fiancée et la tombe," the enforced marriage of Henriette in "La grande dame et le joueur de vielle"), is only a symbolically concrete representation of a gradual emergence from childhood and from innocent prepubertal sexuality. By transforming this emergence into a sudden expulsion, Flaubert idealizes his hero's childhood as a privileged age wholly cut off from his present state of frustration.

But if the hero's awakening to the horror of worldly existence is placed in the past, how can his survival into the present be justified? And if he has until now been able to survive in the unideal world, what more could occur that would serve as the efficient cause for his suicide?

From the point of view of the literary work itself, there is no answer to these questions. The null-praxis, as it appears in *René*, involves the successive taking up and rejection of the manifold of worldly possibilities. True, in *René* this worldly experience can only take place after the expulsion from the home of childhood,[5] but Flaubert's treatment of this theme differs markedly, if not indeed deliberately, from that of Chateaubriand.[6] René's expulsion from the paternal mansion does not negate a priori his possibility of finding a satisfactory praxis in the world; it merely symbolizes his entry into an adulthood in which no specific worldly career has been determined for him:

Plein d'ardeur, je m'élançai seul sur cet orageux océan du monde, dont je ne connaissais ni les ports, ni les écueils. (Chateaubriand, p. 194)

---

[5] "Il fallut quitter le toit paternel" (Chateaubriand, *Atala, René...* [Paris: Garnier, 1958], p. 191.)

[6] The opposition is especially noticeable in the death scene common to both works. In *René* it is the hero's father that dies, and in seeing him on his deathbed René for the first time is convinced of the immortality of the soul: "C'est la première fois que l'immortalité de l'âme s'est présentée clairement à mes yeux" (Chateaubriand, *Atala, René...*, p. 189). In "La dernière heure," the conception of the immortality of Lélia's soul is precisely singled out for ridicule: "Tu as prié pour un souffle, pour un mot, pour le néant, pour son âme enfin! Son âme... je la méprise... Qu'est-ce que ça me fait à moi, son âme? savez-vous ce que c'est que son âme?" (OJ II, 268). For René his father's death holds out to him a promise of future salvation and transcendence of earthly evils, while in "La dernière heure" the death of Lélia destroys the hero's childhood faith.

This allows him to search the world vainly for an unknown "port," and only at the end of this search to discover that his forbidden relationship with his sister was his sole source of earthly happiness. For Flaubert's hero, whose sister dies at the very beginning, a comparable search for a worldly praxis would be pointless and inconsistent; the author accepts the lesson of René's experience a priori. But at the same time, in order to justify his protagonist's suicide, Flaubert is obliged to fill in the ten years that follow his expulsion from childhood with a "disillusioning" experience of the world similar to that of Chateaubriand's hero. The contradiction between the need for and the impossibility of such significant worldly experience could not be and was not in fact resolved; Flaubert was forced to abandon his narrative after a brief, half-hearted attempt at describing the hero's unhappy life at school. For what importance could such experience have after the decisive trauma of his childhood?

From the point of view of Flaubert's own experience, this inconsistency reflects the fact that he himself, like Ohmlin in "Rage et impuissance," has only discovered his "expulsion" *now*, in the frustrations of his adolescence. The distant loss of the childhood idyll is not in itself so crucial as is the author's *present* state of sexual guilt and dissatisfaction. This is revealed in a passage near the end of the work:

Je trouve... que j'aurais dû vivre comme je meurs, gai et tranquille; qu'au lieu de pleurer et de maudire Dieu, j'aurais dû en rire et le braver; j'aurais dû éteindre mes pleurs sous un rire, oublier la réalité et *puisque je n'avais pu trouver l'amour, prendre la volupté!* (OJ II, 270)

Here the hero explicitly states the immediate cause for his suicide—"puisque je n'avais pu trouver l'amour." This unattainable "amour," contrasted with guilty "volupté," is represented as offering the only possible means of preserving the child's original unified existence under the conditions of adult sexuality.

The hero's failure to find this "amour" can be related to the author's own experience, recounted in section xiv of "Mémoires d'un fou," with an English girl to whom he gives his sister's name, Caroline. This autobiographical account describes an abortive love affair which presumably took place in the spring and summer of 1836; Gustave tried to develop a Romantic passion for "Caroline," but did not respond when she made obvious advances to him:

Un jour elle se coucha sur mon canapé dans une position très équivoque; j'étais assis près d'elle sans rien dire. Certes le moment était critique, je n'en profitai pas, je la laissai partir. (OJ I, 523)

That Flaubert gave this girl his sister's name reflects his desire for her

to take his sister's place as a love object in a fashion that would have reconciled his adolescent sexuality with the childhood idyll. This proved impossible when the girl's feelings became such that real sexual desire intruded itself into the relationship—Gustave's inhibitions, reinforced by a sense of superiority to worldly sexuality, were too powerful for him to give himself up to adult sexual experience. Yet the alternative of "volupté," of sexuality without love, remains a temptation for him and for his hero, a possibility of worldly action that escapes the limitations of the null-praxial form.

This fact is of more than merely psychological significance. It is the revelation of the falseness of Romantic "amour" and its assimilation to the degradation of "volupté" that makes up the central theme of *Madame Bovary.* Flaubert was never able to absorb himself in a love affair that could recreate for him the lost childhood paradise. At the same time, aside from merely physical desire, he had too deep a need for recognition as an adult to renounce sexual activity, even if this activity could not be attached to the ideal.[7] This dichotomy presents a model of the relationship between the author and his characters that is found in the mature novels: their worldly "volupté"-oriented activity is perceived as a *necessity,* despite its alienation from the ideal, while at the same time there is no Romantic illusion that this alienation can be transcended (disalienated) through the incorporation of the "volupté" within an ideal "amour."

The central literary problem left over to the author by "La dernière heure" is that of content. The separation of reality from the ideal and the impossibility of any return through worldly activity to the paradise of childhood have already been established, and out of this the null-praxis has been developed. But because worldly praxis has been revealed to be invalid a priori, Flaubert must face the impossibility of finding

---

[7] In "Mémoires d'un fou" Flaubert explains his first sexual experience as caused not by sexual desire but by the need to impress his comrades, which, more than the physical act itself, fills him with remorse and self-contempt:

La vanité me poussa à l'amour, non, à la volupté; pas même à cela, à la chair.

On me raillait de ma chasteté, j'en rougissais, elle me faisait honte, elle me pesait comme si elle eût été de la corruption.

Une femme se présenta à moi, je la pris; et je sortis de ses bras plein de dégoût et d'amertume. Mais alors, je pouvais... dire autant d'obscénités qu'un autre autour d'un bol de punch; j'étais un homme alors, *j'avais été, comme à un devoir, faire du vice,* et puis je m'en étais vanté.... presque tous [les hommes] y ont été poussés par les sens,... *mais il y avait bien plus de dégradation à en faire un calcul, à s'exciter à la corruption,* à aller se jeter dans les bras d'une femme... pour se relever et montrer ses souillures. (OJ I, 524–525)

worldly content in which to "praxialize" the essential structures of his own prepraxial, preworldly experience. This lack of content led to the incompletion of both "La dernière heure" and the following story, "La main de fer." In the final work of the period, "Rêve d'enfer," Flaubert is forced to renounce the null-praxis and accept sexuality as the necessarily unideal ground of his protagonist's worldly career.

Chapter XXII

LA MAIN DE FER (CONTE PHILOSOPHIQUE)
February 1837

I. The city of Saragossa, once vibrant and full of life, now sleeps lazily under the southern sun; "à peine si... quelque fidèle vient s'agenouiller sur la pierre de [ses] cathédrales." Yet occasionally a young man comes to seek faith, to rejuvenate his cynical soul, to take God "comme un amour de jeunesse"; he immerses himself joyfully in the ritual of the church—"il est heureux, car il croit."

II. Such was Manoello, a rich, handsome and pious young nobleman of Saragossa. Melancholy and gentle, "il était né poète sans le savoir." As a child he loved to pick roses, to listen to the sea. Later on he loved a girl of fifteen, but this love passed like his love for the sea. One day when he was nineteen he entered a church. The majesty of the organ, the odor of incense inspired in him a sweet revery, "et il prit dès lors Dieu comme une autre passion." But this love, too, was to pass.

III. From that day on, Manoello spent his time in meditation and prayer. He lived in seclusion with his parents, passionless, "sans amours de femmes." His indifference toward women prompted them to make advances to him, but he remained cold and dispassionate. In society his indifference was interpreted as haughtiness, and "on déchirait sa réputation dans les salons"; the common people too hated him for his "hauteurs." Never did he take part in orgies, never did he applaud "une danse de volupté" in the theatre. Manoello loved only his family, his God, his country. (Unfinished.)

"La main de fer" marks a return to third-person narration and an exotic milieu, in an effort to inject concrete content into a form that remains essentially null-praxial. Like the preceding work it is unfinished, but whereas the plot of "La dernière heure" was fully established by the time it was broken off, "La main de fer" remains no more than a fragment; the author's intentions as to the ultimate fate of his hero, if indeed he ever formulated any, are impossible to discern. Thus what I have spoken of as the "problem of content" in my analysis of "La dernière heure" has now placed in question the very possibility of composing a literary work.

"La main de fer" is an unsuccessful attempt to describe the existence of an adolescent protagonist who has rejected all unideal worldly aims. Its fragmentary nature attests to the overt presence of the conflict that remained at least partially hidden in "La dernière heure": the contradiction between the necessity of dealing with the hero's worldly experience, and the a priori denial of significance to this experience by its situation in the "fallen" world outside the childhood paradise. In "La dernière heure" this worldly content was only necessary to fill in the life of the protagonist after the death of his sister, and to give an immediate cause for his suicide; the author's failure to provide it did not destroy the whole structure of the story. But in "La main de fer," the protagonist undergoes no such traumatic expulsion from childhood as occurred at the death of Lélia. The transition from childhood to adolescence is represented as taking place *gradually*, with no clear-cut line dividing one from the other:

Enfant, il aimait à cueillir des roses, à écouter la mer qui se brise sur les rochers, et couché sur la plage, il s'endormait avec bonheur au bruit des vagues qui le berçaient mollement comme un chant de nourrice.

Plus tard il aima une belle enfant de 15 ans, mais cet amour passa bientôt comme celui de la mer, des coquilles et des roses.

Un jour, il avait 19 ans alors, il entra dans une église, il prêta l'oreille. (OJ II, 272)

This adolescent does not fall irremediably from innocence like the protagonist of "La dernière heure"—his "amour" for the "belle enfant," although like Flaubert's abortive love affair with "Caroline" a sign of his developing adolescent sexuality, remains innocent "comme celui de la mer, des coquilles et des roses," and allows Manoello to return to his former purity through religion. The significance of this is to accentuate the ambiguity of the adolescent's situation between childhood and adulthood. The adolescent heroes of the second period (Garcia, Carlos) are already definitely in the world; their dependent family situation is not a form of security but a worldly imprisonment. The same remains true of the hero of "La dernière heure"; as a result of his sister's death he lost his innocence and was thrown into the adult world. Yet his position became in part ambiguous because he never accepted the world; as long as he lived he remained loyal to the childhood ideal and to the hope of recapturing it in "amour." And because he refused to act in the world, the problem of establishing at the end of the work a worldly motivation for his suicide became unsolvable.

In Manoello the ambiguity of the adolescent's status is intensified. Although at the beginning of the story he is depicted as having lost the unconscious innocence of childhood, his religious devotions return him to his original purity and he experiences adolescence rather as a prolongation of childhood than a separation from it: Manoello is "[une] âme blasée et flétrie" but one who "vient se rajeunir dans l'amour céleste" (OJ II, 272). He maintains a perfect loyalty to the childhood ideal; his youthful love affair, redeemed by his later religious interests, has not separated him in any way from the dependent security of his position in the family. Whereas Ohmlin in "Rage et impuissance" strove desperately to escape his "adolescent" confinement, and the hero of "La dernière heure" chose the tomb only out of despair, Manoello no longer feels any desire to pass beyond his adolescent situation. Thus youth, rather than being a preparation for adulthood, comes to represent an overt refusal of adulthood and of the adult world.

But this means that Manoello's experiences are not worldly at all and consequently cannot make up a genuine praxis. He has been able to reject the world a priori, without experiencing, as did the hero of "La dernière heure," the necessity of finding a place within it:

Jamais la jeunesse de Saragosse ne l'avait vu s'enivrer avec elle, dans une splendide orgie; jamais on ne l'avait vu faire blanchir d'écume sa cavale andalouse aux courses du Prado, ni applaudir au théâtre à une danse de volupté. *Il aimait, à la vérité, sa famille,* son Dieu, sa patrie. (OJ II, 273–274)

Here, at the end of Flaubert's text, the preworldly nature of Manoello's existence becomes explicit. Because the protagonist has no need to live as an adult, no praxis is possible for him; his story can have no further development. And thus Flaubert must leave "La main de fer" unfinished.

The central feature of Manoello's adolescent experiences is his rejection of sexuality; associated with this is his interest in religious practices as a conscious substitute for sexual interests. Such an evolution is already hinted at in the two preceding works: Ohmlin, awakened from his erotic dreams, prays to God to deliver him from the tomb, and the hero of "La dernière heure," his childhood idyll destroyed by the death of his sister, prays that she be returned to life. In both stories religious faith is invoked to bring about a return of the lost ideal state. But in these works faith gives way to violent blasphemy as soon as it becomes apparent that God cannot return the protagonist to the paradise from which he has fallen. In neither does the hero's religion consist of more than a naïve, childlike belief in Providence, with little specifically religious content. In "La main de fer" the situation is quite different. Manoello turns to religion, not as a faith but as an activity, an interest that is to take the place of sexuality:

Pourtant il se trouve parfois un coeur jeune et vierge qui vient se nourrir de la foi, et plus souvent encore quelque âme blasée et flétrie qui vient se rajeunir dans l'amour céleste, se vivifier dans les croyances, se sanctifier dans la prière. Celui-là qui prend Dieu comme un amour de jeunesse et la foi comme une passion, celui-là s'y livre tout entier, *il s'agenouille avec délices, il prie avec ardeur,* il croit par instinct; *la messe des morts* n'est plus pour lui une grotesque psalmodie, *le chant des prêtres* cesse d'être vénal, *l'église* est quelque chose de saint, *l'espérance est pour lui palpable et positive,* il est heureux, car il croit. Que faut-il de plus pour le bonheur? une croyance, il y a tant de gens qui n'en ont pas! (OJ II, 271–272)

It is not the substance of his beliefs so much as the concrete details of worship that preoccupy Manoello. Here Flaubert appears to be recounting a personal experience, a short-lived infatuation with religion which, as he says in a later passage, "passa comme les autres" (OJ II, 273), that is, like his hero's earlier infatuations with girls. Religion offers a refuge from sexuality because in religious devotion the adolescent's developing sensuality can be put to use in the defense of the chastity it originally threatened. Because it contains no explicitly sexual elements, this interest in religion is a less problematic attempt to bring sensuality into the sphere of the ideal than is the impossible "amour" of "La dernière heure," too closely bound up with the dangers of "volupté," and therefore too sharply cutting off the adolescent from childhood. Religion offers Manoello a pure sort of "amour":

Il entra dans une église... Le soleil, pénétrant à travers les vitraux dorés, jetait sur tout cela un jour mystique et azuré qui lui remplit l'âme d'*une douce rêverie de foi et d'amour. Cette rêverie fut sa jeunesse...* (OJ II, 272–273)

And by the end of the work Manoello's love for God is explicitly related to his undiminished loyalty to his family: "Il aima, à la vérité, *sa famille, son Dieu,* sa patrie" (OJ II, 274). But his refusal of sexuality, not his interest in religion, is the central aspect of his present existence:

on vit Manoello dans la cathédrale; il y... passait ses jours dans la médiation et la prière... *Il paraissait sans désirs, sans passions de jeunesse, sans amours de femmes;* son indifférence pour elles les excitait à lui faire des avances, et jamais pour aucune d'elles un regard aimable, une douce parole.... son regard de plomb leur faisait baisser les yeux, et son front pâle les intimidait comme celui d'un vieillard. (OJ II, 273)

In this passage Manoello's religious interests are shown as protecting him from sexual temptation. But the flirtations of the girls never even reach the level of a temptation. Manoello rejects them a priori because, from the standpoint of his purified loyalty to the ideal, the world of sexuality and adulthood can have no temptations to offer him; in his purity he remains unproblematically superior to the evil world. And the ease with which Flaubert was able to reject the flirtations of "Caroline" gives Manoello's indifference to temptation a solid basis in the author's own experience.

But precisely because the content of this story, derived from Flaubert's own adolescent experience, involves a refusal of adulthood, it cannot attain a praxial level and therefore cannot become the basis for a literary work. "La dernière heure" too represented such a refusal, but this attitude was itself put into action in the protagonist's suicide.

Manoello's refusal, because it results merely in a passive remaining within the family, can never become a praxis.

That "La main de fer" does not possess the over-all structure of a "work" should not, however, lead us to neglect its autobiographical content. The following passage is of particular significance:

Sa mélancolie avait quelque chose d'évangélique et de doux, sans ce chagrin âpre et brutal qu'impriment chez les poètes le désespoir et le malheur. Il y avait de la noblesse dans ses paroles, de la fierté dans ses gestes et de la poésie dans son regard, *car il était né poète* sans le savoir; enfant il aimait à cueillir des roses, à écouter la mer qui se brise sur les rochers, et couché sur la plage, il s'endormait avec bonheur au bruit des vagues qui le berçaient mollement comme un chant de nourrice. (OJ II, 272)

Here Flaubert presents the idealized vision of a childhood that is both his hero's and his own. "La main de fer" is the first of Flaubert's works to contain even a summary description of his own childhood or to apply the glorious title of "poète" to its protagonist. Precisely because this story does not aim at transforming the author's own preadult experiences into an adult praxis, because it is grounded on a refusal of adulthood, it can include content taken directly from his own childhood. If adulthood is refused because it has nothing of value to offer, then the age of innocence itself must contain the only possibilities for self-fulfillment. This conception, already apparent in "La dernière heure," has become the entire basis for "La main de fer." Although the child has no praxis, his existence is worthy of particular concern because it alone can be truly disalienated, truly ideal. And Manoello's childhood is of special value because it has retained its primacy for him: he has not cast it off to enter the adult world. It is the exemplary ideality of his childhood experience that makes Manoello a "poète." This signifies not that he is a writer of poems but that his experiences in themselves, because they are not attached to particular worldly goals, possess a universal significance.

But the adolescent's refusal of adulthood cannot be fully unproblematic. It must necessarily imply a strong measure of *ressentiment,* of repressed jealousy against those who enjoy worldly privileges; the emotions that inspired "La peste à Florence" have not simply disappeared. This emotion is quite apparent in Manoello's proud indifference to the "hatred" that surrounds him:

Aussi on le haïssait, en revanche, on déchirait sa réputation dans les salons et dans les cercles de la haute société, sa tristesse passait pour des remords et son indifférence pour un dédain vaniteux; le peuple le haïssait aussi, son laconisme et ses hauteurs semblaient l'insulter. (OJ II, 273)

This unavowed *ressentiment* is symptomatic of the contradiction underlying the adolescent author's attempt to escape the world when his desires for sexual pleasure and social recognition call out in spite of himself to the world. And Flaubert's hatred becomes all the more intense when he finds himself forced to renounce the very story he is writing for lack of a worldly praxis for its protagonist, thereby experiencing his dependency on the world he wishes to reject.

The failure of "La main de fer" to become a true literary work discloses to the author the inadequacy of using his own "exemplary" adolescent existence as fictional subject matter. In his following effort, "Rêve d'enfer," Flaubert accepts worldly sexuality as the basis for his protagonist's praxis. The purity of Manoello's adherence to the childhood ideal must be renounced and a descent made into the everyday adult world. The impossibility of incarnating his own ideal existence in his works leads Flaubert to his discovery of *illusion* as the only basis for worldly action.

CHAPTER XXIII

REVE D'ENFER (CONTE FANTASTIQUE)

March 21, 1837

"C'est souvent avoir une très fausse
opinion de l'esprit d'autrui que de
ne point le nourrir de fadaises."

—La Bruyère

I. (PROLOGUE) The earth was sleeping lethargically when a voice arose from its depths: "Fini le monde! que ce soit aujourd'hui sa dernière heure!" But a voice from heaven replied that one man was still to be created: "les autres hommes se sont plaints de leur faiblesse et de leurs passions; celui-là sera fort et sans passions. Quant à son âme..." And the earthly voice broke into a mocking laugh.

II. Duke Arthur d'Almaroës was an alchemist, a cold, passionless man that people suspected of being a sorcerer, or even the Devil himself. In reality, "cet être infernal ... n'était qu'un esprit pur et intact." Handsome, with flowing blue hair, he was restless and bored on this earth, finding no goals lofty enough for his infinite yearnings, and scorning the caresses of mortal women. Not even suicide was open to him, "car il était condamné à vivre!"

III. Arthur became resigned to his condition and went to live in a crumbling German castle, alone save for his servants. The old castle, its upper stories invaded by bats and owls, and its living room filled with rotting bundles of hay, was tended by an equally decrepit caretaker. There Arthur felt at home; "lui, qui était tombé de si haut pour descendre si bas, il aimait quelque chose de tombé aussi."

IV. Arthur, haggard and tense, is seated in his laboratory when Satan appears to him, "affamé, les flancs creux, avec une tête de chien, des mamelles qui pendent jusqu'à terre." The two go out and pursue their conversation against the howls of a stormy sea. Arthur confides to Satan (who remains skeptical) that he has no soul; when he first arrived on earth, he was still bound to a prior tranquil existence from which he only gradually awakened. And when these distant dreams had evaporated, he found nothing but *ennui*. The soulless Arthur has a body that Satan envies; Satan, being without a real body, has no way of satisfying the violent passions instilled in him by his soul. He vows to prove that Arthur too has a soul by making him fall in love with a peasant girl, but Arthur only laughs scornfully, spreads his green wings and flies away.

V. At sunset the peasant girl Julietta, pensive and melancholy, prepares to return home with her cows. Suddenly, small flames shoot up from the earth and move toward her. A stranger (Satan), richly dressed in black, stands before her. They sit down on the back of her white cow; Julietta, fearful of the stranger, tries to rise but finds that something mysterious is holding her to the animal. Satan tempts her to love Arthur, whom he describes seductively. While they are talking, Arthur passes by. Finally Julietta escapes and runs home. At her mother's request, she goes out to milk the cows. But the pail of milk she brings back to the house has turned to blood.

VI. Julietta and her family, disturbed by these macabre happenings, fall into a fitful sleep. The next day Julietta, possessed by "un amour déchirant,... bondissant, exalté," wanders about in a daze. Suddenly she sees Arthur. She calls to him but he scarcely notices her; she falls on her knees before him. All she can wring from him is a half-hearted promise to meet her the next day on the cliff.

VII. Julietta runs off to the cliff and she is seen no more in the village.

VIII. Once again Satan appears to Arthur; the latter boasts of having remained indifferent to Julietta's cries, but he agrees to go to her on the cliff. Satan refuses to believe that Arthur can have no soul; the latter simply spreads his wings and dares Satan to test his superhuman nature by trying to kill him. Satan enraged, leaps on him, but after several vain attempts, he falls back exhausted. Arthur laughs serenely at his failure.

IX. Julietta has been awaiting Arthur for four years now, and she has grown mad with suffering. "Ses cheveux étaient blancs, car le malheur vieillit." Suddenly Arthur appears to her. She tries to move him by caresses and words of love, but he remains indifferent. Finally, in despair, she leaps off the cliff into the sea. Satan appears; and when he sees that Arthur has remained unmoved by Julietta's suicide, he is forced to admit that Arthur told the truth—he has no soul.

X. (Epilogue) Several centuries have passed. A voice from the earth pleads: "Assez! assez! j'ai trop longtemps souffert... grâce! ne crée point d'autre monde!" And a heavenly voice answers, "Non! c'est pour l'éternité, il n'y aura plus d'autre monde!"

"Rêve d'enfer" is a story of considerable complexity, more than twice as long as any of the others of the period. The question of source material remains open. The prologue and epilogue were, in general conception if not in detail, suggested by the conclusion of *Ahasvérus* by Quinet, but there remain numerous other elements in the text which strongly suggest borrowings from source material as yet undiscovered, notably the Hoffmannesque fantastic rural atmosphere (the location is in Germany), and certain supernatural symbolic touches in the episode dealing with Julietta's encounter with Satan, such as the cow's milk being turned to blood; this type of naïve, "natural" supernatural, so characteristic of Hoffmann, is never found elsewhere in Flaubert's works.[1]

"Rêve d'enfer" represents both the culmination and the transcendence of the null-praxial trend that has been characteristic of the third period. In the supernatural, immortal Arthur d'Almaroës, Flaubert pushes to its maximum the separation of his hero from worldly concerns, while in the story of Julietta which makes up the real action of the work he introduces a purely human protagonist to whom love offers the basis for a worldly career that is no longer "null."

---

[1] My own examination of Hoffmann's (and Nodier's) works has failed to uncover any possible sources. Bruneau, who had access to the journals of the period, does not offer any assistance.

In the character of Arthur, Flaubert, renouncing the attempts at a more or less realistic reproduction of his own adolescent situation that had led to the incompletion of "La dernière heure" and the total failure of "La main de fer," gives full vent to his imagination in describing the ideal conditions of existence for a null-praxial hero. Arthur is, as the prologue explains, a new type of man, an experiment of the Creator:

les autres hommes se sont plaints de leur faiblesse et de leurs passions; celui-là [Arthur] sera fort et sans passions. (OJ I, 163)

Arthur represents the earth's final chance for salvation from the evil of worldly passions; if this final experiment fails, the world will be destroyed. Thus Flaubert gives his hero a supernaturally derived metaphysical mission in the world; this absolves him of the need to elaborate a praxis for him. As could not be true for the adolescent Manoello, Arthur's mere presence on earth is made to be of direct concern to mankind.

Arthur, beneath the physical signs of his extraordinary origin (such as his blue hair and, most notably, his green wings, which he only develops during the first encounter with Satan), is essentially a schematized version of the *ennui*-filled null-praxial heroes of the preceding works. Flaubert devotes nine pages, a full quarter of the text, to a detailed initial description of the peculiarities of Arthur's earthly existence. What is most notable in all this, beyond the grotesque detail of his dilapidated German castle, is that although Arthur is without passions, he retains the purely human *need* for such passions. It is from this unsatisfied longing that his *ennui* is derived; the earthly objects around him are inadequate to his superhuman needs:

Mais lui... esprit céleste... arrivé au milieu des hommes sans être homme comme eux, ayant leurs corps... leurs formes,... mais d'une nature supérieure, d'un coeur plus élevé et *qui ne demandait que des passions pour se nourrir*, et qui, les cherchant sur la terre d'après son instinct, n'avait trouvé que des hommes, —que venait-il donc faire? (OJ I, 166)

And in particular it is sexuality, from which Arthur might have expected the most, that most disappoints him:

Aurait-il compris nos plaisirs charnels, lui qui n'avait de la chair que l'apparence? les chauds embrassements d'une femme, ses bras humides de sueur, ses larmes d'amour, sa gorge nue, tout cela l'aurait-il fait palpiter un matin, lui qui trouvait au fond de son coeur une science infinie, un monde immense? (OJ I, 166)

nue, la femme était pour lui sans beauté... Il n'avait point assez d'air pour sa poitrine,... de lumière pour ses yeux et *d'amour pour son coeur*. (OJ I, 167)

Thus Arthur relives the plight of the hero of "La dernière heure," unable to find "amour," although in addition his superhuman origin removes the alternative possibility of a descent to "volupté."

Arthur's profession of alchemy (which he himself hardly takes seriously), his ruined castle, the baroque details of his appearance and habits merely ornament his situation. Since he can do nothing to modify the terms of his arid earthly existence, even suicide being impossible for him, his "story" considered in itself must end with this preliminary description. By placing his hero beyond the limits of human praxiality, Flaubert has obliged himself to construct his plot out of the activities of other, secondary protagonists. The full significance of this development is only revealed in the episode of Julietta. Before this, however, Flaubert introduces in Satan a supernatural counterfoil to Arthur.

If Arthur is merely an exaggerated version of the other null-praxial protagonists, Satan returns us to the sexual interests of the first period. But here Satan is not a "father" like the Robert-Satan of "La fiancée et la tombe," but a "son" like the *moine des Chartreux,* desiring without the possibility of fulfillment. Satan incarnates Flaubert's longing for "volupté," now for the first time placed in open confrontation with the refusal of sexuality that Arthur represents; Gustave-Satan's sexual frustration cries out under the weight of Gustave-Arthur's oppressive purity. The author's splitting of himself into two parts involves a more total purgation of all sexuality from his ideal self [Arthur] than was possible with the single protagonists of "La dernière heure" or "La main de fer." But at the same time this split denotes a realization that the ideal self cannot occupy the whole stage; once the author has discovered in his own existence the continual struggle between "amour" and "volupté" that was hinted at in "La dernière heure," then even if the baser tendencies are repeatedly defeated they cannot be denied a role in the internal dialectic. For Flaubert has realized that their defeat will never be permanent; sexuality and adulthood cannot be simply renounced once and for all. As is the case with Saint Anthony's temptations, although they can be vanquished without too much difficulty, they will never cease to return.

Satan then embodies the author's repressed, frustrated sexual desires. But this is not all there is to his character. Satan is not only a tempter of the pure Arthur; he is the ruler of the fallen, sinful world dominated by the passions that God had eliminated from Arthur's make-up. Satan controls the soul (*âme*), which in Flaubert's terminology is simply the seat of worldly desires. The peculiarity of this usage is significant: for

Flaubert the separation between the ideal and the worldly is so profound that the mere presence of a soul susceptible to the temptation of worldly desire is sufficient to insure damnation. Arthur, however, in opposition to Satan represents the *corps;* he has no *âme* and thus is not subject to temptation.[2] This *âme-corps* distinction acquires great significance in the second meeting of the pair later in the work.

Thus Satan is what the "femme du monde" represented at the end of the first period—the incarnation of a universal negativity,[3] although unlike the "femme" who stands outside the world, a figure of death that is not herself mortal, Satan has a soul and is subject as well as ruler in his kingdom. Satan's passions make him a far less noble figure than Arthur; there is no question here, as there is in "Danse des morts" and "Smarh," of admiring him as a powerful ruler standing above the helpless protagonist. Flaubert has not yet renounced the pretension, embodied in Arthur, of remaining loyal to the ideal and outside the fallen adult world.[4]

The first meeting between Arthur and Satan consists merely in an exposition of their respective positions: Arthur complains of his *ennui* and Satan of his sexual frustrations; Satan expresses his envy of Arthur for being without a soul, but remains skeptical and announces his intention of tempting him with the love of Julietta. The dialogue between these two superhuman figures is still only a static preliminary to the dynamic portion of the story that deals with Julietta's unhappy love for Arthur.

Julietta is the first of a series of heroines in whom Flaubert has incarnated his own experience of separation from the idyll of childhood and awakening to adolescent sexuality.[5] Although the chief immedi-

---

[2] In the opening description of Arthur, Flaubert seems inconsistently to endow him with an *âme:* "Cet être infernal... n'était qu'un esprit pur et intact," infini et régulier comme une statue de marbre qui penserait,... qui aurait une volonté, une Puissance, *une âme enfin*" (OJ I, 165). Here the author refers to the *âme* as the source of Arthur's unfulfilled yearning for a pure "amour," and of his resulting *ennui.* This inconsistency is not without importance; see below, pp. 149 ff.

[3] This was Satan's role in "Voyage en enfer," at the beginning of the first period, but in that work he merely displayed his "kingdom" to the narrator without explaining the nature of his own relationship to it.

[4] Although in the deepest sense he never truly renounced this pretension, which is at the basis of the vision of his nature novels (and which the victory—still only tentative—of Saint Antoine over Satan in the 1849 *Tentation* reestablishes), during the years of his own first sexual experiences and entry into adulthood, when "La danse des morts" and "Smarh" with their triumphant Satans were produced, Flaubert despaired of the possibility of maintaining himself outside the "Satanic" bourgeois world.

[5] The most important such figures in the later works are the "Chœur des jeunes filles" in "La danse des morts," Marie of "Novembre," and of course Emma Bovary.

ate inspiration for Julietta undoubtedly came from the English girl "Caroline" of whom we have seen traces throughout this period, the flux of new, troubling sensations, the sense of alienation from childhood joys can only be Flaubert's own:

> Il faisait soir et le soleil rougeâtre et mourant éclairait à peine la vallée et les montagnes. C'était à cette heure du crépuscule où l'on voit, dans les prés, des fils blancs qui s'attachent à la chevelure des femmes... ce jour-là, [Julietta] était triste, elle ne courait plus pour cueillir des fleurs et pour les mettre dans ses cheveux.... non! plus de joie ni d'ivresse,... mais au contraire, des soupirs répétés, un air rêveur, des larmes dans les yeux, et une longue promenade, bien rêveuse et bien lente, au milieu des herbes.... Elle était oppressée, *son cœur brûlait, il désirait quelque chose de vague, d'indéterminé,* il s'attachait à tout, quittait tout, il avait l'ennui, le désir, l'incertitude; ennui, rêve du passé, songe sur l'avenir, tout cela passait dans la tête de l'enfant, couchée sur l'herbe et qui regardait le ciel les mains sur son front. *Elle avait peur d'être ainsi seule au milieu des champs, et pourtant elle y avait passé son enfance...* (OJ I, 179–180)[6]

Whereas Satan represented only the guilt-charged physical frustrations of adolescent sexuality, here Julietta's awakening to adolescence is described sympathetically as a positive expansion of the soul beyond the confines of childhood in the process of maturation. It is precisely this positive aspect of adolescence Flaubert had sought to repress in his male heroes which appears here, disguised in the otherness of the opposite sex. Yet even in this form the awakening to sexuality is ultimately guilty, Satanic. As soon as Julietta has become separated from the innocence of childhood, she is visited by Satan himself, who instills in her her fatal passion for Arthur.

At this point in the work a serious problem of interpretation arises. What is the significance of Julietta's choice of the ideal Arthur as a love-object? Does this simply reflect the flirtations of "Caroline" with the

---

The autobiographical works "Mémoires d'un fou," "Smarh," and "Novembre" present masculine versions of this experience.

[6] Cf. "Smarh," where Flaubert-Smarh's awakening from childhood is depicted in quite similar terms:

> Un soir, en revenant, c'était un crépuscule d'été, le soleil était rouge, et des fils blancs s'attachaient aux cheveux; et ce jour-là... il y avait dans son âme bien d'autres tempêtes que celles de l'océan, bien d'autres nuages que ceux du ciel.
>
> Pourquoi donc s'ennuyait-il déjà, le pauvre enfant?
>
> Ce n'était plus assez... de sentir dans ses cheveux le vent de l'automne qui roule les feuilles jaunies et les plumes de la colombe,... rien de tout cela!
>
> Il s'en retournait ainsi, bercé par sa marche et écoutant lui-même le bruit de ses pas dans les herbes, regardant le soleil qui se retirait à l'horizon, et les boeufs couchés à l'ombre et remuant la tête pour chasser les moucherons.
>
> (OJ II, 109–111)

author, here represented by Arthur? Only when we have answered these
questions will we be able to grasp the meaning of Julietta's guilty love.
If Arthur simply represents the author himself, in what sense can we
speak of Flaubert as identifying with the girl's love for his hero?

Among the details of the "seduction" of Julietta by Satan one seemingly minor incident provides us with an important clue. Satan has in-
duced Julietta to sit down with him on the back of a cow lying in the
grass:

Julietta regardait l'étranger avec terreur.... Oh! laisse-moi, laisse-moi; il faut que
je m'en aille...
— Je te laisse libre, Julietta, pars!
Et il laissa tomber son bras qui la tenait vivement étreinte.
Elle ne put se lever, *quelque chose l'attachait au ventre de l'animal* qui geignait
tristement et humectait l'herbe de sa langue baveuse; il râlait et remuait sa tête sur
le sol comme s'il se mourait de douleur.
— Eh bien, Julietta, pars! qui t'empêche?
Elle s'efforça encore, mais rien ne put lui faire faire un mouvement, sa volonté
de fer se brisait devant la fascination de cet homme et son pouvoir magique.
(OJ I, 181–182)

Here it is not merely Satan that attracts Julietta, but the gross material
being of the cow that, more than simply a symbol of fertility, resembles
one of the monsters that fascinates Saint Antoine in the *Tentation*.[7]
Julietta's attachment to the cow, although it results from her sexual
awakening, goes beyond sexuality to "la matière" that later tempts
Antoine.

But if Julietta in this scene is attracted by "la matière," she soon falls
hopelessly in love with Arthur. If we wish to understand the meaning of
Julietta's love for Arthur, we must seek to clarify its connection with
this baser attraction to the cow which links her preoccupations with the
concerns of the author of the *Tentation*. This connection has its roots in
the character of Arthur himself.

---

[7] Cf. from the courtesan Marie's account of her adolescence in "Novembre":
"j'enviais jusqu'au beuglements plaintifs des vaches, quand elles mettent bas... je
jalousais leurs douleurs" (OJ I, 220), and especially the following passage from the
1849 *Tentation de Saint Antoine* (Paris: Conard, 1910):
   LE CATOBLÉPAS, *corps de taureau, terminé par une tête de sanglier...:* Me
   dérange qui voudra! je ne bouge... ma tête est si lourde que je ne peux la
   lever, *je la roule au bout de mon cou: la mâchoire entr'ouverte j'arrache
   les herbes vénéneuses arrosées de mon haleine...* Si je relevais mes paupières,
   Antoine,... et que tu aperçusses mes prunelles... de suite tu mourrais!
   ANTOINE:... Eh bien?... Si j'allais avoir envie de les regarder, ces yeux!"
   (pp. 405–406)
Here Antoine is attracted to the monster despite the danger of death; similar is the
danger of mortal sin in which Julietta now finds herself.

I have already spoken of the duality established by Flaubert between Satan and Arthur as *âme* and *corps*. The equation of the appetitive *âme* with Satan is not difficult to understand if we accept Flaubert's null-praxial rejection of all concrete desire objects: the *âme* as the seat of desire is necessarily Satanic because it can only function to attach its possessor to such objects at the expense of the paradisial ideal that lies in the past, outside the object world. But in what sense is Arthur the *corps?* The real significance of this identification is made clear in the combat of Arthur and Satan that takes place during their second encounter:

Il fallait voir aux prises ces deux créatures toutes bizarres, toutes d'exception, l'une [Satan] toute spirituelle, l'autre [Arthur] charnelle et *divine dans sa matière;* il fallait voir en lutte l'âme et le corps et cette âme, cet esprit pur et aérien, rampant, impuissant et faible devant *la morgue hautaine de la matière brute et stupide....*

C'était deux principes incohérents qui se combattaient en face; l'esprit tomba d'épuisement et de lassitude devant la patience du corps.

Et qu'ils étaient grands et sublimes, ces deux êtres qui, réunis ensemble, auraient fait un Dieu, l'esprit du mal et la force du pouvoir! (OJ I, 191–192)

The italicized passages hold the key to Arthur's position as the object of Julietta's passion. Arthur is not merely the divine, superhuman being with whom the author identifies his ideal self in its resistance to the earthly passion of Julietta-"Caroline"; he is also "la matière brute et stupide," his purity merely a "morgue hautaine."

It is easy to give a superficial, partial explanation of this insulting characterization of the ideal hero. The author's hostility to Arthur can be seen simply as self-criticism for his own inability to choose "la volupté," that is, to respond to the advances of "Caroline"; Flaubert would be expressing here the same "remords" that he spoke of in "La dernière heure":

Une pensée m'est venue, et *c'est le seul remords qui soit venu me troubler...* je trouve donc que j'aurais dû... puisque je n'avais pu trouver l'amour, prendre la volupté. (OJ II, 270)

But this narrow interpretation cannot fully explain the connection between Arthur's materiality and his divinity, or between Julietta's love for him and her attachment to the "matière brute et stupide" of the cow.

Arthur's divinity derives from his incarnation of the preworldly ideal. This ideal was expressed in the works of the first period in sexual terms: the union of Paul and Annette in "La fiancée et la tombe," of Ernest and Henriette in "La grande dame et le joueur de vielle," the "souvenirs de jeunesse et d'amour" of the *moine des Chartreux,* and the like. But in the later null-praxial works, under the influence of the guilt first expressed in "Un parfum à sentir" ("les nuits que l'on passe à pleurer et à maudire sa mère"), Flaubert renounces the description of the paradise in sexual terms. If the first-period heroes were adults with legitimate sexual rights, these new protagonists resemble their creator in being adolescents whose desires cannot be referred to an already existing "fiancée" but are guilty and must accordingly be repressed. In "Rage et impuissance" this desexualization of the ideal is most explicit; Ohmlin's original erotic paradise is revealed to be nothing more than a sham, while his true ideal, once he becomes aware of his imprisonment, is merely "la vie." And what does Ohmlin regret in "la vie"?

Oh! mourir! ne plus rien voir de tout ce qui se passe sur cette terre; la nature, les champs, le ciel, les montagnes... (OJ I, 155)

It is a relationship to nature that is here expressed. And if in "La dernière heure" an innocent prepubertal sexuality appears in the hero's relationship with his sister, nothing of the sort can be found in "La main de fer":

enfant, il aimait à cueillir les roses, à écouter la mer qui se brise sur les rochers, et couché sur la plage, il s'endormait avec bonheur au bruit des vagues qui le berçaient mollement comme un chant de nourrice. (OJ II, 272)

This image of the child's passive, unconscious self-absorption in nature is the vision of the paradise that is found throughout the remainder of the early works, in "La danse des morts," "Mémoires d'un fou," "Smarh," and "Novembre." But what is nature if not *material* reality? The child reposes passively in a purely material unity with "mother" nature. He has no *âme*, no desires, no self-consciousness; in the above-quoted passage this vegetative state is symbolized by sleep: "il s'endormait avec bonheur."[8] And the same is true of Arthur's own vision of his celestial childhood as he describes it to Satan in their first meeting:

il me semblait, lorsque je fermais les yeux et que j'écoutais la mer, retourner vers ces régions supérieures où tout était poésie, silence et amour, et je crus avoir continuellement dormi. *Ce sommeil était lourd et stupide,* mais qu'il était doux et profond! (OJ I, 176)

The repetition of the word "stupide" is no accident. It is in this sense of the child's unconscious unity with nature that the divine ideal that

---

[8] Cf. from "La danse des morts" (the "Choeur des Elus"): "N'est-ce pas que nous avons sur nous comme un voile précieux, une gaze légère couverte de roses *qui nous fait dormir sous des sensations d'amour?*" (OJ I, 428). Or from "Smarh": "Ce n'était plus assez de rester dans le fond de la vieille barque grise, *de se laisser bercer par la marée montante*" (OJ II, 110).

Arthur represents can be spoken of as "la matière brute et stupide." Beneath the insulting tone lies a note of nostalgic envy of the "stupidity," the innocence of childhood.

The null-praxial heroes of the preceding works, like Arthur himself, are unable to find praxis-goals in the world because they remain loyal to the childhood ideal, or, in other terms, to an original, unconscious unity with nature which no worldly object can grant them. But this does not mean that these heroes are themselves children still existing within the confines of the ideal. They are adolescents in whom an *âme*—worldly desire—has already awakened, but who refuse to give themselves up to the unideal aims of this *âme*, and even attempt to ignore its presence. Arthur, the supreme creation of the period, claims to have no *âme* at all.

Yet all is not so simple on this score. At the beginning of "Rêve d'enfer," where Arthur's sublime *ennui* was recounted with such complacency, Flaubert did not insist on his hero's lack of a soul, later to become the very essence of his superhumanity. In one passage, he even implied the opposite. The author must have been at least dimly aware that Arthur's unfulfilled desire for a superhuman "amour" could spring only from the soul as the seat of all desire. It is only at the end of the first encounter with Satan that Arthur's soullessness becomes an undeniable fact. Once Satan has revealed his own frustration, which unlike Arthur's is of an overtly sexual nature, Arthur, who at the beginning of the conversation had spoken at length of his *ennui*, never again brings up the subject; throughout the rest of the story he is described as being in a state of absolute calm.[9] If during their first meeting Arthur and Satan had joined together in bewailing their lot, in the combat that takes up most of their second encounter Arthur remains totally serene and even laughs in triumph at his superiority over Satan. For now Arthur has become simply "la matière." He has ceased to represent the adolescent who has remained loyal to the childhood ideal, and now

---

[9] A most illustrative contrast can be drawn between the two descriptions of Arthur in his room before his meetings with Satan. In the first, Arthur in his gloomy chamber appears as a tortured soul:

> *Aucune lumière n'éclairait l'appartement... L'alchimiste... alla vers son creuset et le considera quelque temps.... C'était bien là un de ces fronts pâles d'alchimistes d'enfer, ses yeux creux et rougis, sa peau blanche et tirée,... tout cela indiquait bien les nuits sans sommeil, les rêves brûlants, les pensées du génie.* (OJ I, 171)

But in the moonlit atmosphere of the second meeting, Arthur is free of any earthbound frustration:

> *la lune... éclairait le cabinet d'Arthur... il se penchait sur la rampe de fer et humait avec délices l'air frais de la nuit.* (OJ I, 189)

appears as an incarnation of that ideal itself. The inconsistency in the original conception of Arthur between his adolescent *ennui* and his childhood soullessness can no longer be hidden once the worldly source of the *ennui* has been revealed; Arthur's ideality can only be maintained by the sacrifice of the unideal adolescent component. The result of this is that Flaubert, who at the beginning of the story had identified strongly with Arthur, now looks at him as an *other*, an ideal figure with whom he as himself an adolescent tempted by sexuality can no longer identify, and whose calm ideality he now resentfully mocks as "la matière brute et stupide."

Yet, although Arthur has become an other to Flaubert, he remains in another sense a part of him; Arthur is *his own* ideal, his own former unity with nature which he can no longer reestablish. Satan's attack on Arthur is a vain attempt to retrieve this unity:

Et qu'ils étaient grands et sublimes, ces deux êtres qui, *réunis ensemble,* auraient fait un Dieu, l'esprit du mal et la force du pouvoir. (OJ I, 192)

The two combatants represent the two halves of Flaubert himself, desire and ideal, hopelessly separated. Superficially Satan is attempting to kill Arthur and thereby destroy the inhibitory force of the ideal, but, as the author indicates, the highest aim of his attack is to incorporate Arthur into himself as "la force du pouvoir," the force of unconscious, guiltless being, possessed by the child whose act is continuous with his desire. Satan's effort is doomed to failure; the fact that he represents "l'esprit du mal" prevents him from ever capturing the guiltless ideal. The two opponents must remain separate entities within the author's psyche, with the real, worldly Gustave-Satan grasping in vain at the ideal Gustave-Arthur.

Now we have arrived at the source of Flaubert's identification with Julietta in her love for Arthur. To be sure, in the battle between Satan and Arthur, the author identifies with Satan's effort to recapture his own lost ideal.[10] But their conflict can only be symbolic and extra-worldly; it cannot itself become a praxis directed toward a concrete end because Satan's goals in this conflict remain purely *internal*. Because Flaubert is himself both Arthur and Satan, the dialogue between them can never come to a conclusion; both will continue to subsist within him, and the end of "Rêve d'enfer" finds both still confronting each other in eternal opposition. But for Julietta, on the con-

---

[10] In the same paragraph in which Arthur was insultingly designated as "la matière brute et stupide" Flaubert showed his favor to Satan by calling him "cet esprit pur et aérien."

trary, the desire for the ideal Arthur can truly become a praxis, for the object of desire is not within the desirer herself but outside her, in the world. Julietta-"Caroline," unlike Gustave, is able to accept her sexuality without losing her attachment to the ideal; in her Romantic passion the love object *incarnates* this ideal.

Flaubert himself is not unaware of the enormous significance of the contrast between the praxial humanity of Julietta and the static immortality of Satan and Arthur. In the following passage he describes the profound physical changes wrought by her love for Arthur:

Julietta attendait le duc [Arthur], elle l'attendait jour et nuit, courant sur les rochers, elle l'attendait en pleurant, elle l'attendait depuis quatre années...

Ses cheveux étaient blancs, car le malheur vieillit; il est comme le temps, il court vite, il pèse lourd et il frappe fort...

Ses cheveux étaient blancs,... ses mains étaient crevassées par le froid;... et puis elle était pâle, amaigrie, avait les yeux creux et ternes... (OJ I, 193–194)

The author exaggerates the effects of Julietta's awaiting of Arthur in order to demonstrate its praxial significance. Her relationship to Arthur is not symbolic and eternal like Satan's, but temporal and life-absorbing. The physical transformation she undergoes parallels the aging of Henriette, the "grande dame," in her twenty-year wait for her son Paul.

The aging of Julietta through the *malheur* of her love has a further significance. By this means she takes on in part the qualities of a mother figure; her love is implicitly assimilated to the ideal love of the mother which the adolescent must renounce in the process of growing to adulthood. Thus Julietta comes to resemble not only the "grande dame" but Marguerite of "Un parfum à sentir," whose ideal love too was rejected by her husband Pedrillo. But in the first period the "mother" Marguerite was rejected for the "girl" Isabellada in a guilty transcendence of maternal love toward adult sexuality; in Julietta the mother and the girl are brought together in a single figure whose love is at once valid and unacceptable.[11]

Julietta's final assault on Arthur before she throws herself into the sea has a considerable, and in part willful, resemblance to that of Satan which preceded it:

elle se traîna sur sa poitrine, elle l'accabla de ses baisers et de ses caresses...

---

[11] A similar duality is embodied in Mme. Arnoux in *Education sentimentale,* whose parting gift to Frédéric of a lock of her white hair symbolizes the ultimate unrealizability of her quasi-maternal love.

Il fallait voir cette femme, s'épuisant d'ardeur,... *Julietta était bondissante d'amour, comme Satan l'était de rage et de colère.* (OJ I, 195–196)

Compare:

Arthur se coucha sur le sol... Satan... s'y traînait...
   Il fallait voir aux prises ces deux créatures...
   Enfin [Satan était] épuisé de rage et de colère... (OJ I, 191–192)

But now the dreamlike, fantastic nature of Satan's combat and of the unrealizable effort at self-reunification that it symbolizes has given way to a concrete manifestation of a woman's love that offers itself as a genuine possibility to Arthur-Gustave:

Elle passa bien des heures sur les joues d'Arthur, qui regardait le ciel azuré, qui pensait sans doute aussi à des rêves sublimes, à des amours, *sans penser qu'il avait là, devant lui, dans ses bras, une réalité céleste,* un amour d'exception, tout brûlant et tout exalté. (OJ I, 196)[12]

Here Arthur is momentarily portrayed as no longer the purely inert "matière" of the combat with Satan but once again the adolescent who, like the hero of "La dernière heure," dreams of "amour." Yet the love that Arthur rejects is not depicted as the mere "volupté" that offered itself to this earlier protagonist (or to Manoello in "La main de fer") but as this very "amour" itself. The idealization of Julietta's love does not simply reflect Flaubert's own regret for having repulsed "Caroline"; it denotes his recognition of the necessary presence of forbidden "volupté" in even the purest earthly love. That her love is "amour" makes Julietta's praxis a true longing for the ideal, a valid possibility of worldly action; but because this love is also "volupté," it cannot be accepted by the ideal Arthur. Thus for Flaubert-as-Arthur there can be no "amour." Love is only a possibility of Flaubert-as-Julietta, of the self as both detached from and attracted by its own ideal, the self that has fallen from its ideal into the world, but at the same time still seeks the ideal in the world. Flaubert never entirely renounces his loyalty to Arthur. But in his works it is only through the representation of Julietta's worldly search that he is able to transform his own internally experienced separation from the ideal—the split between Satan and Arthur—into *praxis.* The Romantic adolescent Flaubert already knows that there is no adequate praxis for him in the world; even his

---

[12] To this we should compare these lines from "Mémoires d'un fou" describing "Caroline's" advances to Gustave:
   Un jour elle se coucha sur mon canapé dans une position très équivoque...
   Certes le moment était critique, je n'en profitai pas, je la laissai partir...
   Je ne pouvais croire qu'elle m'aimait réellement. (OJ I, 523)

passion for Mme. Schlesinger is in essence retrospective, not active and goal-directed.[13] There can only be the praxis of the *other*, the inferior being who chases after the illusion of finding in the world the ideal that Flaubert knows to lie outside it, preserved as a memory in his pure "Arthurian" self.

At the end of "Rêve d'enfer" the earth is finally destroyed. Although Flaubert gives no explanation, we must presume that God's last experiment has failed not because Arthur has succumbed like a mere mortal to earthly passions, but because he was unable to find the superhuman "amour" that could alone have satisfied him. The world has proved inadequate to provide sustenance for the ideal. Arthur himself remains, at the end as at the beginning of the story, an ideal being isolated on earth. But what has been revealed in the working out of the plot is the paralyzing self-contradiction that lies within his very presence on this earth. If even the "réalité céleste" of Julietta's love is insufficient for Arthur, it is because no "réalité" can ever be sufficient; the ideal can have no concrete relationship with the real world.

The world that is destroyed in the conclusion is the Romantic world that, unideal as it may be, still offers a place for the hero to experience his null-praxis of disillusionment. The Romantic God that presides over it and finally destroys it is cruel enough to permit this hero's sufferings, but not so cruel as to deny him the privilege, conferred by these sufferings, of superiority over happier men. With the destruction of this Romantic universe Flaubert enters upon the really critical phase of his development.

It is in "Rêve d'enfer" that the characteristic otherness of the Flaubertian protagonist comes to light for the first time. In the first period Flaubert's heroes are adults superior to himself, fulfilling his own worldly desires, his own future possibilities. In the second and third, his heroes stand on the same adolescent level as he does; their actions fulfill his own present possibilities for revolt against the world or withdrawal from it. This is true of Arthur as well. But, beginning with Julietta, Flaubert's future protagonists stand on a *lower* level than the author himself, seeking worldly goals that he has already renounced even before they offered themselves. This relationship of the author to the praxis of his characters is essentially post-Romantic; for the Romantic, the protagonist's career is always at least a possible road

---

[13] Flaubert himself admits this in "Mémoires d'un fou": "Comment aurait-elle pu en effet voir que je l'aimais, car je ne l'aimais pas alors,... j'ai menti; *c'était maintenant que je l'aimais*" (OJ I, 538). The "maintenant" is two years after Flaubert's first meeting with Mme. Schlesinger, when he had returned alone to Trouville.

to an ideal disalienation. Because it unveils the falseness of this possibility, "Rêve d'enfer" thus marks the end of the unproblematically
Romantic stage of Flaubert's development.

CHAPTER XXIV

UNE LEÇON D'HISTOIRE NATURELLE, GENRE COMMIS

March (?) 1837

AMIDST ALL the scientific activity to date, the *commis* has been sadly neglected, perhaps because no one had sufficiently studied this most interesting of "animals," or perhaps because of the difficulty involved in classifying him. The narrator, however, can speak with the modest authority of a zoologist who has spent much time in offices and who, in the interests of science, has worn out two umbrellas, twelve hats, and six resoled boots.

The *commis* is between the ages of thirty-six and sixty; he is small, round, and fresh. When you sneeze, he says "Dieu vous bénisse." He changes his fur according to the season; in summer he wears a straw hat and a pair of light cotton pants that he is careful to keep clean of ink. In winter he wears a huge overcoat to protect him from the cold.

The *commis* is ordinarily mild mannered, defending himself only when attacked. Usually he is a bachelor and indulges every so often in "le fin cigare de trois sous." Sometimes, however, he is married, in which case he is an upright and peaceable citizen. His wife stays at home, darning socks and reading melodramas.

At the office, the *commis* works in his shirtsleeves. He writes lovingly, savoring the odor of the ink, and carries on perpetual discussions with his colleagues on the weather and the latest civic improvements. This interesting biped adores the heat and his greatest joy is to blaze up the fire in the furnace. Then, sweating and panting, "il rit du rire de l'heureux." If by misfortune you should leave the door open when you enter the office the *commis* flies into a rage, bares his nails, stamps, and swears at you.

Every Sunday he goes to the theatre and during intermissions (if he is young) plays dominoes. Sometimes he loses; then he goes home, breaks a few dinner plates, neglects his dog Azor, and wolfs down the boiled beef left over from the day before.

When the political climate becomes more favorable, concludes the narrator, he will be able to publish the sequel to the present study, consisting of his sociological observations on the diverse species of *commis*.

OF ALL FLAUBERT's works before "Mémoires d'un fou," "Le commis" has undoubtedly attracted the most general interest. One of the two early works published in the Rouen journal, the *Colibri,* and undoubtedly the most professional of the *œuvres de jeunesse,* it has been widely viewed[1] as a prefiguration of *Bouvard et Pécuchet* and as the first clear expression of Flaubert's "realist" tendencies.

The date of its composition is unknown. In a letter to Ernest Chevalier of March 24, 1837 (only three days after the termination of

---

[1] Notably by Edouard Maynial, *Le jeunesse de Flaubert,* 2d ed. (Paris, 1913), pp. 95 ff.

"Rêve d'enfer"), Flaubert mentions that he is about to correct the proofs of "Le commis."[2] The story appeared in the *Colibri* six days later. Since Flaubert had spoken to the editor of the journal about the completed work on March 23, its composition must have antedated the completion of "Rêve d'enfer" (dated March 21), but we have no way of knowing by how much. In the absence of any other evidence, the most plausible hypothesis is that it was written at some time following the publication of "Bibliomanie" in the same journal on February 28, which would make it more or less contemporaneous with "Rêve d'enfer." Since, as Bruneau has observed, "la 'physiologie' du commis s'insère dans une série d'oeuvres du même genre publiées par le *Colibri*" (les *débuts littéraires*, p. 146), it is possible that the inspiration for this work did not originate entirely with Flaubert himself. Nevertheless, its chronological position in his works is far from accidental.

The *physiologie*, to which genre "Le commis" belongs, is less a work of fiction than a form of essay, although in such works as Balzac's *Physiologie du mariage* and particularly in his *Petites misères de la vie conjugale*, a great deal of fictional content can be brought in as illustrative material. The essence of the genre is its generally good-natured ridicule of the reified existence of the bourgeois—the portrayal of a type, usually a professional one, as the unreflective, unfree object of a "scientific" investigation. The depiction of the mannerisms and "idées reçues" of the type in question involves the sort of comic spirit analyzed by Bergson in *Le rire*: the assimilation of human activity to mere mechanism. An analogous critique of bourgeois social types was carried on in the popular lithographs (Monnier, Gavarni, Daumier) of the July monarchy.

Because "Le commis" contains no materials of directly personal significance, it is chiefly important as a manifestation of the keen interest that Flaubert had begun to take at this early stage of his career in the "bêtise" of bourgeois life. Thus, rather than analyzing the specific subject matter of "Le commis," we must examine the sources of this concern with "la bêtise," which was to prove of such great significance throughout Flaubert's lifetime.[3]

_____

[2] "J'ai été hier [March 23] chez Degouve-Denuncques [editor-in-chief of the *Colibri*], mon 'Commis' sera inséré jeudi prochain et mercredi je corrigerai avec lui les épreuves." (*Correspondence* [Paris: Conard, 1910–1933], I, 24.)

[3] [Pour écrire *Bouvard et Pécuchet*] il faut, comme Antoine par le Catoblépas, être attiré par la stupidité... Flaubert savourait, humait, dégustait la bêtise" (Albert Thibaudet, *Gustave Flaubert, 1821–1880: Sa vie, ses romans, son style*, 4th ed. [Paris, 1935], p. 206). It is interesting that Thibaudet chooses for his example the very monster of the Tentation that resembles Julietta's cow in "Rêve d'enfer."

Although this concern is expressed in a form that sharply differentiates "Le commis" from the surrounding Romantic works, its contemporaneous appearance with "Rêve d'enfer" is not simply an accident. In discussing the works of the third period, I have noted the problem of content arising in connection with the protagonists who remain so attached to the ideal of the childhood paradise that they can find no opportunity for action in the real world. In "Rêve d'enfer," with the story of Julietta's worldly love for Arthur, Flaubert finds the way out of the content problem; the world is no longer to be the home of the ideal itself, but only of those who seek, ever in vain, to grasp it.

The manifold consequences of this development are only hinted at in "Rêve d'enfer." But if the world in which the works are located is no longer to be the home of the ideal, then the idealization that characterizes the milieux of almost all the preceding works (including, of course, "Rêve d'enfer" itself) can no longer serve the author's purposes. The function of the milieu is now to make manifest the nonexistence of any worldly ideal, and for this to be best accomplished, the world must be depicted in its everyday, unideal reality. Accordingly in the works that directly follow "Rêve d'enfer"—three brief scenarios, and the stories "Quidquid volueris" and "Passion et vertu"—a strictly contemporary bourgeois milieu is employed throughout, and in both stories the destruction of the protagonist's ideal aspirations by the negativity of this milieu is made fully explicit.[4]

Thus "Le commis" can be said to participate in a general growth of Flaubert's concern with the unideal reality of the bourgeois milieu. But this concern is not sufficient to explain the great interest the author shows in "Le commis" for concrete, trivial manifestations of the *bêtise* of bourgeois life. Flaubert is not merely analyzing the unideality of the *commis* as a member of contemporary society; he is in a positive sense attracted to the minutiae of his "hero's" everyday existence. As has often been observed, "Le commis" represents the first clear-cut manifestation of a lifelong fascination with such details that led Flaubert

---

[4] For example, the following description from "Passion et vertu" of the heroine's lover, who seduces her and then leaves her, explicitly relates his unscrupulousness to a contemporary bourgeois environment:

Loin d'être une de ces âmes d'exception comme il y en a dans les livres et dans les drames, c'était un coeur sec, un esprit juste... Mais il possédait a fond *cette théorie de séductions,... le chic enfin, pour employer le mot vrai et vulgaire,* par lesquels un habile homme en arrive à ses fins.

Ce n'est plus cette méthode pastorale à la Louis XV,... science si bien exposée dans Faublas... *Mais maintenant* un homme s'avance vers une femme, il la lorgne, il la trouve bien, il en fait le pari avec ses amis ; est-elle mariée, la farce n'en sera que meilleure. (OJ I, 241–242)

to compile the *Dictionnaire des idées reçues* and the "Dossier" of *Bouvard et Pécuchet*.

What is the link between this fascination and the subject matter of the contemporaneous "Rêve d'enfer"? We should recall the attraction of Julietta to her monstrous cow:

Quelque chose l'attachait au ventre de l'animal qui geignait tristement et humectait l'herbe de sa langue baveuse; il râlait et remuait sa tête sur le sol comme s'il se mourait de douleur. (OJ I, 182)

This attraction, as my analysis shows, is not unrelated to Julietta's love for the ideal Arthur, who like the cow represents "la matière brute et stupide," but without the animal's repulsive particularity. The similarity between the cow and the *commis* is not difficult to grasp; both fascinate the author by their repulsive detail, and by the naïve, purely "material" shamelessness with which they manifest their monstrousness to the world.

But there is a more direct link between the *commis* and the ideal "matière" of Arthur. In "Chronique normande," the penultimate work of the first period, the final reconcilation of the son with the father took place when the latter renounced the narrow ambitions that had opposed him to the son, who was himself a sleeping child not at all discontent with his dependent position. This reconciliation only became possible as a result of the pair's common possession of a social "being" that did not require them to participate in the "becoming" of a goal-directed praxis, and therefore did not involve them in conflict over worldly objects. The son possessed this being as a still-unconscious child, the father as a "bourgeois," an adult with an established place in the world.

This similarity between child and bourgeois reappears at the end of the third period between the null-praxial hero and the *commis*. These latter two share the unchanging being of "la matière" because both *are* what they are without having to become it. As Arthur's symbolic immortality demonstrated, the null-praxial hero is for Flaubert an essentially static, "eternal" figure. But the *commis* too is "eternal"; like an animal species, his attributes remain unchanged throughout his life. And because of their common indifference to temporality, neither the *commis* nor Arthur has a genuine praxis. The *commis*'s manifold idiosyncrasies at work or at home are no more praxial than Arthur's lackadaisical toying with alchemy. The difference is that what for the latter were merely superfluous operations are for the former the functions of which his very life process consists. But professional functions, like bodily functions, involve no temporal progression toward a goal, no path through the world toward an ultimate disalienation. For Flaubert, the *commis* in his bourgeois security experiences not the slightest degree of alienation.

The story of the *commis,* like that of Arthur—or of Homais—cannot become the subject of a work of fiction because it is not a "story" at all, but a static description. Its source in the author's personality is not his interest in the praxial possibilities for movement through the world, but his fascination with the "being," the "matière" that already *is* in the world. The details of this being attract and tempt Flaubert because, like the "stupidity" of the childhood ideal, the *bêtise* of the *commis* places him in a form of paradise, secure from any possibility of alienation.

This unideal paradise can acquire a greater significance than the ideal one now that the unideal world has replaced the Romantic universe destroyed at the end of "Rêve d'enfer" as the locale of Flaubert's fictions. The reified career of the *commis,* and of the bourgeois in general, is an alternative to authentic praxis that exists not in an inaccessible past but in the real world itself. And in this sense, the *commis* offers, like the Catoblépas for Antoine, a genuine, permanent temptation for the author. The childhood ideal can exist only for the Romantic hero and accordingly plays no part in Flaubert's mature works; but the adult "paradise" of *la bêtise* first revealed in "Le commis" is never renounced.

CONCLUSION

THE FIRST TWO years of Flaubert's literary career have led him through a variety of Romantic forms and structures to an uncovering of his fundamental contradiction with Romanticism. In the first year, the adolescent Flaubert seeks to legitimize his guilt-laden worldly desires by attributing them to adult protagonists. But in "Un parfum à sentir" near the end of this period, the Flaubertian hero divests himself of his spurious adulthood and overtly accepts the dependent adolescent position of his creator. The works of the second year explore in turn the two basic alternatives open to the adolescent hero. The first stories depict him as involved in a guilty revolt against his dependent position; the later ones elaborate the contrary possibility of flight from the evils of the adult bourgeois world into the adolescent's preworldly purity. But whereas the revolt had been renounced because its guilty nature ultimately proved unacceptable to Flaubert, the attempt to imitate René's disillusioned withdrawal from the world was unsuccessful for the opposite reason. The ideal hero could have no genuine interest in the unideal world; he could only recognize its worthlessness from without. And for this reason no concrete worldly career was possible for him; his story could not be made to constitute a literary entity.

In "Rêve d'enfer" at the end of the second year Flaubert is finally driven to replace his inactive unwordly hero with the heroine Julietta, who in her futile quest for worldly happiness is the distant prototype of Emma Bovary. From this point on, Flaubert's protagonists, through their devotion to worldly goals that he himself cannot accept as possible bases for his own career, stand on a lower level than their creator.

The source of this transformation is Flaubert's recognition, implicit in the incompletion of the semiautobiographical stories "La dernière heure" and "La main de fer," that it is impossible to create a worldly praxis out of his own extraworldly situation. This in turn forces him to modify the nature of his identification with his protagonists. His heroes can no longer be idealized models for him because he feels their career to be grounded upon an *illusionary* understanding of the terms of worldly existence, a false hope of attaining ideal happiness in the unideal world. This is indeed an important aspect of the vision of his mature works. And yet neither "Rêve d'enfer" nor the third-year works that develop its insights are in any sense "mature" or post-Romantic. They are instead the last of the early works to remain at all satisfactorily within their Romantic forms. The contradiction discussed in the Introduction between the author's own extraworldly position and the worldly praxis of his Romantic heroes only now begins to enter into the works themselves.

Because Flaubert is an adolescent who has not yet been faced with the necessity of participating in the adult world, he has thus far been able to avoid the question of choosing a particular career for himself. Hence his understanding of the inability of worldly praxis to provide ideal satisfaction remains itself "unworldly," or in other words, wholly *abstract*. Flaubert can feel superior to his protagonists whose devotion to narrow worldly interests cuts them off from the universal posture he assumes, but he is far from recognizing that his own experience of the world must be condemned to the very same narrowness. He can no longer identify with the Romantic hero's assumption of a particular place in the world, but, because his own position has remained that of a "universal" adolescent, he grasps his own experience as divorced from all particularity. Thus his vision of *experience,* as opposed to his conception of *praxis,* remains wholly Romantic.

The experiences of the Romantic hero take place in the world, yet they are not *of* the world but models of universal validity. By the very nature of the Romantic literary method the narrator, who expresses in the work the author's "universal" consciousness, identifies with and affirms the attitudes embodied in the hero's experience. But for Flaubert the identification with the hero in his concrete experiences stands in contrast to his refusal of the romantic hero's illusion-based career *as a whole.*

This dual relationship of the author to his protagonist allowed Flaubert to create Julietta's coherent although schematic praxis in "Rêve d'enfer," and, during the following year, the more highly developed career of the heroine of "Passion et vertu" (December 1837). In this latter work as well as in "Quidquid volueris" (October 1837), the protagonists' careers integrate material taken not merely from the purely internal sexual awakening depicted in "Rêve d'enfer" but from Flaubert's nascent "grand amour" for Elisa Schlésinger,[1] as well as what

---

[1] Flaubert's first meeting with Mme. Schlésinger has been almost universally dated by scholars in the summer of 1836. But it is also known that Flaubert was at Trouville in 1837; in a letter to Ernest Chevalier on September 22 of that year, he makes explicit mention of his visit: *"J'ai d'abord été à Trouville,* puis de là à Nogent" (*Correspondance* [Paris: Conard, 1910–1933], I, 28) Since there is no sign whatever of the famous love affair in the works that precede the summer of 1837, while "Quidquid volueris" (October 1837) contains material offering indisputable parallels with the autobiographical account of the affair in "Mémoires d'un fou" (e.g., the boat ride of the hero, his beloved, and her husband [OJ I, 230–232]; cf. in "Mémoires" [OJ I, 511–513]), we may hazard the hypothesis that even if Flaubert met Mme. Schlésinger for the first time in 1836, it was during the next summer that the significant experiences of the relationship took place.

we may presume to be his first sexual experience;[2] it is this additional material that accounts for the greater richness of these works in comparison with the abstract, allegorical "Rêve d'enfer." But if the contrast of "Rêve d'enfer" between praxis and experiential content is aggravated in a work like "Passion et vertu" where the object of the heroine's love is not an ideal hero but a bourgeois scoundrel, this did not prevent Flaubert from achieving a satisfactory formal unity. For this duality does not in itself run counter to the formal exigencies of the work. The Romantic form becomes inadequate only when the author himself experiences the duality as a contradiction and refuses to incorporate his own experiences within the praxis of the other. And this in turn occurs when he comes to feel an unfulfilled need for a praxis to unify his experiences. This frustration finds expression in "Agonies" (April 1838):

Souvent je me suis demandé pourquoi je vivais, ce que j'étais venu faire au monde, et je n'ai trouvé là dedans qu'un abîme derrière moi, un abîme devant; à droite, à gauche, en haut, en bas, partout des ténèbres.

La gloire même après qui [*sic*] je cours n'est qu'un mensonge. (OJ I, 404–405)

Despair of finding a place in the world is not idealized in a fictional "null-praxis" like that of "La dernière heure," but remains a personal sentiment that demands expression regardless of literary coherency:

Agonies! eh bien, *c'est quelque roman bien hideux et bien noir, je présume; vous vous trompez, c'est plus, c'est tout un immense résumé d'une vie morale bien hideuse et bien noire....* Non, c'est moins que de la poésie, c'est de la prose; moins que de la prose, des cris; mais il y en a de faux, d'aigus, de perçants, de sourds, *toujours de vrais, rarement d'heureux. C'est une œuvre bizarre et indéfinissable* comme ces masques grotesques qui vous font peur. (OJ I, 402)

Flaubert is here concerned to differentiate the autobiographical work

[2] This experience is discussed in "Mémoires d'un fou" in a detailed account with evident similarities to the relation of the heroine's sexual disillusionment in "Passion et vertu." Compare "Mémoires":

Je me demandais si c'était bien là les délices que j'avais rêvées, ces transports de feu que je m'étais imaginés dans la virginité de ce coeur tendre et enfant. Non, jamais on ne pourra dire tous les mystères de l'âme vierge... comme sa déception est amère et cruelle! (OJ I, 525–526)
"Passion et vertu":

Elle pensait aux sensations qu'elle avait éprouvées, et ne trouvait en y pensant, *rien que déception et amertume. 'Oh! ce n'est pas là ce que j'avais rêvé!'* disait-elle. (OJ I, 250)
The similarity of these passages is sufficient evidence that it is the author's own disillusionment that is being related in "Passion et vertu"; the experience that led to it most probably took place not long before this work was written.

he is introducing from a "roman." He wants to tell the truth about his own life, not fabricate as in the past a fictional totality from his experiences. And a few pages further on he expresses his frustration at being unable to make this personal truth the subject of a genuine literary work:

Quel est l'homme qui n'a pas senti son esprit accablé de sensations et d'idées incohérentes, terrifiantes et brûlantes? L'analyse ne saurait les décrire, mais un livre ainsi fait serait la nature. Car qu'est-ce que la poésie, si ce n'est la nature exquise, le coeur et la pensée réunis?

Oh! si j'étais poète, comme je ferais des choses qui seraient belles!

Je me sens dans le cœur une force intime que personne ne peut voir. Serai-je condamné toute ma vie à être comme un muet qui veut parler et écume de rage?

Il y a peu de positions aussi atroces. (OJ I, 405)

Because Flaubert has now come to experience for himself the frustration of lacking any genuine praxial goals in the world, he can no longer identify with the artificial praxis of the other. Thus his most significant works of the next few years are essentially autobiographical: "Mémoires d'un fou," "Smarh," and "Novembre." In each of these works Flaubert attempts to unify his personal experiences in a literary totality, but, despite undoubted stylistic and descriptive merits, as formal creations none are successful. Whatever the significance of Flaubert's own experiences, they cannot form a coherent literary work because he refuses to situate them within the inevitable particularity of a worldly praxis.

Flaubert's escape from the threatening prospect of a bourgeois career as the result of the incapacitating nervous attack of January 1844 permitted him to separate his ideal self entirely from worldly action. Because he could now devote himself entirely to his extraworldly interest in literature, the problem of his own praxis was solved. He was no longer obliged to idealize his worldly experiences in his works; the privilege of ideality was now to be reserved for his extraworldly activities as a writer. These developments are embodied in Flaubert's first full-length novel, the *Education sentimentale* of 1843–1845. In the original conception of the novel Flaubert had hoped to construct a worldly praxis for his hero Henry out of his own experiences with Mme. Schlésinger in Paris and with the Marseilles woman, Eulalie Foucauld, who had earlier served as a model for the courtesan Marie in "Novembre." But after Flaubert's attack the story of Henry was abandoned for that of his contemplative friend Jules. Having become, like the "Romantic" youth Léon in *Madame Bovary,* a successful bourgeois Henry forfeits his claim to the author's interest, and the entire last third of the novel is devoted to Jules's wholly internal evolution toward an aesthetic grasp of the world—an evolution that quite evidently parallels the author's own.

The artist's extraworldly praxis toward which Jules evolves, and which the Antoine of the first *Tentation* incarnates in a symbolic form, cannot offer a genuine literary content to Flaubert. But by choosing it as his subject he renounces the effort exemplified in the creation of Henry to idealize his own worldly experiences and returns on a higher level to his original "adolescent" position outside the world. From this standpoint the world is once again viewed as the "enfer" depicted in the author's first adolescent work; the satisfactions it offers are nothing but the evil temptations that offer themselves to Antoine.

The enslavement of the protagonist by these temptations eventually provides the thematic content of the mature novels, *Madame Bovary* and *Education sentimentale*. Because, like Flaubert, Emma and Frédéric are Romantics, they are driven to refuse the narrowness of any particular place in the bourgeois world; yet because, unlike him, they have been condemned to live in this world, the solutions they choose all prove to be valueless at their very core.

In contrast to his protagonists, the mature Flaubert remains the Romantic hero he always felt himself to be, but only in his unworldly existence as an artist. His own worldly activity is no more ideal than that of his heroes and heroines—it is this he expresses in the celebrated (though possibly apocryphal) *boutade*, "Madame Bovary, c'est moi!" As a worldly individual Flaubert and, indeed, everyone else, is Emma Bovary, basing illusory hopes for ideal satisfaction on desires that can never transcend the particularity of the fallen bourgeois world. But by engaging in the praxis of the artist, by creating works of universal validity, Flaubert is able to retain his adolescent universality. The mature novels, like the early stories, have a Romantic hero; but he is no longer among the protagonists: he is the extraworldly author himself.

APPENDIX

FLAUBERT'S EARLY WORKS, 1835–1837

"Voyage en enfer"	January–March (?) 1835
"Une pensée"	February (?) 1835
"Matteo [sic] Falcone, ou Deux cercueils pour un proscrit"	August–September (?) 1835
"Chevrin et le roi de Prusse, ou L'on prend souvent la tête d'un roi pour celle d'un âne"	August–September (?) 1835
*"Deux amours et deux cercueils: Drame en cinq actes"	Summer (?) 1935
"Mort du duc de Guise"	September 1835**
"Le moine des Chartreux, ou L'anneau du prieur"	September (?) 1835
"Dernière scène de la mort de Marguerite de Bourgogne"	September 1835–January 1836
"Portrait de Lord Byron"	September 1835–January 1836
"San Pietro Ornano (histoire corse)"	September 1835–January 1836
*"La fiancée et la tombe, conte fantastique"	September 1835–January 1836
*"La grande dame et le joueur de vieille [sic] ou La mère et le cercueil"	September 1835–January 1836
"Deux mains sur une couronne, ou Pendant le quinzième siècle (épisodes du règne de Charles VI)"	January 1836**
"Un parfum à sentir, ou Les baladins: conte philosophique, moral, immoral ad libitum"	April 1, 1836**
"Chronique normande du dixième siècle"	May 1836**
"La femme du monde"	June 1–2, 1836**
"Un secret de Philippe le prudent, roi d'Espagne (conte historique)"	September 1836**
"La peste à Florence"	September 1836**
"Bibliomanie"	November 1836**
"Rage et impuissance, conte malsain: Pour les nerfs sensibles et les âmes dévotes"	December 15, 1836**

* Not in the Conard edition of the *Œuvres de jeunesse;* published in Bruneau, *Les débuts littéraires.*

** Dated by Flaubert.

"La dernière heure (conte philosophique)"	January 1837**
"La main de fer (conte philosophique)"	February 1837**
"Rêve d'enfer (conte fantastique)"	March 21, 1837**
"Une leçon d'histoire naturelle, genre commis"	March (?) 1937

** Dated by Flaubert.

WORKS OF GUSTAVE FLAUBERT

Bertrand, Louis, ed. "Les Carnets de Gustave Flaubert," *Revue des deux mondes,* July 15, 1910, pp. 371–392.

Bruneau, Jean. *Les débuts littéraires de Gustave Flaubert.* Paris, 1962. With the exception of "La fiancée et la tombe," first published in facsimile in *Le manuscrit autographe* (January–February 1929, pp. 1–5), all of the following works were previously unpublished.

"Trois pages d'un Cahier d'Ecolier ou Œuvres choisies de Gustave F***" (pp. 40–41)

"Madame d'Ecouy" (pp. 99–100)

"Deux amours et deux cercueils: Drame en cinq actes" (pp. 122–123)

"La Grande Dame et le joueur de vieille [*sic*], ou La mère et le cercueil" (pp. 124–126)

Two (untitled) scenarios (pp. 142–144)

"La fiancée et la tombe: conte fantastique" (pp. 162–165)

Dubosc, Georges. "Une composition d'histoire et géographie par Gustave Flaubert en 1837," *Trois Normands: Pierre Corneille, Gustave Flaubert, Guy de Maupassant: Etudes documentaires.* Rouen, 1917, pp. 110–122.

Flaubert, Gustave. *Œuvres complètes.* 2 vols. Paris: Ed. du Seuil, 1964.

———. *Œuvres complètes.* 22 vols. Paris: Conard, 1910–1933. This includes the nine-volume edition of Flaubert's *Correspondance.* It also includes the *Œuvres de jeunesse* (OJ). 3 vols. 1910.

———. *Œuvres complètes: Correspondance (Supplement).* 4 vols. Paris: Conard, 1954.

———.*Premières œuvres.* 2 vols. Paris: Bibliothèque Charpentier, 1925.

———. *Souvenirs, notes et pensées intimes.* Paris, 1965.

Vinaver, Eugène. "Un inédit de Flaubert: L'influence des Arabes d'Espagne sur la civilisation française du Moyen-Age (mars 1837)," *French Studies,* January 1947, pp. 37–43.